Formal Models of Domestic Politics

Formal Models of Domestic Politics offers the first unified and accessible treatment of canonical and important new formal models of domestic politics. Intended for students in political science and economics who have already taken a course in game theory, the text covers eight classes of models: electoral competition under certainty and uncertainty, special interest politics, veto players, delegation, coalitions, political agency, and regime change. Political economists, comparativists, and Americanists alike will find models here central to their research interests.

The text assumes no mathematical knowledge beyond basic calculus, with an emphasis placed on clarity of presentation. Political scientists will appreciate the simplification of economic environments to focus on the political logic of models; economists will discover many important models of politics published outside of their discipline; and both instructors and students will value the numerous classroom-tested exercises.

Scott Gehlbach is Professor of Political Science, Lyons Family Faculty Fellow, and Romnes Faculty Fellow at the University of Wisconsin–Madison; Senior Research Fellow at the International Center for the Study of Institutions and Development at the Higher School of Economics, Moscow; and Research Associate of the Centre for Economic and Financial Research at the New Economic School in Moscow. A specialist in Russia, Professor Gehlbach has made fundamental contributions to the study of economic reform and other issues in political economy. Known for employing a wide range of research methods in his work, Gehlbach is the author of the award-winning *Representation through Taxation: Revenue, Politics, and Development in Postcommunist States* (Cambridge Studies in Comparative Politics) and numerous articles in top journals, including the *American Political Science Review*, the *American Journal of Political Science*, and the *Journal of Politics*. His work has been supported by two Fulbright-Hays Fellowships and many other grants. Professor Gehlbach received his Ph.D. in political science and economics from the University of California–Berkeley.

Analytical Methods for Social Research

Analytical Methods for Social Research presents texts on empirical and formal methods for the social sciences. Volumes in the series address both the theoretical underpinnings of analytical techniques as well as their application in social research. Some series volumes are broad in scope, cutting across a number of disciplines. Others focus mainly on methodological applications within specific fields such as political science, sociology, demography, and public health. The series serves a mix of students and researchers in the social sciences and statistics.

Series Editors:

R. Michael Alvarez, California Institute of Technology
Nathaniel L. Beck, New York University
Lawrence L. Wu, New York University
Stephen L. Morgan, Cornell University

Other Titles in the Series:

Event History Modeling: A Guide for Social Scientists,
    by Janet M. Box-Steffensmeier and Bradford S. Jones
Ecological Inference: New Methodological Strategies, edited by Gary King,
    Ori Rosen, and Martin A. Tanner
Spatial Models of Parliamentary Voting, by Keith T. Poole
Essential Mathematics for Political and Social Research, by Jeff Gill
Data Analysis Using Regression and Multilevel/Hierarchical Models,
    by Andrew Gelman and Jennifer Hill
Political Game Theory: An Introduction, by Nolan McCarty and
    Adam Meirowitz
*Counterfactuals and Causal Inference: Methods and Principles for Social
    Research,* by Stephen L. Morgan and Christopher Winship

Formal Models of Domestic Politics

SCOTT GEHLBACH

University of Wisconsin–Madison

CAMBRIDGE
UNIVERSITY PRESS

CAMBRIDGE UNIVERSITY PRESS
Cambridge, New York, Melbourne, Madrid, Cape Town,
Singapore, São Paulo, Delhi, Mexico City

Cambridge University Press
32 Avenue of the Americas, New York, NY 10013-2473, USA

www.cambridge.org
Information on this title: www.cambridge.org/9781107610422

First published 2013

Printed in the United States of America

A catalog record for this publication is available from the British Library.

Library of Congress Cataloging in Publication Data

Gehlbach, Scott.
Formal models of domestic politics / Scott Gehlbach, University of Wisconsin,
Madison.
    pages   cm. – (Analytical methods for social research)
Includes bibliographical references and index.
ISBN 978-0-521-76715-6 – ISBN 978-1-107-61042-2 (pbk.)
    1. Elections – United States – Mathematical models.   2. Political participation –
United States – Mathematical models.   3. Game theory.   I. Title.
JK1976.G44   2012
324.973001′51 – dc23   2012036928

ISBN 978-0-521-76715-6 Hardback
ISBN 978-1-107-61042-2 Paperback

Additional resources for this publication at www.cambridge.org/gehlbach

To Masha

Contents

Illustrations and Table

Acknowledgments

My primary thanks go to the many students who have enrolled in the course on which this text is based. I would not have written this book if not for you, and I could not have done it without your help. Thank you, Yasushi Asako, Adam Auerbach, Sanja Badanjak, Nick Barnes, Eric Becker, Galina Belokurova, Jennifer Brick Murtazashvili, Jason Brozek, Bugrahan Budak, Meina Cai, Maria del Pilar Casal, Hannah Chapman, Josh Cutler, Mason Delang, Matthew Dimick, William Egar, Jason Engle, Dylan Fitz, John Geis, Petr Gocev, Marko Grdesic, Jesse Gubb, Kyle Hanniman, Marlies Hilbrink, Lauren Jankovic, Patrick Kearney, Dimitri Kelly, Insoo Kim, Rachid Laajaj, Akos Lada, Stéphane Lavertu, Yoon Jin Lee, Ruoxi Li, Kuen-Da Lin, Jinjie Liu, Richard Loeza, Georgy Loginov, Kyle Marquardt, John Marshall, Rogerio Mazali, John Morrow, Luciana Moscoso Boedo, Susanne Mueller, Ilia Murtazashvili, Robert Naramore, Peter Nasuti, Sarah Niebler, Tom O'Grady, David Ohls, Max Palmer, Jonathan Phillips, Ryan Powers, Marc Ratkovic, Megan Ritz, Maria Fernanda Rodrigo, Emily Sellars, Rajen Subramanian, Joanna Syrda, Mark Toukan, Carly Urban, Kristin Vekasi, Samantha Vortherms, Caleb White, Jennifer Williams, Steven Wilson, Jessica Winchell, and Yiqing Xu.

A few students provided help outside the classroom as well as inside it. Emily Sellars read the first essentially complete manuscript in its entirety, providing numerous comments on substance and presentation. Jonathan Phillips did the same for key portions of the final manuscript. Lauren Jankovic produced many of the diagrams in the text, and Ryan Powers helped with some last editing.

Along the way, I received helpful advice and encouragement from a number of colleagues and friends, including Alex Debs, Georgy Egorov, David Laitin, Eddy Malesky, Ken Shepsle, Konstantin Sonin, Milan Svolik, and David Weimer. I am also grateful to Scott Ashworth, Luciana Moscoso Boedo, Monika Nalepa, and Alejandro Saporiti, each of whom tried out draft versions of the manuscript on their students. Not least, I am indebted to Tim Colton for arranging for me to teach the text one last time to his students and to Harvard's Davis Center for Russian and Eurasian Studies for hosting me while I was doing so.

At Cambridge University Press, Ed Parsons set this project in motion, Lew Bateman saw it to completion, the series editors Michael Alvarez and Neal Beck provided support throughout, and Russell Hahn shepherded the final manuscript through production. I am grateful for the painless process and—not least—the excellent choice of reviewers, whose suggestions made this a better book.

Financial and institutional support was provided by the International Center for the Study of Institutions and Development at the Higher School of Economics, Moscow; by Jeffrey and Susanne Lyons through their establishment of the Lyons Family Faculty Fellowship; and by the Graduate School at UW Madison through an H. I. Romnes Faculty Fellowship.

This book is dedicated to Masha, who secured us life in the same town and brought us Adrian while I was putting the finishing touches on the manuscript. Masha, you are my hero.

Preface

This book is an introduction to formal models of domestic politics. It is based on a course I have taught at Wisconsin since 2004 (and at Harvard in 2012), and I expect that readers of the text will have the background that students in my course have had: a semester of game theory at the level of Osborne (2004) or McCarty and Meirowitz (2007) and familiarity with basic differential and integral calculus. My course is in the Political Science Department but has always attracted a few economists, and I anticipate that the book will similarly be useful to scholars in both disciplines.

Notwithstanding this claim to interdisciplinarity, a primary goal in writing this book has been to strip away some of the economics from well known models of political economy. I cut my teeth in graduate school on Persson and Tabellini (2000), from which I learned much, but I quickly learned that I would need to teach a lot of economics if I were to use that text in a political science course. More generally, formal models of domestic politics are as likely today to appear in economics as in political science journals, and some translation is necessary if they are to be accessible beyond the economics discipline. Conversely, there are numerous important models published in political science journals that are not well known among economists; this text provides an introduction.

Other than Persson and Tabellini (2000), the only other contemporary texts covering related material are McCarty and Meirowitz (2007) and Austen-Smith and Banks (2005), but these serve purposes different from my own. (Two earlier texts—Ordeshook, 1986, and Morrow, 1994—predate many of the models covered here.) As already indicated, McCarty and Meirowitz (2007) is primarily a game theory text, albeit one targeted to political scientists; my book is intended for students who know some game theory and want to learn particular classes of models.

Austen-Smith and Banks (2005) provides a thorough treatment of select strategic models of politics, but it assumes a far stronger technical background than does this book. (I do not cover social choice theory, which is the topic of Austen-Smith and Banks, 1999.) Finally, my aim is different from that of Weingast and Wittman (2006) and various other handbooks, which are superb resources but not textbooks per se.

In writing what is essentially the first textbook of its type, I have faced some choices. In principle, I could have attempted an exhaustive but cursory summary of several decades' work, leaving readers to go back to the original papers once they had discovered a model to their liking. I opted instead for the other extreme: a hopefully careful treatment of canonical models of domestic politics, together with some important models from the more recent literature. The field is vast, and I apologize to the authors of papers not covered. In some cases (e.g., the rapidly proliferating work on nondemocratic politics), it was my judgment that the literature was just too fresh for an authoritative treatment. I fully anticipate that many instructors will find certain models missing, and I expect that some of them will choose to supplement this text with other readings.

That said, most graduate students do not have the background to fully absorb the typical research paper in formal theory. In economics, textbooks have long served as a bridge between introductory training and the literature. In similar fashion, I have endeavored to extract the essential insights from sometimes intricate models so that they could be presented and solved in the classroom. (A useful exercise is to have students choose one or two of the original papers to see what has been lost in the textbook treatment.) There is not an equation here that has not been written on a blackboard. Similarly, all exercises—some of them also based on research papers—have been tested in problem sets and exams. A solutions manual is available to instructors upon request.

The text is organized around eight classes of models, each of which constitutes a single chapter: electoral competition under certainty and uncertainty, special interest politics, veto players, delegation, coalitions, political agency, and regime change. Instructors wishing to rely solely on this book should find more than enough to fill a semester. Very roughly speaking, the material in later chapters is more difficult than what comes before. In a few places, I have further set off sections that in my judgment are more demanding than a preceding discussion of the same topic. Such material, which might be omitted from an introductory course, can be identified by italicized section titles.

1

Electoral Competition under Certainty

We begin with models of electoral competition. This chapter explores electoral competition when voting behavior is deterministic; the following chapter considers electoral competition under uncertainty.

A frequent assertion in two-party systems is that there is little substantive difference between the positions chosen by the parties. The economist Harold Hotelling was the first to offer a theoretical explanation for this phenomenon (Hotelling, 1929). Parties, Hotelling argued, choose positions along a left-right continuum (an example of a **policy space**), much as gas stations or drug stores choose a location along Main Street. When there are two parties, the logic of political competition compels each to adopt a position in the center of the ideological spectrum, just as we often observe gas stations located across the street from each other in the center of town. Anthony Downs popularized and extended Hotelling's argument in *An Economic Theory of Democracy* (Downs, 1957).

We thus initiate our discussion of electoral competition with the Hotelling-Downs model, where parties adopt positions to maximize their probability of winning. We then take up an alternative model in which parties are motivated not to win office for its own sake, but to achieve the best possible policy outcome. Following this, we explore electoral competition when more than two parties compete. Finally, we endogenize the number of parties (or candidates) in the election by considering various models of entry.

1.1 The Hotelling-Downs Model

1.1.1 Euclidean Preferences

The Hotelling-Downs model is most easily expressed as a static game of complete information, where two parties simultaneously choose positions and the election outcome follows mechanically and deterministically from those policy choices.[1] The implicit assumption of the Hotelling-Downs model is that parties are able to credibly commit to implementing whatever policy they have promised during the election campaign. One motivation for this assumption is that parties are long-lived and therefore have an incentive to acquire a reputation for keeping campaign promises (Alesina and Spear, 1988; Cox and McCubbins, 1994; Aldrich, 1995).

We focus for now on the special case of a one-dimensional policy space, which for simplicity we assume to be the entire real number line $\Re$; we denote any generic policy by x. In this model, there are two players, parties labeled $P = A, B$. Each party P has the same strategy space, choosing a position $x_P \in \Re$. Further, each party prefers outcomes that imply a higher probability of winning to those that imply a lower probability, where $\pi(x_A, x_B)$ is the probability that party A wins, given that party A and party B have chosen positions x_A and x_B, respectively.

To define $\pi(x_A, x_B)$, we describe voters' preferences and behavior and the electoral rule:

(i) There is a continuum of voters, indexed by i, each with unique **ideal point** (most-preferred policy) $x_i \in \Re$. The distribution of ideal points is continuous and strictly increasing on some interval, so that there is a unique median ideal point, which we denote x_m. Voters have **Euclidean preferences** over policy, so that a voter always prefers a policy closer to her ideal point to one further away. These preferences can be represented by the utility function

$$u_i(x) = -|x - x_i|.$$

(ii) Voters vote sincerely, choosing the party whose policy they most prefer. Voters who are indifferent between the two parties abstain.

(iii) The election is plurality-rule: the party with the most votes wins.

---

[1] Equivalently, we can think of the Hotelling-Downs model as an extensive game of complete information, where a finite number of voters vote strategically after parties have chosen positions. In this alternative formulation, we assume that voters play weakly undominated strategies, which, as discussed later, implies that voters in equilibrium vote for the party whose position they most prefer.

If the two parties receive the same vote, then the election winner is chosen by a fair lottery.

Given these assumptions, $\pi(x_A, x_B)$ equals one if the fraction of voters who strictly prefer x_A to x_B is greater than one-half, equals zero if the fraction of voters who strictly prefer x_B to x_A is greater than one-half, and equals one-half otherwise.

To derive a prediction for the play of actors in this strategic environment, we look for the set of Nash equilibria. We begin by deriving the best-response correspondence for party B, that is, we find the set of optimal policy choices for party B, given x_A. Consider, for example, the optimal x_B when $x_A < x_m$. Party B can win with certainty by adopting any position closer to x_m than is x_A. (To see this, note that because voters prefer policies closer to their ideal points to those further away, party B is preferred by all voters with ideal point $x_i > \frac{x_A + x_B}{2}$, which is more than one-half of all voters given that $\frac{x_A + x_B}{2} < x_m$.) In contrast, choosing either i) x_A or ii) a position the same distance from x_m as x_A but on the other side of x_m gives a probability of winning of one-half: in (i) all voters are indifferent between party A and party B and so abstain, whereas in (ii) voters divide evenly between party A and party B. Finally, choosing a position further away from x_m than is x_A means that party B loses with certainty.

A similar logic applies when $x_A > x_m$. Thus, when $x_A \neq x_m$, any position closer to x_m than is x_A is a best response. Finally, when $x_A = x_m$, only x_m is a best response: choosing $x_B = x_m$ results in a probability of winning of one-half, whereas any other position entails losing with certainty.

Party A's best-response correspondence is analogous: if $x_B \neq x_m$, any position closer to x_m than is x_B is a best response, whereas if $x_B = x_m$, the best response is x_m. Each party's best response is therefore to choose a position closer to x_m than is the other party's position, when that is possible. Clearly, the two parties are playing a best response to each other only when $x_A = x_B = x_m$. Thus, the unique Nash equilibrium is

$$x_A^* = x_B^* = x_m.$$

The logic of political competition forces each party to adopt the median ideal point, as only when that is the case is neither party able to increase its probability of winning.

1.1.2 Single-peaked Preferences

The assumption that voters have Euclidean preferences, though convenient, is restrictive. In many policy environments, it is natural for voters to have asymmetric preferences, valuing differences to one side of their ideal point more than those to the other. We should therefore ask whether the result obtained in the previous section—that in equilibrium parties each adopt the median ideal point—carries through if we assume more generally that voters have single-peaked preferences, which we define as follows:

*Voters have **single-peaked preferences** over policies in $\Re$ if and only if, for each voter i, there is a unique ideal point x_i and the following condition holds for all $x', x'' \in \Re$:*

$$\text{if } x'' < x' < x_i \text{ or } x'' > x' > x_i, \text{ then } x' \succ_i x'',$$

where $\succ$ is the strict preference relation.

Preferences are single-peaked with respect to policies along the real number line if and only if each voter has a unique ideal point and—among positions *on the same side* of that ideal point—prefers positions that are closer to the ideal point to those further away. Clearly, Euclidean preferences are a special case of single-peaked preferences.

Social choice theory tells us that if individuals have single-peaked preferences, then an alternative is a **Condorcet winner** (an alternative such that no other alternative is strictly preferred by a majority) if and only if it is a median ideal point. The same logic implies that if voters in a Hotelling-Downs environment have single-peaked preferences, then the parties converge to a median ideal point, as any other position can be beaten.

To see this, assume as before that the distribution of voters' ideal points is continuous and strictly increasing on some interval, so that there is a unique median ideal point. Our intuition is that (x_m, x_m) is the unique Nash equilibrium, that is, that this strategy profile is a Nash equilibrium and no others are. We first demonstrate existence $((x_m, x_m)$ is a Nash equilibrium) and then uniqueness (no other strategy profile is a Nash equilibrium).

(i) Existence: When the parties adopt (x_m, x_m), each party wins with probability one-half. If either party deviates to any other position, then it wins with probability zero.[2] Thus, there is no profitable deviation.

(ii) Uniqueness: We prove that (x_m, x_m) is the unique Nash equilibrium by showing that for all other strategy profiles at least one party has an incentive to deviate. Consider three mutually exclusive and exhaustive cases:

(a) *One of the parties wins with certainty.* But then the losing party can adopt the position chosen by the winning party and win with probability one-half. Thus, this is not a Nash equilibrium.

(b) *Parties A and B each win with probability one-half, with $x_A = x_B \neq x_m$.* But then either party can win with certainty by instead adopting x_m. Thus, this is not a Nash equilibrium.

(c) *Parties A and B each win with probability one-half, with $x_A < x_m < x_B$ or $x_B < x_m < x_A$.* But then either party can win with certainty by instead adopting x_m. Thus, this is not a Nash equilibrium.

The logic of the proof illustrates another insight of the Hotelling-Downs model: two-party elections are often close. So long as parties have the freedom to commit to any position in the policy space, either party can guarantee itself a tie by adopting the position chosen by the other. In equilibrium, therefore, each party wins with probability one-half.

1.1.3 Hotelling-Downs Competition in a Multidimensional Policy Space

We are conditioned to think of politics as one-dimensional. Politicians and journalists speak of "liberal" and "conservative" policies, and parties throughout the world are labeled "leftist" or "rightist." Yet even simple policy environments may be inherently multidimensional. Consider, for example, the "pie-splitting" environment, where three individuals must decide how to divide a "pie" of size 1. Let q_1 be the share received by individual 1 and q_2 that received by individual 2, so that individual 3 receives $1 - q_1 - q_2$. Assume that individuals prefer more pie to less.

---

[2] This may seem obvious, but showing this rigorously takes a bit of work. The logic of the argument is that if either party deviates to some other position x', then *some* positive fraction of voters with ideal points between x_m and x' prefer the party that has not deviated, as do all voters with ideal points equal to and to the other side of x_m; together, these groups constitute a strict majority. See, for example, Roemer (2001, Section 1.2). We use the same argument throughout the proof whenever we need to establish that a party that adopts x_m receives a strict majority of the vote against a party that adopts some other position.

There is no Condorcet winner (i.e., no policy that beats or ties any other policy) in this environment. To see this, assume to the contrary that a Condorcet winner (q_1, q_2) exists. Because the shares of the three individuals sum to one, it must be true that at least one individual receives something from this policy. But then that individual's share could be divided between the remaining two players, who would clearly prefer this alternative division (q'_1, q'_2) to (q_1, q_2).

A similar logic applies in the context of electoral competition. Consider the Hotelling-Downs model, but now assume that the parties compete by proposing a division of a "pie" of size one among three groups, labeled $g = 1, 2, 3$. Let α_g be the size of group g, with $\sum \alpha_g = 1$ and $\alpha_g < \frac{1}{2}$ for all g; thus, any two groups constitute a majority. Again, individuals prefer more pie to less. We denote by (q_{1P}, q_{2P}) the policy offered by party P.

There is no Nash equilibrium of this game. To see this, assume to the contrary that there is some strategy pair $((q_{1A}, q_{2A}), (q_{1B}, q_{2B}))$ that is a Nash equilibrium. Note that in this equilibrium either one party wins with certainty or the two parties each win with probability one-half. In the first case, the losing party can increase its probability of winning to one-half by choosing the same policy as that chosen by the other party. In the second case, either party can increase its probability of winning to one by adopting a policy preferred by two groups to the policy chosen by the other party; by the argument already given, such a policy exists. Thus, there is no Nash equilibrium.

Intuitively, when there is no Condorcet winner, then there is no equilibrium to the Hotelling-Downs model, as any policy can be beaten by some other policy. As we show in the following chapter, however, this result is sensitive to the assumption that individuals' voting decisions follow deterministically from their policy preferences.

1.2 The Wittman Model

Up to now, we have assumed that parties care only about winning. We might defend this assumption by arguing that the nonpolicy benefits of holding office (prestige, patronage power, etc.) are paramount. The universality of this argument, however, is questionable: many politicians appear to enter politics not for the perks of office but because of their strong policy preferences. It is intuitive that parties made up of such politicians would be less likely to compromise on policy for the sake of winning office.

Donald Wittman was the first to formulate a model with **policy-seeking** rather than **office-seeking** parties (Wittman, 1973).[3] Surprisingly, our intuition that policy-seeking parties may be less inclined to adopt centrist positions does not hold in the basic Wittman model: as in the Hotelling-Downs model, the unique equilibrium is for each party to adopt the median ideal point. Intuitively, even though parties care about policy, they can implement policy only by winning office. The logic of political competition therefore drives them to adopt the same centrist policies they would choose if they were instead motivated to win office for its own sake.

To focus the discussion, assume as in the model of Section 1.1.1 that voters have Euclidean preferences over $x \in \Re$. There are two parties, $P = L, R$, which have von Neumann-Morgenstern preferences over lotteries over policy outcomes, where L receives a payoff equal to $-|x|$ and R a payoff equal to $-|x - 1|$ if policy x is implemented (i.e., the parties have ideal points 0 and 1, respectively). We assume $0 < x_m < 1$, so that the parties are "polarized." Parties L and R maximize expected utility by choosing positions x_L and x_R, respectively. Thus, letting $\pi(x_L, x_R)$ be the probability that L wins, given (x_L, x_R), L solves

$$\max_{x_L} \pi(x_L, x_R)(-|x_L|) + [1 - \pi(x_L, x_R)](-|x_R|),$$

whereas R solves

$$\max_{x_R} \pi(x_L, x_R)(-|x_L - 1|) + [1 - \pi(x_L, x_R)](-|x_R - 1|).$$

There is a Nash equilibrium of this game in which each party chooses x_m. Proving this is easy: if either party deviates to some other position, then that party loses with certainty rather than winning with probability one-half. Because losing to a party that has adopted x_m gives the same expected utility as winning with probability one-half when each party has adopted x_m, there is no profitable deviation.

Moreover, this is the unique Nash equilibrium, though showing that involves a few more steps. The basic logic can be seen by assuming that the parties have chosen positions $0 < x_L < x_m < x_R < 1$, with $|x_L - x_m| = |x_m - x_R|$. Because the median voter is indifferent between

---

[3] In general, the literature assumes that parties are either all office-seeking or all policy-seeking. An exception is Callander (2008a), who considers heterogeneous motivations.

the two parties, each party wins with probability one-half. Thus, for example, L has expected utility $-\frac{1}{2}(x_L + x_R) = -x_m$. However, L can
profitably deviate by moving some infinitesimal ϵ to the right, increasing its probability of winning from one-half to one, and thus receiving
expected utility $-(x_L + \epsilon) > -x_m$. Intuitively, divergence is not a Nash
equilibrium, as there is always an incentive to move a bit closer to the
center and thus win for sure. As we will see in the next chapter, this
incentive is softened when policy preferences map stochastically onto
voting decisions, as then a small move toward the center results in only
a small increase in the probability of winning.

1.3 Multiparty Competition

Our discussion so far has been limited to models of two-party competition. Such models were the focus of most early formal work on electoral
competition, perhaps due to the predominance of two-party competition
in the United States. However, in many political environments, more
than two parties compete for the vote. Following the literature, we refer
to this as multiparty competition, though a literal interpretation of this
term would also include two-party competition.

As a point of departure, consider the Hotelling-Downs model with
one-dimensional policy competition, but now assume that the election
is contested by three parties, $P = A, B, C$, each of which maximizes its
probability of winning. We continue to assume that voters vote mechanically for the party they most prefer, though this assumption is far less
innocuous in a multiparty setting. We take up the question of strategic
voting later this chapter. Further, we adapt the model of voter behavior
from that considered earlier by assuming that if voters are indifferent
among two or more parties, then they choose a party from among those
they most prefer using an equal-probability rule (e.g., they flip a fair
coin if they are indifferent between two parties) rather than abstaining.

One might expect that each party would adopt the median ideal point,
as with two-party competition. However, this is not a Nash equilibrium:
any party could profitably deviate by adopting a position some arbitrarily small distance from x_m and thus receiving almost half the vote,
leaving its two competitors to divide the remaining half. As this is a
plurality-rule election, any party that deviated in this way would win
with certainty.

So is there a Nash equilibrium of this game? Yes, for certain distributions of voter preferences. Assume, for example, that voters have Euclidean preferences with ideal points distributed uniformly on $[0, 1]$. Then the following configuration of positions is a Nash equilibrium:

$$x_A = x_B = \frac{1}{3},$$
$$x_C = \frac{2}{3}.$$

To see this, note that in equilibrium party C receives one-half of the vote and wins with certainty, so that party C has no incentive to deviate. Consider possible deviations by party A; the same arguments apply to party B:

- Adopting any $x_A < \frac{1}{3}$ leaves party C with one-half of the vote while dividing the other half between parties A and B, so that party C continues to win with certainty.
- Adopting some $x_A \in \left(\frac{1}{3}, \frac{2}{3}\right)$ provides one-sixth of the vote and divides the remaining five-sixths between parties B and C. Thus either party B or C wins with certainty or, if $x_A = \frac{1}{2}$, parties B and C each win with probability one-half.
- Adopting $x_A = \frac{2}{3}$ divides one-half of the vote between parties A and C, so that party B wins with certainty.
- Adopting $x_A > \frac{2}{3}$ provides party B with one-half of the vote while dividing the other half between parties A and C, so that party B wins with certainty.

The equilibrium in this example is nonetheless unattractive as an empirical prediction. If both parties A and B expect to lose, then we may ask why they entered the race to begin with. The answer may be that the fixed cost of competing in this particular electoral arena was previously sunk. In that case, parties may choose to contest elections even when they expect to lose so that they survive to contest future elections, or so that they may contest elections in other arenas. We turn to the question of endogenous entry in elections later in this chapter.

Further, we may ask why party C is content merely to win, when moving toward $x = \frac{1}{3}$ would increase party C's vote share. Clearly, this configuration of positions is not a Nash equilibrium when parties maximize vote share, which seems to be the more natural assumption in a proportional-representation setting. Moreover, there is no Nash equilibrium of this game, even in the special environment of the previous example. To see this, consider the following list of conditions, which Cox

(1987b) establishes are necessary for any Nash equilibrium when parties maximize vote share:[4]

(i) No more than two parties occupy any one position.

(ii) Each extremist position (meaning a position leftmost or rightmost among those occupied by the parties, not leftmost or rightmost among all positions that could be occupied) is occupied by exactly two parties.

(iii) If two parties occupy the same position x, then the share of voters to the left of x who most prefer x among all positions that have been adopted is equal to the share of voters to the right of x who most prefer x among all positions that have been adopted.

With three parties, Condition (ii) cannot be satisfied.

What is the appropriate objective for office-seeking parties in multiparty competition? In two-party competition maximizing (expected) vote share and maximizing the probability of winning are often equivalent. However, as the example just given suggests, this is not generally the case in multiparty competition. Choosing the appropriate objective therefore boils down to whether one believes that a larger vote share translates into additional post-election benefits. In most environments, it seems that it must. In parliamentary systems, for example, a large vote share may increase the probability that a party controls the policy agenda, a consideration we take up when examining models of legislative bargaining in Chapter 6. For the remainder of this section we therefore assume that parties maximize vote share rather than their probability of winning.

The conditions just listed ensure that there is no equilibrium in three-party competition when parties maximize vote share. What about four-party competition? For certain distributions of voter preferences, such an equilibrium may exist, with parties adopting divergent positions. Assume, for example, that citizens have Euclidean preferences and ideal points distributed uniformly on $[0, 1]$. Then the following configuration of positions is a Nash equilibrium of the Hotelling-Downs model with four-party competition:

---

[4] These conditions hold not only when parties maximize vote share, but also when they maximize the margin of victory relative to the second-place finisher and when they maximize their "total" margin of victory relative to all other parties.

$$x_A = x_B = \frac{1}{4},$$

$$x_C = x_D = \frac{3}{4}.$$

To see this, note that in equilibrium every party receives one-fourth of the vote. Without loss of generality, focus on possible deviations by party A. Adopting any $x_A < \frac{1}{4}$ or $x_A > \frac{3}{4}$ provides less than one-fourth of the vote; adopting any $x_A \in \left(\frac{1}{4}, \frac{3}{4}\right)$ gives exactly one-fourth of the vote; and adopting $x_A = \frac{3}{4}$ provides one-sixth of the vote. Thus, party A has no incentive to deviate.

An equilibrium exists in this example because the parties are spaced in such a way that no party can increase its vote share by adopting a position arbitrarily close to that of another party. However, equilibrium existence is sensitive to the distribution of voters' ideal points, as demonstrated by another example. Assume that citizens have Euclidean preferences and ideal points x_i distributed on $[0, 1]$ according to a triangular distribution with distribution function $F(x_i) = 2x_i - x_i^2$. The first two conditions given earlier imply that the parties must be paired, with two parties occupying one position x_L and the other two parties occupying some other position $x_R > x_L$. Let $\hat{x} = \frac{x_L + x_R}{2}$ be the ideal point of voters who are indifferent between the positions adopted by the four parties. Then the third condition implies that $F(x_L) = F(\hat{x}) - F(x_L)$, and $F(x_R) - F(\hat{x}) = 1 - F(x_R)$.

Figure 1.1 shows the necessary relationships among different subpopulations: the fraction of voters to the left of x_L (which we denote by a) must equal that between x_L and $\hat{x}$ (which we denote by b), and the fraction of voters between $\hat{x}$ and x_R (which we denote by c) must equal that between x_R and 1 (which we denote by d). Further, for this to be an equilibrium, it must be the case that neither of the two parties at x_R can profitably deviate by adopting a position some arbitrarily small distance ϵ to the left of x_L, gaining nearly all the voters with ideal points between 0 and x_L (i.e., gaining a) while losing $\frac{1}{2}(c + d) = c$, and neither party at x_L can profitably deviate by adopting a position some ϵ just to the left of x_R, gaining c but losing a. Thus, it must be true that $a = c$. Together, these conditions imply $a = b = c = d$, so that one-quarter of the voters fall into each group. But this is not possible with the given distribution, given that $\hat{x} - x_L = x_R - \hat{x}$. Thus, there is no Nash equilibrium.

As in deterministic models of two-party *multidimensional* competition, an equilibrium does not exist in this example because parties

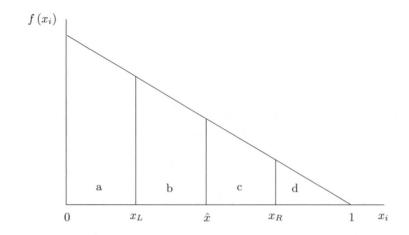

Figure 1.1. Equilibrium requires $a = b$, $c = d$, and $\hat{x} = \frac{x_L + x_R}{2}$.

are able to "steal" large blocks of voters by adopting a position only marginally different from that of some other party. This extreme sensitivity to party positions rests critically on the assumption that voters care only about policy. The following chapter shows how this assumption may be relaxed in a probabilistic model of electoral competition.

1.4 Entry

Thus far, we have treated the number of parties on the ballot as exogenous. Various factors, however, may act to restrict the number of parties that participate in an election. Citizens may vote strategically, choosing only among those parties they believe have a realistic chance of winning. And parties with no chance of winning may choose not to compete. Duverger (1954) famously argued that these considerations explain the predominance of two-party systems in electoral environments characterized by single-member districts and plurality-rule elections, an observation known today as **Duverger's Law** (Riker, 1982).

Early formal treatment of these issues tended to treat strategic entry and strategic voting as distinct phenomena. Palfrey (1984), for example, adapted the Hotelling-Downs model to incorporate entry by a third party after platform choice by two "dominant" parties, whereas work on strategic voting examined how voters could "make votes count"

(Cox, 1997), given that certain parties contested the election.[5] As Shepsle (1991) argues, however, these phenomena are best studied jointly, as the knife-edge conditions that must hold in order for strategic voters to divide their votes among more than two parties may emerge endogenously when parties decide whether to enter the race.

In this section, we therefore consider two models of endogenous entry, contrasting strategic and sincere voting behavior in each. The first model is a straightforward extension of the Hotelling-Downs model to allow for endogenous entry and strategic voting. The second is a sharper departure from the models considered earlier, as it assumes a single set of "citizens" who are both voters and potential candidates for office, where any candidate is expected to implement the policy she most prefers if elected. We begin with a brief discussion of strategic voting.

1.4.1 Strategic Voting

Strategic voting is the idea that voters are strategic players who condition their strategies on beliefs about others' strategies. Strategic voting is typically contrasted with **sincere voting**, where voters mechanically vote for the party whose position they most prefer, whatever they expect others to do. Colloquially, the term "strategic voting" is often used to refer to *outcomes* in which voters misrepresent their preferences by voting for a party other than the one they most prefer, but this is incorrect usage: in equilibrium, strategic voters may vote for their most-preferred party, so long as that is optimal given what they expect other voters to do.

Strategic voting is an attractive concept because it treats the voter like any other actor in a model. Depending on the context, however, one might be skeptical about drawing predictions from the *equilibria* of voting games with strategic voters, as any such equilibrium requires coordination among a typically large number of players. Such coordination may be facilitated in mature democracies by well-established party systems, reasonably accurate and well-publicized pre-election polling, and other mechanisms that serve to coordinate expectations (Fey, 1997). In other institutional environments, coordination seems less likely.[6]

Models with strategic voting typically assume that the population of

---

[5] Seminal contributions to the literature on strategic voting include Cox (1987a), Austen-Smith and Banks (1988), and Palfrey (1989).

[6] Voters may also differ in their inclination or capacity to vote strategically. Callander (2005) presents a model in which only some voters are strategic.

voters is finite: this ensures that an individual's vote may be pivotal, providing an incentive to condition one's vote on what other voters are expected to do.[7] In contrast, we may assume a continuum of voters when voting is sincere; at times this assumption is convenient.

In two-party elections, sincere and strategic voting are equivalent so long as we assume that strategic voters play **weakly undominated voting strategies**. To see this, note that voting for the party whose position one prefers less can never be better in a two-party election (at best, a voter is indifferent between voting for the less-preferred party and voting for the other if—given expectations about how others will vote—she does not expect her vote to affect the election outcome), and it may be worse (if the voter expects her vote to be pivotal). Absent this assumption, implausible equilibria are possible. As an example, if we do not rule out weakly undominated voting strategies, then it is an equilibrium for all voters to vote for the same party. Clearly, no individual's vote is pivotal in this equilibrium, and so each voter is indifferent between voting for one party and voting for the other.

1.4.2 Entry with Position-taking Candidates

We begin our analysis of strategic entry by considering a model of electoral competition by Feddersen, Sened, and Wright (1990). The Feddersen-Sened-Wright model is precisely the Hotelling-Downs model of Section 1.1, with the following exceptions.

First, there are N potential candidates who may compete in the election, where N is arbitrarily large. (In what follows, we use the term "candidate" rather than "party" both to emphasize the ephemeral nature of a candidacy and to foreshadow our discussion of citizen-candidates.) Each potential candidate chooses whether to participate in the campaign and, if so, what position to adopt. Formally, a strategy for potential candidate P is $x_P \in \Re \cup \{Stay\ out\}$. Each candidate bears a cost $\delta > 0$ if she enters the race and receives a payoff of $v > \delta$ if she wins the election.

Second, the set of voters is finite, where each voter has preferences over policy represented by a strictly concave utility function. The assumption of concave utility implies that voters are **risk-averse**. Thus, for example, any voter would prefer a candidate who adopted some position x to a lottery over two candidates who adopted $x - \Delta$ and $x + \Delta$, respec-

---

[7] The strategic model of turnout buying presented in Section 2.5 assumes a continuum of voters, but a voter need not be pivotal to prefer to cast a vote in that setting.

tively. Voters behave strategically, voting for precisely one candidate to maximize their expected utility, given other voters' expected strategies. For reasons just discussed, we restrict attention to weakly undominated voting strategies. If two or more candidates tie for first place, then the election winner is chosen by a fair lottery over the candidates with the most votes.

In analyzing the model, we restrict attention to pure-strategy equilibria. The assumption that candidates are office-seeking and that entry is costly implies that all candidates who enter receive the same number of votes; otherwise, the losing candidate(s) would deviate by staying out. Moreover, the cost of running and the benefit of holding office place an upper bound on the number of candidates possible in equilibrium. To see this, let M be the equilibrium number of candidates. Then for it to be a best response for these candidates to enter, $\frac{v}{M} - \delta$, which is the expected utility in equilibrium for those candidates, must be greater than zero, the expected utility from staying out. Simplifying, we see that the equilibrium number of candidates $M \leq \frac{v}{\delta}$. Intuitively, when the benefit from holding office is small and the cost of running is large, then few candidates enter the race.

Another way of thinking about entry is that the cost of running borne by all candidates ($M\delta$) offsets the benefit of holding office for the election winner. An election is a type of **tournament**, where the rent earned by the tournament winner draws entrants until the rent is dissipated. That said, the assumption that the set of voters is finite implies that the number of voters N must be divisible by the equilibrium number of candidates M, which may lead to incomplete dissipation of rents. If, for example, there are 200 voters and $3 \leq \frac{v}{\delta} < 4$, then only two candidates are possible in equilibrium, even though the benefit from holding office is large enough to support three candidates. This **integer constraint** is a nuisance of deterministic models with a finite number of voters and should probably not be overinterpreted. In the next chapter we show how the introduction of uncertainty about whether voters will actually cast their ballots can solve this "problem."

An additional insight of the Feddersen-Sened-Wright model is that all voters cast their ballots in equilibrium for a candidate whose position they most prefer. Given that each candidate receives the same number of votes, all voters are pivotal in equilibrium. This implies that any voter must vote for one of her most-preferred candidates, as otherwise she could tip the election to such a candidate by changing her vote. Thus, the Feddersen-Sened-Wright model illustrates that strategic voting need not result in preference misrepresentation.

A surprising conclusion of the model is that there exist equilibria in which all candidates adopt the median position. Such equilibria are supported by the following voting strategies off the equilibrium path: if any potential candidate—either one already at x_m or one who has chosen to stay out—deviates to a position other than x_m, then all voters with ideal points equal to or to the other side of x_m vote for one of the candidates who remains at x_m. Thus, voters coordinate on one of their preferred candidates if faced with an entrant who is supported by a plurality but not a majority of the electorate.

Moreover, there are no equilibria in which any position other than x_m is adopted. To gain insight into why only convergent equilibria exist, consider the following two examples:

(i) Suppose that there are three voters with ideal points 0, $\frac{1}{2}$, and 1, respectively, and that three candidates have entered at these ideal points. Given that voters in equilibrium vote for their most-preferred candidate, each candidate wins with probability one-third, resulting in an expected policy outcome of $\frac{1}{2}$. But then either the voter with ideal point 0 or the one with ideal point 1 could deviate to voting for the candidate at $\frac{1}{2}$, resulting in that candidate's election with certainty. Given that voters are risk-averse, this is a profitable deviation.

(ii) Suppose that voters have ideal points uniformly distributed (i.e., evenly spaced) on the interval $[0,1]$, where the number of voters is divisible by four, and suppose that two candidates have entered at $\frac{1}{4}$ and two at $\frac{3}{4}$. In Section 1.3 we showed that this configuration of positions was a Nash equilibrium of the Hotelling-Downs model with four candidates and sincere voting. For this to be an equilibrium with strategic voting, voters must divide equally between the four candidates, where each voter votes for one of the candidates she most prefers. But then the voter with ideal point equal to 0 could profitably deviate by voting for the other candidate at $\frac{1}{4}$, resulting in that candidate's election with certainty.

The Feddersen-Sened-Wright model assumes strategic voting. It is useful to compare the equilibrium outcome to the case where voting is sincere. For simplicity, assume a continuum of voters so that we do not need to worry about the integer constraint. If we assume that voters choose a candidate from among those they most prefer using an equal-probability rule, as in Section 1.3, then there is no convergent equilibrium with more than two candidates: any candidate who entered could profitably deviate by adopting a position arbitrarily close to that of the other candidates (and in the direction of x_m, if x_m was not the original position). We could, of course, support a convergent equilibrium at x_m by assuming that voters coordinate on one of the candidates that remains at x_m in the event of a deviation, but this is ad hoc. In contrast, coordination off the equilibrium path is a mutual best response when voting is strategic.

Indeed, for certain parameter values, a pure-strategy Nash equilibrium may fail to exist when voting is sincere.[8] To see this, assume $3 \leq \frac{v}{\delta} < 4$, which implies that the benefit of holding office is sufficiently large to support three but not four candidates. Clearly, there is no equilibrium with one candidate, as any other potential candidate could profitably deviate by adopting the same position and winning with probability one-half, gaining $\frac{v}{2} - \delta > 0$. Further, there is no equilibrium with two candidates. By the logic of the Hotelling-Downs model, any such equilibrium would require that both candidates locate at x_m. But then a third potential candidate could profitably deviate by entering and adopting a position arbitrarily close to x_m. Finally, there is no equilibrium with three candidates. In any such equilibrium, the candidates each receive one-third of the vote, requiring either that a) all candidates locate at the same position, or b) at least one candidate occupy a position alone to the left or right of the position(s) adopted by the other two candidates. We dispensed with (a) in the previous paragraph. To see that (b) is not a mutual best response, observe that the loner candidate could increase her vote share, and thus win with certainty, by moving to a position arbitrarily close to that occupied by the nearest candidate(s).

Osborne (1993) further demonstrates that a Nash equilibrium with four or more candidates "almost never" exists, that is, only for knife-edge distributions of voter preferences. Thus, endogenizing the entry decision is not sufficient to guarantee equilibrium existence in models with three or more potential candidates. As the Feddersen-Sened-Wright model demonstrates, however, endogenous entry and strategic voting together generate predictions similar in spirit to the basic Hotelling-Downs model.

---

[8] The logic of the proof here follows Osborne (2004), Exercise 74.1. Osborne (1993) shows that this result can be derived from a more general proposition that establishes conditions similar to those provided by Cox (1987b) for the game in which entry is fixed, as discussed earlier.

1.4.3 Citizen-candidates

Up to now, we have assumed that political parties or candidates are able to make binding campaign promises, regardless of whether they have office-seeking or policy-seeking preferences. The models of entry we consider here take a different tack, assuming that candidates have policy-seeking preferences and are unable to make binding campaign promises. In these models, there is no sharp distinction between candidates and voters. Rather, there is a single set of "citizens," who are both potential candidates for office and voters. The preferences of citizens are common knowledge, so that voters are able to infer the policy that would be implemented after the election by any candidate in the race.

Such **citizen-candidate** models were first proposed by Osborne and Slivinski (1996) and Besley and Coate (1997). The two papers differ primarily in what they assume about voter behavior: Osborne and Slivinski assume sincere voting, whereas Besley and Coate assume strategic voting. As we will see, different equilibrium entry decisions are possible depending on whether voters behave sincerely or strategically.

We adopt the following general setup. There is a population of citizens who play two roles: they may enter the election campaign as candidates, and they vote over those candidates who have entered. For concreteness, assume that the policy space is the real number line $\Re$ and assume that any citizen i receives payoff $-|x - x_i|$ if policy $x \in \Re$ is implemented by the election winner. As discussed earlier, these preferences are common knowledge. Depending on the context, the population of voters may be either a continuum or finite. In either case, assume that there is a unique median ideal point x_m.

As in Section 1.4.2, we assume a common cost $\delta > 0$ of participating in the election. We further assume that citizens may value office for its own sake (i.e., in addition to any policy benefits), where $v \geq 0$ denotes the common exogenous payoff from holding office.

The timing of events is as follows:

(i) Entry. Each citizen chooses between entering and staying out of the race.

(ii) Voting. Each citizen (even if a candidate) votes for one of the candidates or abstains. The winner is decided by plurality rule, with ties settled by a fair lottery.

(iii) Policy choice. The winning candidate chooses a policy $x \in \Re$. In the event that no candidate has entered the race, a status quo policy $\bar{x} \in \Re$ is implemented.

Given the absence of any commitment technology, the choice in (iii) is degenerate: the winning candidate implements her most-preferred policy. Voting in (ii) may be either sincere or strategic; we will be explicit about which we assume. When voting is strategic, we rule out certain implausible voting profiles by assuming that citizens play only weakly undominated voting strategies. As already discussed, this implies that citizens vote for their most-preferred candidate in two-candidate elections.

We begin by deriving the condition for existence of a "median-voter" equilibrium in which a citizen with ideal point x_m enters the race alone. To fix ideas, assume a continuum of citizens who vote sincerely, and assume that citizens abstain if indifferent among all candidates who have entered. In checking that this is an equilibrium, we must verify that the citizen-candidate indeed prefers to enter, given that nobody else does, and that nobody else wants to enter, given that only a median citizen has entered. The first of these two conditions holds when

$$-|x_m - x_m| + v - \delta \geq -|\bar{x} - x_m|.$$

The left-hand side of this inequality is the payoff in equilibrium: the citizen implements her most-preferred policy and receives the exogenous payoff from holding office v, but she bears the cost of entry δ. The right-hand side is the payoff from not entering, given that no other citizen has: there is no cost of entry, but the citizen forfeits the payoff v and must accept the status quo policy $\bar{x}$. Simplifying gives

$$\delta \leq |\bar{x} - x_m| + v. \tag{1.1}$$

Thus, we see that a median individual is more likely to enter the race, given that nobody else has, when the cost of entry δ is low, the status quo policy is far from the median ideal point, and the exogenous payoff from winning v is large.

To verify that no other citizen would want to deviate by entering, given that only a median individual has entered, we consider three sets of citizens:

(i) Citizens with $x_i < x_m$. It is not profitable for any such citizen to deviate by entering, as she would lose the election to the median individual, thus suffering the same policy loss while incurring the entry cost δ.

(ii) Citizens with $x_i > x_m$. By the same argument, it is not not profitable for any such citizen to deviate by entering.

(iii) Citizens with $x_i = x_m$. Given that another median citizen has entered, any citizen with ideal point x_m who deviated by entering would win with probability one-half. The condition for any such citizen not to enter, given that another median citizen has, is therefore

$$- |x_m - x_m| \geq \frac{1}{2} \left(- |x_m - x_m| + v \right) + \frac{1}{2} \left(- |x_m - x_m| \right) - \delta,$$

or

$$\delta \geq \frac{v}{2}. \tag{1.2}$$

Entering does not change the expected policy payoff, but it does provide a chance to win the exogenous payoff from holding office v.

Comparing Conditions 1.1 and 1.2, the condition for existence of an equilibrium where only a median individual enters can be summarized as

$$\frac{v}{2} \leq \delta \leq |\bar{x} - x_m| + v.$$

The cost of entry must be high enough to deter entry by a second candidate, but low enough for the one candidate to actually want to enter. With respect to the exogenous payoff from holding office v:

(i) For v sufficiently high, there is no δ that satisfies the condition, as a second median individual enters the race to try to win the exogenous rent from holding office.

(ii) When there is no independent benefit from holding office, that is, when $v = 0$, then for δ sufficiently low this one-candidate equilibrium exists so long as $x_m \neq \bar{x}$.

Thus, as in various models already considered, for certain parameter values there is an equilibrium in which political competition results in adoption of the median ideal point. The equilibrium here is not the only possible one-candidate equilibrium, however. Exercise 1.4 derives the set of all one-candidate equilibria, given v, δ, x_m, and $\bar{x}$.

For certain regions of the parameter space, there also exist equilibria with two candidates, even when there are no office-seeking benefits. To show this, we restrict attention to the case where $v = 0$.

Observe first that in any two-candidate equilibrium, the candidates must tie. Otherwise, the losing candidate would deviate by not entering, receiving the same policy payoff (as the other candidate wins regardless of whether the losing candidate stays in the race) while saving the cost of entry δ. In addition, it must be the case that the two candidates have different ideal points. Otherwise, given that $v = 0$, either of the two candidates would prefer to withdraw, receiving the same policy payoff while saving the cost of entry δ.

These considerations imply that in any two-candidate equilibrium, the two candidates must have ideal points equidistant from and on opposite sides of the median ideal point x_m: the absence of office-seeking benefits implies divergence. (In Section 2.4, we show that we can relax the requirement of a "just-so" configuration of ideal points by assuming that citizens fail to vote with some small probability.) Let Δ denote the distance in a given equilibrium between the candidates' ideal points and the median ideal point, and denote the ideal points of the two candidates by x_L and x_R, respectively, where $x_L < x_R$. Thus, $x_L = x_m - \Delta$ and $x_R = x_m + \Delta$. In what follows, we fix Δ and derive the conditions for no citizen to have an incentive to deviate from her equilibrium strategy. These conditions place bounds on Δ, which measures divergence between the two candidates, as a function of parameters of the model.

We check first that no citizen has an incentive to deviate from her equilibrium strategy in the entry stage of the game. Without loss of generality, focus on L, that is, the candidate who has entered to the left. In equilibrium, L ties with R, so that x_L and x_R are each implemented with probability one-half. In contrast, if L deviated by staying out of the race, x_R would be implemented with certainty. Thus, L has no incentive to deviate from her equilibrium strategy if

$$\frac{1}{2}\left(-|x_L - x_L|\right) + \frac{1}{2}\left(-|x_R - x_L|\right) - \delta \geq -|x_R - x_L|.$$

Recalling that $x_R - x_L = 2\Delta$, this can be simplified to $\delta \leq \Delta$. Thus, the candidates must be sufficiently far apart, relative to the cost of entry, for it to be worthwhile to stay in the race.

To see that no other citizen has an incentive to enter, we must be more specific about whether citizens vote sincerely or strategically, as with more than two candidates strategic voting may imply that a citizen votes for one of her less-preferred candidates. We consider each case in turn.

Sincere Voting. In principle, citizens of one of three types might have an incentive to deviate by entering against L and R: those with ideal points $x_i \leq x_L$, those with $x_i \geq x_R$, and those with x_i such that $x_L < x_i < x_R$. However, neither of the first two types would choose to enter, as doing so would take votes away from the candidate they most prefer, resulting in a victory for their less-preferred candidate. In contrast, a citizen with ideal point between x_L and x_R might be tempted to enter if x_L and x_R were far enough apart that a plurality of voters would prefer the new candidate. Thus, x_L and x_R must be sufficiently close to each other to deter entry. Together with the condition that $\delta \leq \Delta$, this implies that any two-candidate equilibrium must satisfy a "Goldilocks" condition, with the candidates neither too close to each other nor too far apart.

Strategic Voting. In subgames off the equilibrium path with three candidates, there may be configurations of candidates such that it is an equilibrium for some citizens to vote for a candidate whose ideal point they do not most prefer. Consider, for example, an environment where a large, odd number of citizens have distinct ideal points uniformly distributed on the unit interval, and assume that three candidates with ideal points $\left(0, \frac{1}{2}, 1\right)$ have entered. It is a voting equilibrium in this example for any citizen i with ideal point $x_i < \frac{1}{2}$ to vote for the candidate on the left, for any citizen i with ideal point $x_i > \frac{1}{2}$ to vote for the candidate on the right, and for the citizen with ideal point $x_i = \frac{1}{2}$ to vote for herself. In this equilibrium, the two "extremist" candidates each win with probability one-half. No voter with $x_i \neq \frac{1}{2}$ wants to change her vote, even if she prefers some other candidate, as that would swing the election to the extremist candidate she less prefers. Anticipating this outcome, the citizen with ideal point $\frac{1}{2}$ would not enter.

Thus, in contrast to the case of sincere voting, extremist candidates—where x_L and x_R are far apart—are possible with strategic voting. Even though a plurality may prefer a hypothetical centrist candidate, a coordination failure among centrist voters prevents that individual from achieving a plurality should she enter. This may be especially likely if the potential centrist candidate does not have the backing of a political party or other institutional mechanism that could help centrist voters overcome their coordination problem.

Equilibria with three or more candidates are also possible for certain regions of the parameter space. Moreover, as Exercise 1.5 demonstrates, such equilibria are possible even with sincere voting. Essentially, the absence of commitment power gives candidates a limited repertoire of responses to other candidates' expected actions, thus ruling out the type of vote-stealing deviations used to demonstrate the nonexistence of three-candidate equilibria with sincere voting in Section 1.4.2.

Exercises

1.1 Consider three-party competition in an election governed by a
runoff rule: if no party receives a majority of votes in the first
round of voting, then there is a second (runoff) round of voting. In
the second round, voters choose among the top two vote-getters in
the first round. If all three parties receive the same vote total in the
first round, then two parties are chosen using an equal-probability
rule to compete in the second round (so that the probability that
any party enters the second round equals two-thirds). If two parties tie for second in the first round, then one of the tying parties is
chosen by a fair coin toss to compete in the second round. Assume
that parties cannot change their positions between the first and
second rounds. Voters have Euclidean preferences over policies on
the real number line, with ideal points distributed such that there
is a unique median ideal point x_m. Parties maximize their probability of winning.

Argue that it is a Nash equilibrium for all three parties to choose
the median position x_m. Explain why such an equilibrium exists
under the runoff rule but not plurality rule.

1.2 Consider the following generalization of the Hotelling-Downs and
Wittman models, where parties are both office-seeking and policy-
seeking. The environment is identical to that presented in Section
1.2, with the following exception: each party $P = L, R$ receives an
exogenous benefit $v > 0$ from election. Thus, party L solves

$$\max_{x_L} \pi(x_L, x_R)(-|x_L| + v) + [1 - \pi(x_L, x_R)](-|x_R|),$$

whereas party R solves

$$\max_{x_R} \pi(x_L, x_R)(-|x_L - 1|) + [1 - \pi(x_L, x_R)](-|x_R - 1| + v).$$

Complete the following steps to show that $(x_L, x_R) = (x_m, x_m)$
is the unique Nash equilibrium of this game.

(a) Existence: Show that $(x_L, x_R) = (x_m, x_m)$ is a Nash equilibrium of this game.

(b) Uniqueness: Show that no other (x_L, x_R) is a Nash equilibrium
of this game by examining the following three mutually exclusive and exhaustive cases, showing that for each case some
party has an incentive to deviate:

(1) One of the parties wins with certainty. (Note that this implies that at least one party P has adopted some $x_P \neq x_m$.)

(2) Parties L and R each win with probability one-half, with $x_L = x_R \neq x_m$.

(3) Parties L and R each win with probability one-half, with x_L and x_R some distance Δ on either side of x_m.

1.3   Consider the Wittman model described in Section 1.2, but now assume that $x_m > 1$, so that the parties' ideal points lie on the same side of the median ideal point. Show that $(x_L, x_R) = (1, 1)$ is a Nash equilibrium. Is this the unique Nash equilibrium?

1.4   Consider the following special case of the citizen-candidate model presented in Section 1.4.3. Citizens vote sincerely, with ideal points distributed continuously on some interval of the real number line and unique median ideal point $x_m = \frac{1}{2}$. Assume that the cost of entry $\delta = \frac{1}{4}$ and that the exogenous payoff from winning $v = 0$. Let the default policy $\bar{x} = 0$.

Derive the set of one-candidate equilibria of this game as follows:

(a) Find the set of citizens whose ideal points are such that, if any such citizen enters alone, all other citizens prefer not to enter.

(b) Check that all citizens in this set indeed prefer to enter, given that no other citizen has.

1.5   Consider the following special case of the citizen-candidate model presented in Section 1.4.3. Citizens vote sincerely, with ideal points distributed uniformly on the interval $[0, 1]$. Demonstrate as follows that there exists an equilibrium with three candidates with ideal points $\left(\frac{1}{6}, \frac{1}{2}, \frac{5}{6}\right)$ if $v \geq 3\delta$.

(a) Show that no candidate prefers to deviate by staying out of the race, given the profile of other citizens' strategies:

(1) Show that the two candidates with "extreme" ideal points prefer to remain in the race.

(2) Show that the candidate with ideal point $\frac{1}{2}$ prefers to remain in the race.

(b) Show that no other citizen prefers to deviate by entering the race, given the profile of other citizens' strategies:

(1) Show that no citizen i with ideal point $x_i \leq \frac{1}{6}$ (similarly, $x_i \geq \frac{5}{6}$) prefers to deviate by entering the race.

(2) Show that no citizen i with ideal point $\frac{1}{6} < x_i < \frac{1}{2}$ (similarly, $\frac{1}{2} < x_i < \frac{5}{6}$) prefers to deviate by entering the race.

(3) Show that no citizen i with ideal point $x_i = \frac{1}{2}$ prefers to deviate by entering the race.

1.6 Consider the following special case of the citizen-candidate model presented in Section 1.4.3. There is a large, finite set of citizens who vote strategically and play weakly undominated voting strategies. Further, for simplicity, restrict attention to equilibria in which citizens abstain from voting if all candidates have the same ideal point. Two-thirds of all citizens have ideal point 0; the remaining one-third have ideal point 1. The status quo policy $\bar{x} = 1$, and the exogenous payoff from holding office $v \geq 0$.

(a) How, if at all, does the set of one-candidate equilibria of this model differ from that of the otherwise identical model with sincere voting? (You need not actually solve for the equilibria of either model to answer this question.)

(b) Derive the condition for existence of a two-candidate equilibrium in which two citizens with ideal point 0 have entered, given the following outcome off the equilibrium path: if two citizens with ideal point 0 and one citizen with ideal point 1 have entered, then one of the candidates with ideal point 0 wins with certainty.

(c) Describe voting strategies such that the outcome off the equilibrium path in part (b) is a Nash equilibrium of the analogous subgame.

1.7 This problem follows Gehlbach, Sonin, and Zhuravskaya (2010) in modeling entry under alternative institutions. Assume a large but finite number of potential candidates and a continuum of voters. Each potential candidate decides whether to enter the campaign or not, bearing a cost $\delta > 0$ if she does so. Following this decision, any candidate announces a position $x \in \{\hat{x}, \bar{x}\}$, where all voters strictly prefer $\hat{x}$ to $\bar{x}$. Voters then cast their ballots for the candidate whose expected policy choice (which may or may not be the policy previously announced by the candidate) they most prefer, choosing according to an equal-probability rule if indifferent. Voting is by plurality rule. Finally, the election winner implements a policy $x' \in \{\hat{x}, \bar{x}\}$, receiving a payoff $R > 0$ if $x' = \bar{x}$. In addition to this endogenous rent, the election winner receives a payoff $v > 0$

regardless of the policy x' chosen. We assume that $\delta < \frac{v}{2}$, which implies that there are at least two candidates in equilibrium.

We model differences in institutions as follows. Under strong democratic institutions, the election winner is constrained to implement the policy she announced during the campaign. In contrast, under weak democratic institutions, the election winner may choose any $x' \in \{\hat{x}, \bar{x}\}$, regardless of the policy announced during the campaign.

Consider first equilibrium behavior under strong democratic institutions.

(a) What policy is implemented in equilibrium by any election winner?

(b) Denote by M the equilibrium number of candidates. Derive the condition such that any candidate who has entered prefers not to deviate by not entering.

(c) Derive the condition such that any potential candidate who has not entered prefers not to deviate by entering.

(d) Use your solution to the previous two parts of the problem to derive a condition for the equilibrium number of candidates M, given parameters of the model.

Now consider equilibrium behavior under weak democratic institutions.

(e) What policy is implemented in equilibrium by any election winner?

(f) Denote by M the equilibrium number of candidates. Derive the condition such that any candidate who has entered prefers not to deviate by not entering.

(g) Derive the condition such that any potential candidate who has not entered prefers not to deviate by entering.

(h) Use your solution to the previous two parts of the problem to derive a condition for the number of candidates in equilibrium, given parameters of the model.

How does candidate entry compare under strong and weak democratic institutions?

2

Electoral Competition under Uncertainty

In this chapter we examine electoral competition under various forms of uncertainty. The models here depart from those in the previous chapter in assuming that voters behave stochastically—in how they cast their vote, or even in whether they vote at all. As we will see, the incorporation of stochastic voting behavior can resolve many of the issues associated with the models in the previous chapter, including nonexistence of equilibrium and full convergence of campaign platforms in equilibrium.

In considering the models here, a useful distinction can be drawn between **individual uncertainty** and **aggregate uncertainty**. For models with individual uncertainty only, stochastic behavior at the level of individual voters averages out in large polities. In contrast, with aggregate uncertainty, parties are uncertain about the general electoral environment at the time key decisions are made.

We begin by considering extensions of the Hotelling-Downs and Wittman models to incorporate individual and aggregate uncertainty, and we show how multiparty competition can be modeled in a random-utility framework. We then explore entry when the decision to vote is uncertain. Finally, we ask why citizens choose to vote at all.

2.1 Multidimensional Policy Conflict

In the last chapter we showed that multidimensional policy choice arises naturally in redistributive environments. As is well known from the theory of social choice, any division of a "pie" among a group of individuals can be beaten in a pairwise vote by some other division. In the context of electoral competition, this implies that there is no Nash equilibrium

27

of the Hotelling-Downs model when policy is redistributive and voting is deterministic.

Lindbeck and Weibull (1987) and Dixit and Londregan (1996) provide a solution to this nonexistence problem that assumes that voter preferences over redistributive transfers map stochastically onto their vote for one of the two parties, given unobserved **affinities** for one party over the other. Such affinities may reflect voter socialization or the inability of policy-seeking parties to make binding campaign promises. Persson and Tabellini (2000) subsequently showed how such "probabilistic" models could be applied to a variety of applications.[1] We begin by assuming that there is only individual uncertainty. We then extend the model to incorporate aggregate uncertainty.

2.1.1 Individual but Not Aggregate Uncertainty

Let a population of mass one be partitioned into discrete groups, where g indexes groups and the proportion of individuals in group g is α_g. Assume that $\alpha_g < \frac{1}{2}$ for all groups g, so that no group constitutes a majority. There are two parties, labeled $P = A, B$. Each party P names a vector of intergroup transfers $\mathbf{t}_P$, where t_{gP} is the per capita transfer proposed for voters in group g. If $t_{gP} > 0$, then party P has proposed that individuals in group g receive transfers from other groups, whereas if $t_{gP} < 0$, then party P has proposed that individuals in group g be taxed to support transfers to other groups. Proposed transfers must be budget-balancing—the government cannot redistribute more money than is available in the economy and cannot use tax revenues for any purpose other than redistribution—so that $\sum \alpha_g t_g = 0$. As an example, suppose that there are three groups in the economy, with $\alpha_1 = \frac{1}{4}, \alpha_2 = \frac{3}{8}, \alpha_3 = \frac{3}{8}$. Then the following set of transfers satisfies budget balance: $t_1 = \frac{1}{2}, t_2 = -\frac{1}{3}, t_3 = 0$.

Each voter in group g receives $u_g(t_{gP})$ from transfer t_{gP}, where u_g is twice-differentiable, increasing, and strictly concave. In addition, voters have idiosyncratic affinities for the two parties unrelated to their policy platforms. We assume in particular that voter i in group g votes for

---

[1] Seminal models of probabilistic voting include Hinich, Ledyard, and Ordeshook (1972), Hinich (1977), and Coughlin and Nitzan (1981); see Coughlin (1992). Enelow and Hinich (1982) foreshadow the treatment in Lindbeck and Weibull (1987) and Dixit and Londregan (1996) by assuming that voter utility is additively separable in a policy payoff and a stochastic term.

party A if

$$u_g\left(t_{gA}\right) > u_g\left(t_{gB}\right) + \eta_{ig},$$

and for party B otherwise. Thus, when the two parties propose identical transfers to group g, voters in group g with $\eta_{ig} > 0$ prefer party B, whereas those with $\eta_{ig} < 0$ prefer party A. The magnitude of η_{ig} indicates the strength of the preference, so that voters with large $|\eta_{ig}|$ require larger transfers from one party to overcome their inherent preference for the other. Following Persson and Tabellini (2000), we adopt the simplifying assumption that η_{ig} is distributed independently across groups and uniformly on the interval $\left[-\frac{1}{2\omega_g}, \frac{1}{2\omega_g}\right]$. The parameter ω_g represents the degree of preference homogeneity within group g. When ω_g is large, then voters in group g differ little in their relative preference for party B over party A.

To generate insight into the relationship between income and redistributive transfers, we assume a particular functional form for u_g, with $u_g\left(t_{gP}\right) = v\left(y_g + t_{gP}\right)$, where the parameter y_g is the pre-transfer income of voters in group g. We denote the first and second derivatives of v by v' and v'', respectively.[2] Thus, the condition for voter i in group g to support party A may be rewritten as

$$v\left(y_g + t_{gA}\right) > v\left(y_g + t_{gB}\right) + \eta_{ig}.$$

We assume that parties maximize their probability of winning, as in the Hotelling-Downs model of the last chapter. However, for purposes of analysis it is convenient to proceed under the alternative assumption that parties maximize vote share. With a continuum of voters, individual uncertainty averages out, so that any pair of redistributive platforms implies a particular vote share for each party. Clearly, a party that maximizes its vote share maximizes its probability of winning, as the probability of winning depends only on the vote. Further, unlike the case with three or more parties examined in Section 1.3, there are no equilibria in which a party maximizes its probability of winning but not its vote share.

We begin by aggregating up from individual votes, given a pair of platforms $(\mathbf{t}_A, \mathbf{t}_B)$. Within any group g, any voter i with

$$\eta_{ig} < v\left(y_g + t_{gA}\right) - v\left(y_g + t_{gB}\right)$$

---

[2] In addition, to ensure an interior solution, assume that $v'\left(y_g + t_{gP}\right)$ approaches infinity as $y_g + t_{gP}$ approaches 0 and approaches zero as $y_g + t_{gP}$ approaches infinity. This implies that in equilibrium both parties have an incentive to leave each group g with positive net income.

votes for party A rather than party B. Assume preliminarily that the share of voters supporting party A is strictly between zero and one; we will show that this condition holds in equilibrium. Then, because η_{ig} is distributed uniformly on $\left[-\frac{1}{2\omega_g}, \frac{1}{2\omega_g}\right]$, the share of voters in group g supporting party A is

$$\omega_g \left[v\left(y_g + t_{gA}\right) - v\left(y_g + t_{gB}\right) - \left(-\frac{1}{2\omega_g}\right)\right]$$

$$= \frac{1}{2} + \omega_g \left[v\left(y_g + t_{gA}\right) - v\left(y_g + t_{gB}\right)\right].$$

Given that the size of each group g is α_g, the share of all voters supporting party A is therefore

$$\frac{1}{2} + \sum \alpha_g \omega_g \left[v\left(y_g + t_{gA}\right) - v\left(y_g + t_{gB}\right)\right].$$

Party A's problem is to maximize this expression given the constraint $\sum \alpha_g t_{gA} = 0$, that is, given budget balance. We solve for the optimal $\mathbf{t}_A$ by writing down the Lagrangian,

$$\frac{1}{2} + \sum \alpha_g \omega_g \left[v\left(y_g + t_{gA}\right) - v\left(y_g + t_{gB}\right)\right] - \lambda \left(\sum \alpha_g t_{gA}\right),$$

and setting the derivative of this expression with respect to t_{gA} equal to zero for all g. Doing so gives

$$\alpha_g \omega_g v'\left(y_g + t_{gA}^*\right) - \lambda \alpha_g = 0,$$

that is,

$$\omega_g v'\left(y_g + t_{gA}^*\right) = \lambda. \qquad (2.1)$$

The incentives for party B are identical to those for party A, as each party cares only about winning. Thus, each party adopts the same vector of redistributive transfers $\mathbf{t}^* = \mathbf{t}_A^* = \mathbf{t}_B^*$ and receives one-half of the vote, winning with probability one-half. Note that the Lagrange multiplier λ can be interpreted as follows: if either party had an additional dollar available to spend on redistribution, then it would be able to increase its vote share by λ.

To understand the nature of equilibrium redistribution, consider the relationship between the transfers offered to any two groups g and h:

$$\omega_g v'\left(y_g + t_g^*\right) = \omega_h v'\left(y_h + t_h^*\right),$$

which follows immediately from Equation 2.1. In equilibrium, each party chooses policy to equalize the marginal vote share from all groups. For the special case in which the distribution of idiosyncratic affinities is identical across groups (i.e., $\omega_g = \omega$ for all g), this implies that transfers are chosen to equalize citizens' marginal utility of post-transfer income:

$$v'\left(y_g + t_g^*\right) = v'\left(y_h + t_h^*\right).$$

Thus, for example, if there were two groups, with $y_g > y_h$, then group g would be taxed to subsidize group h; intuitively, the poor could be "bought" more cheaply than the rich.

The following interpretation may also be useful. When preference heterogeneity is identical within each group, the party acts as a **Benthamite social planner**. A Benthamite, or utilitarian, social welfare function is the sum of all individuals' utilities. When groups have identical preference heterogeneity, that is, when $\omega_g = \omega$ for all g, then party A's vote share is

$$\frac{1}{2} + \sum \alpha_g \omega \left[v\left(y_g + t_{gA}\right) - v\left(y_g + t_{gB}\right)\right].$$

Maximizing this expression with respect to $\mathbf{t}_A$ (given budget balance) is equivalent to maximizing

$$\sum \alpha_g v\left(y_g + t_{gA}\right),$$

which is the utilitarian social welfare function for the environment here.

More generally, when parties maximize their probability of winning and there is individual uncertainty of the form assumed here, then parties maximize the utility of the *average* (i.e., mean, not median) voter. This average is unweighted when preference heterogeneity is identical across groups, whereas it is weighted by ω_g when preference heterogeneity varies across groups. This result extends beyond the redistributive setting of this model to a more general policy environment, so that if each party chooses a policy vector $\mathbf{x} \in \mathbf{X}$, then the equilibrium policy maximizes

$$\sum \alpha_g \omega_g u_g\left(\mathbf{x}\right).$$

2.1.2 Aggregate Uncertainty

The model in the previous section demonstrates that individual uncertainty is sufficient to guarantee existence of a Nash equilibrium in the

Hotelling-Downs model with multidimensional competition. We now add aggregate uncertainty to the model by assuming that the distribution of η_{ig} is not known with certainty at the time that parties adopt their platforms, using a formulation suggested by Persson and Tabellini (2000).

We adapt the model of the previous section to assume that η_{ig} is distributed uniformly on the interval $\left[\eta - \frac{1}{2\omega_g}, \eta + \frac{1}{2\omega_g}\right]$, where η is a random variable distributed uniformly on the interval $\left[-\frac{1}{2\psi}, \frac{1}{2\psi}\right]$ that is realized after the parties have adopted their policy platforms. One interpretation of this timing assumption is that parties are uncertain about what information (e.g., about the state of the economy) voters will acquire in the period between platform choice and the election, and thus that they are uncertain about which party voters will be inclined to support. A realization of $\eta < 0$ means that voters are on average inclined to support party A, whereas a realization of $\eta > 0$ implies that voters are on average inclined to support party B.

We assume that parties maximize their probability of winning. To solve for the equilibrium, we first derive an expression for $\pi(\mathbf{t}_A, \mathbf{t}_B)$, the probability that party A wins, given vectors of proposed transfers $\mathbf{t}_A$ and $\mathbf{t}_B$. With η_{ig} distributed uniformly on the interval $\left[\eta - \frac{1}{2\omega_g}, \eta + \frac{1}{2\omega_g}\right]$, the (random) share of voters in group g who support party A is

$$\omega_g \left[v(y_g + t_{gA}) - v(y_g + t_{gB}) - \left(\eta - \frac{1}{2\omega_g}\right)\right]$$

$$= \frac{1}{2} - \eta\omega_g + \omega_g \left[v(y_g + t_{gA}) - v(y_g + t_{gB})\right].$$

Summing across groups g, the share of all voters supporting party A as a function of η is thus

$$\frac{1}{2} - \eta \sum \alpha_g \omega_g + \sum \alpha_g \omega_g \left[v(y_g + t_{gA}) - v(y_g + t_{gB})\right].$$

Finally, the probability that party A wins is the probability that its total vote share is greater than one-half,

$$\Pr\left(\frac{1}{2} - \eta \sum \alpha_g \omega_g + \sum \alpha_g \omega_g \left[v(y_g + t_{gA}) - v(y_g + t_{gB})\right] > \frac{1}{2}\right)$$

$$= \Pr\left(\eta < \frac{1}{\sum \alpha_g \omega_g} \sum \alpha_g \omega_g \left[v(y_g + t_{gA}) - v(y_g + t_{gB})\right]\right)$$

Using the assumption that η is distributed uniformly on $\left[-\frac{1}{2\psi}, \frac{1}{2\psi}\right]$, this expression can be rewritten as

$$\psi \left[\frac{1}{\sum \alpha_g \omega_g} \sum \alpha_g \omega_g \left[v\left(y_g + t_{gA}\right) - v\left(y_g + t_{gB}\right) \right] - \left(-\frac{1}{2\psi} \right) \right]$$

$$= \frac{1}{2} + \frac{\psi}{\sum \alpha_g \omega_g} \sum \alpha_g \omega_g \left[v\left(y_g + t_{gA}\right) - v\left(y_g + t_{gB}\right) \right].$$

Maximizing this expression with respect to $\mathbf{t}_A$ (given the constraint of budget balance) is equivalent to maximizing

$$\sum \alpha_g \omega_g v\left(y_g + t_{gA}\right).$$

As in the model with individual uncertainty only, party A chooses $\mathbf{t}_A$ to maximize a weighted utilitarian social welfare function, where the weights ω_g measure the responsiveness of groups to redistributive policy.

Extending the model of Section 2.1.1 to incorporate aggregate uncertainty thus produces no change in the equilibrium behavior of the parties. Intuitively, aggregate uncertainty that is unrelated to parties' policy platforms does not alter parties' incentives when they care only about winning.

Nonetheless, the extension to aggregate uncertainty produces an important insight. Although election outcomes are determined in equilibrium by factors beyond the parties' control (e.g., the state of the economy), this does not imply that voters are insensitive to the positions taken by the parties. Rather, if one of the parties were to deviate from the equilibrium platform, the consequence would be a reduction in its probability of winning, with the election outcome now determined both by party platforms and by the aggregate shock. As we will see in Section 3.2, where we extend the model here to incorporate campaign finance, a similar insight helps to explain why there is not more money in politics.

2.2 Divergence

The deterministic models covered in the last chapter offer insight into why parties often adopt similar positions. Clearly, however, parties are not identical in the eyes of voters: Republicans adopt "Republican" positions and Democrats adopt "Democratic" positions. What accounts for such divergence? Our discussion of the Wittman model in the last chapter, and the Lindbeck-Weibull/Dixit-Londgregan model in Section 2.1, showed that neither policy-seeking parties nor aggregate uncertainty alone is sufficient to produce divergence in party platforms, a result due to Calvert (1985). However, when parties care about policy *and* are uncertain about the mapping from policy platforms to electoral outcomes, then divergence may occur. Parties face a trade-off. On the one hand, they want to adopt positions closer to their ideal points to increase their payoff should they win the election. On the other, they have an incentive to adopt positions further away from their most-preferred positions to increase their probability of winning. In equilibrium, parties balance these two considerations, adopting positions distinct from their ideal points but different from each other.

To understand this logic, we return to the Wittman model of Section 1.2, only we now assume that parties do not know with certainty the position of the median ideal point x_m when they choose their policy positions. (This modeling approach follows Roemer, 1994, 1997.) There are various ways to motivate this assumption. One is to think of the distribution of voters' preferences as fixed but not known with certainty to the parties. In this case, we might expect uncertainty about x_m to be greater at times or in places with relatively poor polling technology. Alternatively, we might think of the distribution of voters' preferences as vulnerable to shocks between the time that party platforms are chosen and election day.

Assume for concreteness that x_m is a random variable distributed uniformly on the interval $[\mu - a, \mu + a]$, where $\mu - a > 0$ and $\mu + a < 1$. Recalling from Section 1.2 that parties L and R have ideal points normalized to 0 and 1, respectively, this implies that the parties are "polarized" whatever the realization of x_m.

As before, party L chooses x_L to maximize

$$\pi\left(x_L, x_R\right)\left(-\left|x_L\right|\right) + \left[1 - \pi\left(x_L, x_R\right)\right]\left(-\left|x_R\right|\right),$$

though now we derive $\pi\left(x_L, x_R\right)$ as follows. Assume preliminarily that $0 < x_L < x_R < 1$ and that $\frac{x_L + x_R}{2} \in [\mu - a, \mu + a]$; we will show shortly that this condition holds in equilibrium. Given that voters have Euclidean preferences, all voters i with ideal point $x_i < \frac{x_L + x_R}{2}$ strictly prefer party L to party R. These voters constitute a majority when $x_m < \frac{x_L + x_R}{2}$ (as precisely half of all voters have ideal point $x_i < x_m$), so that the probability that L wins, $\pi\left(x_L, x_R\right) = \Pr\left(x_m < \frac{x_L + x_R}{2}\right)$. Recalling that x_m is distributed uniformly on $[\mu - a, \mu + a]$, so that the density of the distribution of x_m is $\frac{1}{2a}$, $\pi(x_L, x_R)$ can be derived as

$$\frac{1}{2a}\left[\frac{x_L + x_R}{2} - (\mu - a)\right] = \frac{1}{2} + \frac{x_L + x_R}{4a} - \frac{\mu}{2a}.$$

Using this expression, and exploiting the preliminary assumption that $0 < x_L < x_R < 1$ to dispense with the absolute-value signs, party L's problem can be rewritten as

$$\max_{x_L} \left(\frac{1}{2} + \frac{x_L + x_R}{4a} - \frac{\mu}{2a}\right)(x_R - x_L).$$

This is a concave problem, with the first-order condition sufficient for a solution:

$$x_L^* = \mu - a.$$

Similarly,

$$x_R^* = \mu + a.$$

As preliminarily assumed, $0 < x_L^* < x_R^* < 1$, and $\frac{x_L^* + x_R^*}{2} = \mu \in [\mu - a, \mu + a]$.

The parties diverge from the expected position of the median voter, μ, with the degree of divergence proportional to the degree of uncertainty about the position of the median voter, which is measured by a. Intuitively, each party finds the position that balances the trade-off between increasing the probability of winning and increasing the payoff from winning. The greater the uncertainty about the position of the median voter, the less responsive is the probability of winning to a change in position, and thus the closer to its ideal point will be a party's optimal position.

2.3 Multiparty Competition

In the Lindbeck-Weibull/Dixit-Londregan model considered in Section 2.1, voters were assumed to care about policy and to have an exogenous preference for one party over another, represented by the term η_i (here we ignore group membership for simplicity). Alternatively, we could have assumed that voters receive utility from choosing party P of

$$\tilde{u}_i(\mathbf{x}_P, P) = u_i(\mathbf{x}_P) + \epsilon_{iP}, \tag{2.2}$$

where $\mathbf{x}_P$ is the position adopted by party P in a possibly multidimensional policy space, and ϵ_{iP} is a random variable generated independently for each party $P = A, B$. Then if we define $\eta_i \equiv \epsilon_{iB} - \epsilon_{iA}$, the assumption that voter i votes for party A if $\eta_i < u_i(\mathbf{x}_A) - u_i(\mathbf{x}_B)$ is equivalent to the assumption that voter i votes for party A if $\tilde{u}_i(\mathbf{x}_A, A) > \tilde{u}_i(\mathbf{x}_B, B)$.

In principle, we could specify the same **random-utility model** for multiparty competition. However, with three or more parties, a voter's exogenous preference over parties cannot be represented by a single random variable η_i. Nonetheless, there is a tractable formulation, which relies on the assumption of the conditional logit model that the random variable ϵ_{iP} is generated from a Type I extreme-value distribution. (This distribution approximates a normal distribution in shape, though the density is skewed toward "extreme" values at one end of the distribution or the other.) With this assumption, it can be shown that the probability that any voter i votes for party P is

$$\frac{\exp(u_i(\mathbf{x}_P))}{\sum \exp(u_i(\mathbf{x}_Q))},$$

where the summation is over all parties Q in the contest. Thus, for example, voter i is twice as likely to vote for party 1 as for party 2 if

$$\frac{\exp(u_i(\mathbf{x}_1))}{\exp(u_i(\mathbf{x}_2))} = 2.$$

The key characteristic of this formulation is that a slight change in the position chosen by a party produces only a slight change in the probability that voters choose that party. For example, if $x \in \Re$, then a voter with utility function

$$\tilde{u}_i(x_P, P) = -|1 - x_P| + \epsilon_{iP}$$

would be equally likely to vote for two parties A and B that had adopted positions $x_A = x_B = 2$, but only slightly more likely to vote for party A if party A deviated to $x_A = 1.9$:

$$\frac{\exp(-|1 - 1.9|)}{\exp(-|1 - 2|)} \approx 1.1.$$

Consequently, as with other models in this chapter, parties are not able to "steal" large numbers of voters by adopting a position arbitrarily close to that of another party. Exercise 5 illustrates this point in a simple model with three parties and five voters.

When voter utility is given by Equation 2.2, convergent equilibria generally exist with multiple parties, a result established by Lin, Enelow, and Durussen (1999). As McKelvey and Patty (2006) show, this holds even when voters vote strategically, that is, when voters condition their voting decision on their expectation of what other voters will do. Nonetheless, the convergent equilibrium may not be unique. Moreover, with more than two parties, convergence breaks down when voters also have (ex ante) observable preferences for one party over another that are unrelated to the policies that parties adopt. Then parties diverge toward positions favored by their partisans, that is, those voters who are known ex ante to favor them for nonpolicy reasons.

In general (i.e., with the exception of convergent equilibria, where they exist), analytical solutions to probabilistic models of multiparty competition do not exist. However, computational methods may be used to find equilibria. Adams, Merrill, and Grofman (2005) provide an algorithm for computing equilibrium positions for the general case where voters have both policy and nonpolicy preferences that are observable by parties before they choose positions.

2.4 Entry

The models of entry in Section 1.4 are similar to the other models of electoral competition in Chapter 1 in that candidate positions (represented by candidate identity in the citizen-candidate models of Section 1.4.3) map deterministically onto votes. This implies some peculiar results when the set of voters is finite. First, as shown in Section 1.4.2, an "integer constraint," such that the number of candidates must be divisible by the number of voters, may limit the number of candidates in equilibrium. Second, as demonstrated in Section 1.4.3, the existence of multicandidate equilibria may rely on "just-so" configurations of ideal points, as when a divergent two-candidate equilibrium requires that two citizens have ideal points equidistant from the median ideal point.

As with the oddities of other models in Chapter 1, these "problems" can be solved by assuming some stochastic behavior on the part of voters. Eguia (2007) demonstrates this approach in the context of a citizen-candidate model. Adopting a formulation suggested by Myerson (1993), Eguia draws a distinction between supporting a candidate and voting for that candidate, assuming that with common probability μ any citizen fails to cast her vote. Thus, for example, μ might capture the probability that some work or family obligation prevents a citizen from getting to the polls. In contrast to prior models in this chapter, there is no uncertainty about voters' preferences, only about whether they will actually vote. Under this assumption, candidates who do not have the support of a majority may nonetheless win if their supporters turn out in greater numbers.

In particular, a candidate who has the support of $n - 1$ voters has nearly the same probability of winning as a candidate with the support of n voters when n is large. Thus, for example, in a model like that in Section 1.4.2, there may exist a convergent three-candidate equilibrium even if the number of voters is not divisible by three, as the probability of winning will be approximately one-third for each candidate. Further, in a citizen-candidate model with this form of uncertainty, two candidates with positions "nearly" equidistant from the median ideal point may each win with probability approximately one-half, perhaps justifying the entry decision for both candidates.

At the same time, the introduction of this form of uncertainty may render certain equilibria more vulnerable to entry by another candidate. Consider, for example, a citizen-candidate model with a finite number of citizens. Further, assume that there is only one citizen with ideal point x_m. Then by the argument in Section 1.4.3, if voting is deterministic, a one-candidate "median-voter" equilibrium exists if and only if

$$\delta \leq |x_m - \bar{x}| + v.$$

Because no other citizen has a chance of winning against the citizen with the median ideal point, the necessary and sufficient condition for existence of the equilibrium is that the citizen-candidate prefer to enter, given that nobody else has. In contrast, if voting is uncertain, then those citizens just to the left and right of the median citizen must be deterred from entering. When the electorate is large, any such citizen would win with probability close to one-half against the median citizen, so that if $\delta < \frac{v}{2}$, there is no one-candidate equilibrium. Thus, the conditions for existence of one-candidate equilibria are more restrictive with uncertainty than with certainty.

2.5 The Calculus of Voting

The model of the previous section takes a reduced-form approach to electoral participation, assuming that voters have independent and identical probabilities of casting their votes. Here we examine the microfoundations of participation, comparing the costs and benefits of voting.

To explore this issue, consider a model in which a finite number of citizens have strict preferences over two candidates: an incumbent candidate (I) and an opposition candidate (O). In particular, any citizen i receives utility equal to $u_i(P)$ when candidate P wins, where $P \in \{I, O\}$ and $u_i(I) \neq u_i(O)$ for all i. The candidates themselves are not strategic players. One interpretation is that the model represents the subgame that follows position choices by the incumbent and opposition candidates during an election campaign.

Each citizen i chooses $\sigma_i \in \{0, 1\}$, where $\sigma_i = 1$ indicates that citizen i votes for her preferred candidate, and $\sigma_i = 0$ indicates that she abstains. (Following the discussion in Section 1.4.1, voting for the less preferred candidate is weakly dominated, so we ignore this possibility.) Citizen i bears an idiosyncratic cost $c_i > 0$ if and only if she chooses $\sigma_i = 1$. We denote by $\pi_i(\sigma)$ the probability that citizen i assigns to an incumbent victory, given the profile of voting strategies σ. This formulation allows for preferences over the two candidates to be private knowledge, so that even if there were no strategic uncertainty about how other citizens would vote, citizen i would be uncertain about the election outcome.[3]

Consider the best response of citizen i. For concreteness, assume that citizen i supports the incumbent; the logic is analogous for an opposition supporter. The expected utility of voting is

$$\pi_i(1, \sigma_{-i}) u_i(I) + [1 - \pi_i(1, \sigma_{-i})] u_i(O) - c_i,$$

where $\pi(1, \sigma_{-i})$ is the probability that the incumbent wins when citizen i chooses $\sigma_i = 1$, given the strategy profile σ_{-i} for all citizens $k \neq i$. In contrast, the expected utility of not voting is

$$\pi_i(0, \sigma_{-i}) u_i(I) + [1 - \pi_i(0, \sigma_{-i})] u_i(O).$$

Citizen i therefore prefers to vote if

$$[\pi_i(1, \sigma_{-i}) - \pi_i(0, \sigma_{-i})][u_i(I) - u_i(O)] \geq c_i.$$

The **paradox of voting** is that in general $\pi_i(1, \sigma_{-i}) \approx \pi_i(0, \sigma_{-i})$ if the number of other citizens choosing to vote is at all large. To support even moderately high levels of turnout in equilibrium, the model therefore requires that, for many citizens i, $|u_i(I) - u_i(O)|$ be very large or c_i be very small.

---

[3] In this case, a strategy σ_i is a mapping from type to $\{0, 1\}$, and the expected-utility calculation presented here integrates over the type space.

Riker and Ordeshook (1968) propose a solution to this puzzle by suggesting that citizens perceive a duty to vote, implying a benefit of voting that does not depend on the election outcome. To see how this alters the calculus of voting, assume that any citizen i receives a payoff $d > 0$ if and only if $\sigma_i = 1$; the idiosyncratic cost of voting c_i remains unchanged from the previous discussion. Clearly, if d is sufficiently large, then voting is a dominant strategy for any citizen i with $c_i < d$. High levels of turnout are therefore possible in equilibrium.

Riker and Ordeshook's solution is not without its critics. Barry (1978, p. 15), for example, states that it "is no trick to restate all behavior in terms of 'rewards' and 'costs'." Similarly, Green and Shapiro (1996, pp. 51–52) argue that "[h]aving merely *stipulated* that the act of voting is more gratifying than costly, these authors solve the paradox of voter turnout by reducing it to the same logical status as the paradox of attendance at free concerts or the paradox of strolls along public beaches." Still, there is evidence that civic duty plays a role in how citizens think about the decision to vote (e.g., Verba, Schlozman, and Brady, 1995, Chapter 4), an empirical pattern that might have attracted less notice had not Riker and Ordeshook offered their solution.

Schwartz (1987) presents an alternative solution to the paradox of voting, suggesting that party machines direct selective benefits to citizens to compensate for the cost of voting. When benefits can be targeted to known supporters, this strategy—which Nichter (2008) terms **turnout buying**—has the advantage of requiring that only the act of voting be observed, not the vote itself. Even when this is not possible, benefits can often be directed to small jurisdictions (e.g., precincts), where there is a nontrivial probability that any individual's vote is pivotal.

As Simpser (2012) demonstrates, strategic interaction among voters can exacerbate the effect of turnout buying or its mirror image, turnout suppression. The key assumption of Simpser's model is that sanctions (e.g., loss of government jobs) can be targeted to known opposition supporters who turn out to vote, but only if the incumbent wins reelection. This changes the calculus of voting: opposition supporters now prefer to vote if and only if they expect enough other opposition supporters to vote that the incumbent is likely to lose.

To fix ideas, assume that the set of voters is a continuum, which implies that $\pi_i(1, \sigma_{-i}) = \pi_i(0, \sigma_{-i})$ for all i and all σ_{-i}. We denote the proportion of incumbent and opposition supporters, respectively, by α_I and α_O, where $\alpha_O > \alpha_I$. All citizens share a common benefit d of voting.

Given these assumptions, the election outcome depends only on the relative size of the two groups and on the cost of voting within each group. Assume that for any opposition or incumbent supporter i, the *election-day* cost of voting is a random variable c_i drawn from a uniform distribution on the interval $[0, 1]$. Further, assume $d < 1$. Then absent the threat of post-election sanction, any citizen votes with probability d. With α_I incumbent supporters and α_O opposition supporters, this implies a vote for the incumbent and opposition candidates of $\alpha_I d$ and $\alpha_O d$, respectively.

In addition, however, we assume that any opposition supporter who votes rather than abstains bears a cost $s > 0$ if and only if the incumbent wins. Then the payoff to any opposition supporter i who votes (ignoring the probability-weighted policy payoff, which is unaffected by the decision to vote) is

$$d - c_i - \pi(\sigma) s,$$

where $\pi(\sigma)$ is the probability that the incumbent wins, given the profile of voting strategies σ, whereas the payoff from abstaining is 0. We assume

$$\frac{d(\alpha_O - \alpha_I)}{\alpha_O} < s < d, \tag{2.3}$$

which says that the sanction is not sufficient to deter all opposition supporters but may be sufficient to prevent opposition victory.

There are two pure-strategy Nash equilibria of this game. In the first, high-turnout equilibrium, all opposition (and all incumbent) supporters with $c_i < d$ vote, and the opposition wins, given the assumption $\alpha_O > \alpha_I$. In this equilibrium, no sanction is imposed, as the incumbent loses office. In the second, low-turnout equilibrium, all opposition supporters with $c_i < d-s$ vote, resulting in opposition turnout of $\alpha_O(d - s)$. Given Condition 2.3, $\alpha_O(d - s) < \alpha_I d$, so that the incumbent wins and imposes the sanction. This in turn justifies the voting behavior of opposition supporters.

A key insight of Simpser's framework is that strategic interaction among voters can lead to an unnecessarily large margin of victory by the incumbent. So long as the incumbent is expected to win, many opposition supporters choose to stay home rather than vote for the opposition. Similarly, if the sanction is based on an individual's actual vote, rather than (as here) on the act of voting, then the expectation of an incumbent victory may lead opposition supporters to vote for the incumbent.

Exercises

2.1 Consider a special case of the model in Section 2.1.1:

- There are three groups, $g = 1, 2, 3$.
- Voters in group 1 have income $y_1 = 1$, voters in group 2 have income $y_2 = \frac{1}{2}$, and voters in group 3 have income $y_3 = 0$.
- Voters' payoffs from redistributive transfers are given by

$$u_g\left(t_{gP}\right) = v\left(y_g + t_{gP}\right) = \ln\left(y_g + t_{gP}\right).$$

Find the policy $\mathbf{t}_P$ adopted by each party P in equilibrium.

2.2 Consider a special case of the model in Section 2.1.1, where we follow Dixit and Londregan (1996) in assuming that redistribution takes places with a "leaky bucket."

- There are two groups, $g = 1, 2$.
- Voters in group 1 have income $y_1 = 1$, and voters in group 2 have income $y_2 = \frac{1}{2}$.
- The distribution of voters' affinities for the two parties is the same for each group, with η_{ig} distributed uniformly on $\left[-\frac{1}{2\omega}, \frac{1}{2\omega}\right]$.
- Voters' payoffs from redistributive transfers are given by

$$u_g\left(t_{gP}\right) = \ln\left(y_g + \beta t_{gP}\right) \text{ if } t_{gP} > 0, \text{ and}$$
$$u_g\left(t_{gP}\right) = \ln\left(y_g + t_{gP}\right) \text{ otherwise.}$$

The parameter $\beta \in \left(\frac{1}{2}, 1\right)$, which enters the utility function only if the group receives positive transfers, measures the redistributive capacity of the state: the larger is β, the greater the proportion of funds that "get through" to voters.

Find the policy $\mathbf{t}_P$ adopted by each party P in equilibrium. (Hint: Which group g receives positive transfers in equilibrium?) Interpret your result.

2.3 Modify the model in Section 2.2 so that two parties, $P = A, B$, are office-seeking rather than policy-seeking. Each party maximizes its probability of winning. Assume for simplicity that the distribution F of the random variable x_m is absolutely continuous and strictly increasing for all $x_m \in \Re$. Let γ be the "median median," that is, $F\left(\gamma\right) = \frac{1}{2}$. Find the Nash equilibria of this model as follows:

(a) Without loss of generality, find party A's best response (if it exists) to all $x_B \in \Re$. (Consider three cases: $x_B < \gamma$, $x_B > \gamma$, and $x_B = \gamma$.)

(b) Identify the set of Nash equilibria.

(c) Contrast the predictions of this model with those of the model in Section 2.2.

2.4 Consider the following electoral environment. Policy takes one of two values, $x \in \{0, 1\}$. Two parties compete by adopting positions in this policy space. Citizens vote for the party whose position they most prefer and abstain if indifferent. With probability $\gamma \in \left(\frac{1}{2}, 1\right)$, the median citizen most prefers $x = 0$; thus, with probability $1 - \gamma$, the median citizen most prefers $x = 1$. The election is by plurality rule, with the winner chosen by an equal-probability rule in the event of a tie.

(a) Office-motivated parties: Find all pure-strategy Nash equilibria of the game in which parties care only about maximizing their probability of winning. (There are four strategy profiles to consider.)

(b) Policy-motivated parties: Label the parties $P = L, R$, and assume that party L most prefers $x = 0$, whereas party R most prefers $x = 1$. Party L chooses x_L to maximize

$$\pi\left(x_L, x_R\right)\left(-\left|x_L\right|\right) + \left[1 - \pi\left(x_L, x_R\right)\right]\left(-\left|x_R\right|\right),$$

whereas party R chooses x_R to maximize

$$\pi\left(x_L, x_R\right)\left(-\left|x_L - 1\right|\right) + \left[1 - \pi\left(x_L, x_R\right)\right]\left(-\left|x_R - 1\right|\right),$$

where $\pi\left(x_L, x_R\right)$ is the probability that party L wins, given positions x_L and x_R. Find all pure-strategy Nash equilibria of this game.

2.5 Consider three-party competition in a population of five voters. Assume first that voters vote deterministically for the party whose position they most prefer, using an equal-probability rule to choose from among parties over which they are indifferent. In particular, assume that any voter i receives utility from the position $x_P \in \Re$ announced by party P of

$$u_i\left(x_P\right) = -\left(x_i - x_P\right)^2,$$

where x_i is voter i's ideal point. Voters 1 and 2 have ideal points $x_1 = x_2 = 0$, voter 3 has ideal point $x_3 = 1$, and voters 4 and 5 have ideal points $x_4 = x_5 = 2$.

(a) Assume that each party P has adopted $x_P = 1$. For each voter i, find the probability that voter i votes for party P. Average these probabilities across all voters to find the expected vote share for each party P.

(b) Assume that party A has adopted $x_A = .95$ and parties B and C have adopted $x_B = x_C = 1$. For each voter, find the probability that that voter votes for party P. Average these probabilities across all voters to find the expected vote share for each party P.

Now repeat these steps for a random-utility model as in Section 2.3, where any voter i receives utility from voting for party P of

$$\tilde{u}_i(x_P, P) = -(x_i - x_P)^2 + \epsilon_{iP},$$

where ϵ_{iP} is a random variable independently generated from a Type I extreme value distribution. Voters have the same ideal points as before. Compare your results from the models with certainty and uncertainty. How would your answers change if there were four parties?

2.6 A key question of this and the preceding chapter is the degree of convergence among political parties and candidates. Are voters better off with convergence or divergence? To explore this question, consider the following example from Bernhardt, Duggan, and Squintani (2009). There is a continuum of voters, indexed by i. Voter i has ideal point $x_i = \eta_i + \eta$, where η_i is distributed symmetrically around zero and η is a random variable that takes two values, -1 and 1, with equal probability.

(a) Suppose that two parties, A and B, have adopted $x_A = x_B = 0$, the expected value of the median ideal point.

   (1) Consider the realization $\eta = -1$, so that x_i is distributed symmetrically around -1. For any voter i with $\eta_i \geq 0$ (the argument is symmetric for voters with $\eta_i \leq 0$), how far is x_i from zero, the platform adopted by both parties? (Your answer to this and the following parts of this problem should be a function of η_i.)

   (2) Consider the realization $\eta = 1$, so that x_i is distributed symmetrically around 1. For any voter i with $\delta_i \geq 0$, how far is x_i from zero, the platform adopted by both parties?

(b) Now suppose that two parties, L and R, have adopted $x_L = -1$ and $x_R = 1$, respectively.

   (1) Consider the realization $\delta = -1$, so that x_i is distributed

symmetrically around -1 and L wins. For any voter i with $\delta_i \geq 0$, how far is x_i from the winning party's platform?

(2) Consider the realization $\delta = 1$, so that x_i is distributed symmetrically around 1 and R wins. For any voter i with $\delta_i \geq 0$, how far is x_i from the winning party's platform?

(c) Given your answers to parts (a) and (b), derive the expected distance (i.e., before voters know δ) between a voter's ideal point and the position adopted by the winning party (parties) when parties converge and diverge, respectively. In this example, are voters better off with convergence or divergence?

3

Special Interest Politics

The models in the previous two chapters assume that voting in elections is the only avenue by which citizens may influence policy. Groups of individuals who have overcome their collective-action problems, however, may have other opportunities to exert influence. In this chapter, we examine various models of special interest politics, taking the organization of those interests as given. We first consider a model of pure campaign finance, where campaign spending is the only choice variable. We then explore the interaction between campaign finance and policy choice in a model of electoral competition. Both models simply assume that campaign spending influences voter behavior; we unpack this assumption in a model of informative advertising. We then move to an environment in which organized groups bargain with public officials over policy. We conclude by considering competition for influence in a lobbying model with several organized groups.

3.1 A Model of Pure Campaign Finance

We begin with a model of pure campaign finance. We abstract from the relationship between politicians and organized groups by assuming two parties, $P = A, B$, each of which chooses a campaign expenditure $C_P \in [0, \infty)$. Let $\pi(C_A, C_B)$ denote the probability that party A wins, given campaign expenditures C_A and C_B; the probability that party B wins is therefore $1 - \pi(C_A, C_B)$. We assume that π is weakly increasing in C_A and weakly decreasing in C_B. Each party receives a payoff from winning normalized to one, and each party P incurs a cost of raising campaign funds equal to γC_P, where $\gamma > 0$.

There are various plausible functional forms for $\pi(C_A, C_B)$. As a first example, consider

$$\pi\left(C_A, C_B\right) = \frac{\alpha C_A}{\alpha C_A + (1-\alpha)\,C_B} \quad \text{if } C_A + C_B > 0, \qquad (3.1)$$

$$= \alpha \text{ if } C_A + C_B = 0, \qquad (3.2)$$

where $\alpha \in (0,1)$. This functional form, variants of which are common in the conflict and rent-seeking literatures, implies that the probability that a party wins is strictly increasing in its expenditure.[1] The parameter α measures the natural advantage of party A: when $C_A = C_B$, then party A wins with probability α.

As a first step to analyzing the problem with this functional form, observe that there is no equilibrium in which $C_A = C_B = 0$. Either party could profitably deviate by spending an infinitesimally small amount, thus discontinuously increasing its probability of winning to 1 while bearing essentially no cost of funding the campaign. Further, there is no equilibrium in which one party spends a positive amount while the other spends nothing, as the winning party could reduce its contribution to a smaller positive amount and still win with certainty.

Consider, then, party A's best response when party B chooses some $C_B > 0$. Party A solves

$$\max_{C_A} \frac{\alpha C_A}{\alpha C_A + (1-\alpha)\,C_B} - \gamma C_A.$$

This is a concave problem, the first-order condition for which is

$$\frac{\alpha\,(1-\alpha)\,C_B}{\left[\alpha\tilde{C}_A + (1-\alpha)\,C_B\right]^2} - \gamma = 0,$$

where $\tilde{C}_A$ denotes the optimal C_A, given C_B. This can be rewritten as

$$\frac{1}{\tilde{C}_A}\left[\frac{\alpha\tilde{C}_A}{\alpha\tilde{C}_A + (1-\alpha)\,C_B}\right]\left[\frac{(1-\alpha)\,C_B}{\alpha\tilde{C}_A + (1-\alpha)\,C_B}\right] = \gamma,$$

which, using the definition of $\pi\left(C_A, C_B\right)$ in Equation 3.1, simplifies to

$$\tilde{C}_A = \frac{\pi\left(\tilde{C}_A, C_B\right)\left[1 - \pi\left(\tilde{C}_A, C_B\right)\right]}{\gamma}.$$

---

[1] Snyder (1989) considers a generalization of this functional form and allows for spending decisions across multiple districts.

Solving the analogous problem for party B gives

$$\tilde{C}_B = \frac{\pi\left(C_A, \tilde{C}_B\right)\left[1 - \pi\left(C_A, \tilde{C}_B\right)\right]}{\gamma}.$$

In equilibrium, each party plays a best response to the other's strategy, implying

$$C_A^* = C_B^* = \frac{\pi\left(C_A^*, C_B^*\right)\left[1 - \pi\left(C_A^*, C_B^*\right)\right]}{\gamma} = \frac{\alpha\left(1 - \alpha\right)}{\gamma}, \qquad (3.3)$$

where the last equality uses the fact that $\pi\left(C_A^*, C_B^*\right) = \alpha$ when the parties choose identical expenditure levels. Thus, the parties converge to the same campaign expenditure, even when one party possesses a natural advantage over the other (i.e., when $\alpha \neq \frac{1}{2}$). Total campaign expenditures are greatest when the parties are evenly matched (i.e., when $\alpha = \frac{1}{2}$), and of course they are larger when campaign funds can be raised cheaply (i.e., when γ is small).

It is interesting to compare these results to those with a second functional form,

$$\pi\left(C_A, C_B\right) = 1 \text{ if } C_A + \alpha \geq C_B, \qquad (3.4)$$
$$= 0 \text{ if } C_A + \alpha < C_B.$$

For any choice of C_A and C_B, one party wins with certainty.[2] As before, the parameter $\alpha \geq 0$ measures party A's natural advantage: A can spend α less than B and still win.

Meirowitz (2008) shows that there is no pure-strategy Nash equilibrium of this game if $\alpha < \frac{1}{\gamma}$. To understand this result, assume for simplicity that $\alpha = 0$, and consider the following mutually exclusive and exhaustive cases:

(i) $C_A > C_B$. Party A can profitably deviate by reducing its contribution by some $\epsilon \leq C_A - C_B$, in which case party A still wins, but its campaign expenditure is smaller.

(ii) $C_B > C_A$. By the same argument, party B can profitably deviate by reducing its contribution by some $\epsilon < C_B - C_A$.

---

[2] The sharp competition in Equation 3.4 can by motivated by assuming that the candidates have chosen identical policy platforms, so that only campaign finance determines the election outcome. As Ashworth and Bueno de Mesquita (2009) show in a model with aggregate uncertainty about voter policy preferences, parties can soften this competition—and thus minimize campaign expenditures—by differentiating themselves on policy.

(iii) $C_A = C_B$. Party B can profitably deviate by increasing its contribution by some $\epsilon < \frac{1}{\gamma}$. To see this, note that if $C_A = C_B = C$, where $C \geq 0$, then party B's payoff is $-\gamma C$. In contrast, if B increases its contribution to $C + \epsilon$, its payoff is $1 - \gamma(C + \epsilon)$. This deviation is profitable if

$$1 - \gamma(C + \epsilon) > -\gamma C,$$

that is, if $\epsilon < \frac{1}{\gamma}$.

There is, however, a mixed-strategy Nash equilibrium of this game, where each party mixes according to the uniform distribution on $\left[0, \frac{1}{\gamma}\right]$. Consider party A. For this mixture to be a best response, A must be indifferent over all $C_A \in \left[0, \frac{1}{\gamma}\right]$, given B's strategy. Party A's expected utility is

$$U_A = \Pr(C_B \leq C_A) - \gamma C_A.$$

Given that B mixes according to the uniform distribution on $\left[0, \frac{1}{\gamma}\right]$, $\Pr(C_B \leq C_A) = \gamma C_A$ for any $C_A \in \left[0, \frac{1}{\gamma}\right]$, implying $U_A = 0$ for all C_A in this interval. An analogous argument holds for party B. Finally, note that for either party P, the expected utility from choosing some $C_P > \frac{1}{\gamma}$ is negative: the party wins with certainty, but it could achieve this result at a lower cost by choosing $C_P = \frac{1}{\gamma}$.

An interesting implication of this analysis is that the rents from office are competed away in equilibrium when the parties are evenly matched (i.e., when $\alpha = 0$). This result does not hold when $\pi(C_A, C_B)$ is given by Equation 3.1. To see this, note that given Equation 3.3, party A's expected utility in equilibrium is

$$\pi(C_A^*, C_B^*) - \gamma C_A^* = \alpha - \gamma\left[\frac{\alpha(1-\alpha)}{\gamma}\right] = \alpha^2 > 0.$$

The larger is party A's natural advantage, the larger its expected utility. Similarly, party B's expected utility is $(1 - \alpha)^2$. The sum of these two values takes its minimum at $\alpha = \frac{1}{2}$ (i.e., when the parties are evenly matched), but both parties always earn positive rents in equilibrium. Thus, the first functional form considered here perhaps implies greater incentive for parties to participate in a model with endogenous entry.

Meirowitz (2008) presents results for the more general case in which $\alpha \geq 0$, where he interprets α as a measure of party A's incumbency advantage. In addition, he considers an alternative form of incumbency advantage, in which it is less expensive for party A to raise campaign funds (i.e., $\gamma_A < \gamma_B$). Exercises 3.1 and 3.2 explore these two perspectives.

3.2 Campaign Finance and Policy Choice

We now place more structure on the environment to examine the influence of organized groups on campaign promises, adapting the model of electoral competition with aggregate uncertainty in Section 2.1.2 to incorporate campaign finance. The formalization here incorporates elements of Baron (1994), Grossman and Helpman (1996, 2001), and Persson and Tabellini (2000).

For simplicity, assume that there are two groups of voters, $g = 1, 2$, where group 1 is organized and group 2 is not; Exercise 3.3 generalizes the model to an arbitrary number of organized and unorganized groups. As before, α_g denotes the proportion of voters in group g. We model the role of campaign finance by assuming that each group has both "informed" and "uninformed" voters, where informed voters are influenced by parties' policy positions and uninformed voters by campaign expenditures. In particular, informed voters receive utility $u_g(\mathbf{x})$ from policy $\mathbf{x} \in \mathbf{X}$, where $\mathbf{X}$ is some possibly multidimensional policy space,[3] so that any informed voter i in group g votes for party A if

$$u_g(\mathbf{x}_A) > u_g(\mathbf{x}_B) + \eta_{ig},$$

where we recall that η_{ig} represents the voter's idiosyncratic affinity for the two parties. In contrast, any uninformed voter i in group g votes for party A if

$$sC_A > sC_B + \eta_{ig},$$

where C_P is total campaign spending in support of party P and s is a parameter that measures the importance of campaign expenditures, relative to party affinities. To focus on the role of campaign finance, assume that the proportion of informed and uninformed voters is the same in each group, with fraction β of voters informed. Further, assume that informed and uninformed voters are distributed randomly within each group, so that informed voters are on average no more or less biased

---

[3] For example, in the redistributive environment of Section 2.1,

$$\mathbf{X} = \left\{ \mathbf{x} \mid \sum \alpha_g x_g = 0 \right\}.$$

in favor of the incumbent than are uninformed voters. Finally, assume that the distribution of voters' idiosyncratic preferences over the two parties is the same in each group, with η_{ig} distributed uniformly on $\left[\eta - \frac{1}{2\omega}, \eta + \frac{1}{2\omega}\right]$; as before, η is a random variable distributed uniformly on $\left[-\frac{1}{2\psi}, \frac{1}{2\psi}\right]$, realized just prior to voting.

Group 1 is represented by a lobby that maximizes the aggregate utility of its members. After policy positions have been chosen, but before the random variable η has been realized and voters vote, the lobby chooses a campaign expenditure C_P in support of each party P. (Note that this is the total expenditure for the group, not the per capita expenditure.) We assume that the cost of campaign finance is convex in the quantity $C_A + C_B$, which can be motivated by assuming that the lobby initially targets those group members who are most inclined to contribute and then moves on to other members. For simplicity, let this cost be equal to $\frac{(C_A+C_B)^2}{2}$. Given that voters in group 1 are ex ante predisposed to favor neither party A nor party B, the lobby thus chooses C_A and C_B to maximize

$$\pi\left(\mathbf{x}_A, \mathbf{x}_B, C_A, C_B\right)\left[\alpha_1 u_1\left(\mathbf{x}_A\right)\right] +$$

$$\left(1 - \pi\left(\mathbf{x}_A, \mathbf{x}_B, C_A, C_B\right)\right)\left[\alpha_1 u_1\left(\mathbf{x}_B\right)\right] - \frac{\left(C_A + C_B\right)^2}{2},$$

where $\pi\left(\mathbf{x}_A, \mathbf{x}_B, C_A, C_B\right)$ is the probability that party A wins, given party platforms $\mathbf{x}_A$ and $\mathbf{x}_B$ and campaign expenditures C_A and C_B. This is equivalent to maximizing

$$\pi\left(\mathbf{x}_A, \mathbf{x}_B, C_A, C_B\right)\left[\alpha_1\left(u_1\left(\mathbf{x}_A\right) - u_1\left(\mathbf{x}_B\right)\right)\right] - \frac{\left(C_A + C_B\right)^2}{2}. \quad (3.5)$$

(We assume that uninformed voters value policy as do informed voters, even though they do not take the parties' policy platforms into consideration in deciding how to vote.)

We solve the game by backward induction, beginning with the voting decision. Informed voters choose which party to support as in Section 2.1.2, so the proportion of informed voters in group g who support party A is

$$\frac{1}{2} - \eta\omega + \omega\left(u_g\left(\mathbf{x}_A\right) - u_g\left(\mathbf{x}_B\right)\right).$$

In contrast, the proportion of uninformed voters who support party A is

$$\frac{1}{2} - \eta\omega + \omega s\left(C_A - C_B\right).$$

Given that proportion β of voters are informed, the share of all voters in group g who support party A is

$$\frac{1}{2} - \eta\omega + \beta\omega\left(u_g\left(\mathbf{x}_A\right) - u_g\left(\mathbf{x}_B\right)\right) + (1 - \beta)\omega s\left(C_A - C_B\right).$$

Summing across both groups, the total vote received by party A (as a function of the random variable η) is

$$\frac{1}{2} - \eta\omega + \beta\omega\sum\alpha_g\left(u_g\left(\mathbf{x}_A\right) - u_g\left(\mathbf{x}_B\right)\right) + (1 - \beta)\omega s\left(C_A - C_B\right).$$

The probability that party A wins is the probability that this expression is greater than one-half, that is,

$$\Pr\left(\eta < \beta\sum\alpha_g\left(u_g\left(\mathbf{x}_A\right) - u_g\left(\mathbf{x}_B\right)\right) + (1 - \beta)s\left(C_A - C_B\right)\right).$$

Using the assumption that η is distributed uniformly on $\left[-\frac{1}{2\psi}, \frac{1}{2\psi}\right]$, this simplifies to

$$\frac{1}{2} + \psi\left[\beta\sum\alpha_g\left(u_g\left(\mathbf{x}_A\right) - u_g\left(\mathbf{x}_B\right)\right) + (1 - \beta)s\left(C_A - C_B\right)\right].$$

Plugging this expression into the maximization problem for group 1's lobby (3.5) gives

$$\max_{C_A, C_B}\left[\frac{1}{2} + \psi\left[\beta\sum\alpha_g\left(u_g\left(\mathbf{x}_A\right) - u_g\left(\mathbf{x}_B\right)\right) + (1 - \beta)s\left(C_A - C_B\right)\right]\right]$$
$$\cdot\left[\alpha_1\left(u_1\left(\mathbf{x}_A\right) - u_1\left(\mathbf{x}_B\right)\right)\right] - \frac{\left(C_A + C_B\right)^2}{2},$$

which, after expanding and eliminating terms that do not depend on C_A and C_B, is equivalent to

$$\max_{C_A, C_B}\ \psi\left(1 - \beta\right)s\left(C_A - C_B\right)\alpha_1\left(u_1\left(\mathbf{x}_A\right) - u_1\left(\mathbf{x}_B\right)\right) - \frac{\left(C_A + C_B\right)^2}{2}.$$

Observe that the derivative of the first term with respect to C_A is positive if and only if $u_1\left(\mathbf{x}_A\right) > u_1\left(\mathbf{x}_B\right)$, whereas the derivative with respect to C_B is positive if and only if $u_1\left(\mathbf{x}_A\right) < u_1\left(\mathbf{x}_B\right)$. Group 1's lobby thus contributes to the party P that promises the most attractive policy $\mathbf{x}_P$. Solving for the optimal contributions gives

$$C_A = \psi\left(1 - \beta\right)s\alpha_1\left(u_1\left(\mathbf{x}_A\right) - u_1\left(\mathbf{x}_B\right)\right), C_B = 0 \text{ if } u_1\left(\mathbf{x}_A\right) \geq u_1\left(\mathbf{x}_B\right);$$
$$C_A = 0, C_B = \psi\left(1 - \beta\right)s\alpha_1\left(u_1\left(\mathbf{x}_B\right) - u_1\left(\mathbf{x}_A\right)\right) \text{ if } u_1\left(\mathbf{x}_B\right) \geq u_1\left(\mathbf{x}_A\right).$$

Given these expressions, the net campaign expenditure for party A is

$$C_A - C_B = \psi\left(1 - \beta\right)s\alpha_1\left(u_1\left(\mathbf{x}_A\right) - u_1\left(\mathbf{x}_B\right)\right),$$

which implies that the probability that party A wins as a function of the policies chosen by each party is

$$\frac{1}{2} + \psi\beta \sum \alpha_g \left(u_g\left(\mathbf{x}_A\right) - u_g\left(\mathbf{x}_B\right)\right)$$
$$+ \left(1 - \beta\right)^2 s^2 \psi^2 \alpha_1 \left(u_1\left(\mathbf{x}_A\right) - u_1\left(\mathbf{x}_B\right)\right),$$

that is,

$$\frac{1}{2} + \psi\alpha_1 \left[\beta + \left(1 - \beta\right)^2 s^2 \psi\right] \left(u_1\left(\mathbf{x}_A\right) - u_1\left(\mathbf{x}_B\right)\right)$$
$$+ \psi\alpha_2\beta \left(u_2\left(\mathbf{x}_A\right) - u_2\left(\mathbf{x}_B\right)\right).$$

Recalling that party A wants to maximize, and party B minimize, $\pi\left(\mathbf{x}_A, \mathbf{x}_B\right)$, the parties converge to

$$\mathbf{x}_A^* = \mathbf{x}_B^* = \arg\max_{\mathbf{x}} \; \alpha_1 \left[\beta + \left(1 - \beta\right)^2 s^2 \psi\right] u_1\left(\mathbf{x}\right) + \alpha_2\beta u_2\left(\mathbf{x}\right). \quad (3.6)$$

Thus, in equilibrium, policy is biased toward group 1, with the bias increasing in the share $(1 - \beta)$ of uninformed voters and the effectiveness of campaign spending (as captured by s and ψ). This bias, however, comes at no cost to group 1, as equilibrium contributions are zero, given that $\mathbf{x}_A^* = \mathbf{x}_B^*$. In this model, campaign contributions are entirely off the equilibrium path. Intuitively, each party biases its platform toward group 1 to prevent campaign funds from flowing to the other party.

The model thus provides a theoretical explanation for the empirical observation that campaign contributions are often small relative to the stakes involved (Ansolabehere, de Figueiredo, and Snyder, 2003). Other models provide insight into the campaign spending that does occur. Grossman and Helpman (1996, 2001), for example, show that equilibrium contributions may be positive when organized groups can bargain with candidates over policy *prior* to platform choice.

This said, it is worth stressing that the model presented here, like many of those in the previous two chapters, assumes that parties can make binding campaign promises. Differences in expected policy implementation may be greater when parties and other democratic institutions are weak, as in many new democracies (Robinson and Verdier, 2002; Keefer, 2007; Gehlbach et al., 2010). To the extent that is the case, campaign expenditures may be correspondingly large.

3.3 Informative Campaign Finance

The models just presented take a "black box" approach to campaign finance, simply assuming that the election outcome can be manipulated through campaign spending. In this section, we show how this assumption can be rationalized. The model presented here, which is a simplified version of Ashworth (2006), assumes that voters are uncertain about a candidate's type. "Good" types have verifiable information about their type that can be transmitted to voters through advertising. An incumbent, for example, might advertise actions that she has taken to benefit her constituents during her time in office. The candidate, however, has no independent access to campaign finance, and so she must raise funds from organized interests by promising to provide special favors if elected. Seeing that a candidate has advertised, voters therefore infer that the candidate is a good type but also that she has made promises that they might not want her to keep.

The model has the structure of a simple signaling game. There are two strategic players, an incumbent and a representative voter. The incumbent's type, which may be either good or bad, is private information. The incumbent runs against a challenger, who is a passive player of unknown type. The voter's prior belief is that the incumbent is good with probability $p \in \left[\frac{1}{2}, 1\right)$, where p is a parameter of the model, and that the challenger is good with probability one-half. The assumption that $p \geq \frac{1}{2}$ captures a form of incumbency advantage: the incumbent's reputation is at least as good as the challenger's. This can be motivated by selection, as the incumbent is unlikely to have been elected in the first place if she were not perceived to be of above-average quality. Election of a good type provides a payoff to the voter of $\theta > 0$, whereas election of a bad type provides a payoff normalized to zero.

A good incumbent has verifiable information that can be communicated to the voter through advertising. As just mentioned, however, advertising requires that the incumbent raise campaign funds by promising favors to organized groups whose interests are not necessarily aligned with those of the voter. Rather than model this process explicitly (we take up bargaining between politicians and organized groups in the following sections), we assume that the voter suffers a cost $\phi > 0$ if an incumbent who advertises is elected. We assume that the good incumbent prefers to advertise if and only if doing so results in a strictly higher probability of reelection (e.g., because raising campaign funds requires effort or because she dislikes granting favors to special interests). As we

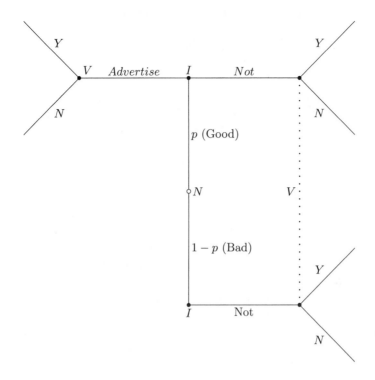

Figure 3.1. The structure of the model in Section 3.3.

will show, the existence of an equilibrium in which the incumbent advertises depends on the relationship between θ and ϕ, which respectively capture the positive and negative consequences of campaign advertising.

Figure 3.1 illustrates the timing of events. Nature (N) initially determines the incumbent's type. A good incumbent (I) may either advertise or not; a bad incumbent has nothing to advertise. The voter (V) observes whether the incumbent advertises but not her type, following which the voter decides whether to reelect the incumbent (Y) or not (N).

We introduce aggregate uncertainty about the election outcome by assuming that there is a random shock to the voter's preferences after the incumbent's move but before the voter decides for whom to vote. In particular, assume that the voter's payoff from electing the challenger is augmented by ϵ, where ϵ is a random variable with strictly increasing distribution F on the real number line. This implies that the incumbent's probability of winning is strictly between zero and one for all possible advertising decisions and inferences about her type.

We look for a separating equilibrium, where the good type advertises and the bad type does not. We begin by considering the voter's decision, given the incumbent's observed action $a \in \{0, 1\}$, where $a = 1$ indicates advertising and $a = 0$ indicates not advertising. Let $\mu(a)$ denote the voter's posterior belief that the incumbent is good, given her action a. Then the voter prefers to reelect the incumbent if

$$\mu(a)\theta - a\phi \geq \frac{1}{2}\theta + \epsilon. \tag{3.7}$$

The left-hand side of this inequality is the expected payoff from voting for the incumbent: with probability $\mu(a)$ the incumbent is the good type, who provides a benefit of θ if elected, but this benefit is at least partially offset by the cost ϕ of the favor (implicitly) granted to special interests if the incumbent has raised campaign funds to advertise. The right-hand side is the expected payoff from electing the challenger, who is the good type with probability one-half.

Clearly, $\mu(1) = 1$ in any equilibrium, as only the good type has verifiable information to advertise. Substituting these beliefs into Condition 3.7, the probability that the incumbent wins in a separating equilibrium, given that she advertises, is

$$\Pr\left(\theta - \phi \geq \frac{1}{2}\theta + \epsilon\right) = F\left(\frac{1}{2}\theta - \phi\right).$$

Further, in a separating equilibrium, $\mu(0) = 0$, as the voter's beliefs must be consistent with the incumbent's equilibrium strategy. The probability that a good incumbent wins if she deviates to not advertising is therefore

$$\Pr\left(0 \geq \frac{1}{2}\theta + \epsilon\right) = F\left(-\frac{1}{2}\theta\right).$$

It is thus a best response for a good incumbent to advertise if and only if

$$F\left(\frac{1}{2}\theta - \phi\right) > F\left(-\frac{1}{2}\theta\right).$$

(Recall that the incumbent prefers to advertise if and only if doing so strictly increases her probability of winning.) Using the assumption that F is strictly increasing, this simplifies to

$$\frac{1}{2}\theta - \phi > -\frac{1}{2}\theta,$$

or $\theta > \phi$.

Intuitively, for a good incumbent to want to signal her type by advertising, the benefit to voters from electing a good candidate must be large enough to offset the cost of promises made to secure campaign funds. A system of public financing can eliminate this trade-off by providing good candidates the opportunity to signal their type without making promises to organized groups. Whether this is good for voters depends on various factors, including whether public financing encourages informative advertising that would otherwise not take place, as well as the relative cost to voters of financing public campaigns.

There are many ways to model the impact of campaign spending on voter behavior. Coate (2004) adopts an approach similar to that taken here, assuming that campaign advertising is directly informative about a candidate's quality (see also Austen-Smith [1987] for an early contribution). Both the Ashworth and Coate models assume that advertisements convey verifiable information about the candidate doing the advertising; Exercise 3.5 explores the converse case, where candidates have verifiable information about their opponents' quality that can be communicated through advertising. Gerber (1996) and Prat (2002), in contrast, show that campaign advertising can be indirectly informative if contributors are able to directly observe candidate type: voters infer that candidates who advertise have been observed by funders to be of high quality.

3.4 Bargaining over Policy

Section 3.2 examines influence by organized groups when two parties compete in an election. Here we assume instead a single policy maker—elected politician, bureaucrat, autocrat—with the ability to unilaterally set policy. For simplicity, we refer to this actor as a "politician" (P). Further, we assume the presence of a single lobby (L) that represents some organized group. In the following section we consider lobbying by multiple organized groups.

The politician has **control rights** over policy—the decision is hers—but the lobby may influence policy by providing a contribution C to the politician in return for implementing a policy to its liking. For concreteness, assume that the policy space is the real number line, with generic policy x, and assume that the politician and lobby have preferences over

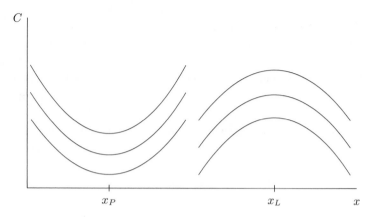

Figure 3.2. Representative indifference curves for the politician and lobby.

policy and contributions represented by

$$u_P = -\gamma_P \left(x - x_P\right)^2 + C, \qquad (3.8)$$

$$u_L = -\gamma_L \left(x - x_L\right)^2 - C, \qquad (3.9)$$

respectively. Thus, x_L and x_P are the lobby's and politician's most-preferred policies, and $\gamma_L, \gamma_P > 0$ represent the degree to which the lobby and politician value policy over contributions. This **quasilinear form** (so called because only the contribution enters linearly into the utility function) is clearly special, though it is common in the literature. Intuitively, there are no wealth effects: the marginal benefit of a change in x is independent of C.

These preferences can be represented graphically by plotting indifference curves in (x, C) space, as in Figure 3.2. (In the figure, $x_L > x_P$, but nothing in the model requires that.) The curves on the left are representative indifference curves for the politician. The quasilinear form of the utility function implies that the indifference curves are parallel, and the convex shape follows from the assumption of quadratic policy loss: as policy moves away from x_P, the politician must receive an increasingly large contribution to remain indifferent between that policy and her most-preferred policy x_P. Similarly, the concave curves on the right are representative indifference curves for the lobby, the peaks of which are at x_L. Both politician and lobby prefer points on an indifference curve to those "outside" it.

In principle, we could model the bargaining process explicitly as an extensive-form game between the politician and lobby. In many such models (e.g., Rubinstein's [1982] model of alternating offers), the bargaining outcome is **Pareto efficient**: there is no other outcome such that both actors are at least as well off and one is strictly better off. In applied work, it is therefore common to abstract from the details of the bargaining process and simply assume that bargaining is efficient. In the setting here, this implies that the outcome will be some point (x, C) such that the politician's and lobby's indifference curves through (x, C) are tangent to each other.

Formally, an efficient bargaining outcome must solve

$$\max_{x,C} \; - \gamma_L \left(x - x_L\right)^2 - C \tag{3.10}$$

$$\text{s.t.} \; - \gamma_P \left(x - x_P\right)^2 + C \geq \bar{u}_P,$$

where $\bar{u}_P$ is some constant. Neither actor can be made better off without making the other worse off. (Equivalently, we could write the problem as maximizing the politician's utility, given the constraint that the lobby be left with some $\bar{u}_L$.) Clearly, the constraint must hold with equality, as otherwise the lobby could increase its utility by reducing its contribution to the politician, so

$$C = \bar{u}_P + \gamma_P \left(x - x_P\right)^2.$$

Substituting this value into the objective function simplifies the problem to finding the x that maximizes the joint utility of the lobby and the politician:

$$-\gamma_L \left(x - x_L\right)^2 - \gamma_P \left(x - x_P\right)^2.$$

(We ignore $\bar{u}_P$, which does not depend on x.) The solution to this problem is

$$\frac{\gamma_P}{\gamma_L + \gamma_P} x_P + \frac{\gamma_L}{\gamma_L + \gamma_P} x_L. \tag{3.11}$$

Given quasilinear utility, any efficient bargaining process results in a policy that is a weighted average of the politician's and lobby's most-preferred policies, where the weights correspond to the value each places on policy relative to contributions. In particular, when policy is relatively important to the politician (γ_P is large relative to γ_L), then the equilibrium policy is close to x_P. Conversely, when the politician is more concerned with the compensation provided by the lobby (γ_P is small relative to γ_L), then the equilibrium policy is close to x_L.

The preferences represented by Equations 3.8 and 3.9 imply that utility can be freely transferred from the lobby to the politician, which is a strong assumption. For example, the cost to the lobby of organizing a mailing on the politician's behalf might be greater than the value of that mailing to the politician. Such **transaction costs** (Coase, 1937, 1960; Williamson, 1985) can easily be incorporated into the framework here by assuming that it costs the lobby $(1 + \kappa) C$ to provide a contribution of C to the politician, where $\kappa \geq 0$. Then the lobby's preferences can be represented by the function

$$\tilde{u}_L = -\gamma_L (x - x_L)^2 - (1 + \kappa) C,$$

which is equivalent to

$$-\left(\frac{\gamma_L}{1 + \kappa}\right) (x - x_L)^2 - C,$$

given that utility functions are unique up to a **positive affine transformation**.[4] The analysis then goes through as before, so that the equilibrium policy is

$$\frac{\gamma_P}{\tilde{\gamma}_L + \gamma_P} x_P + \frac{\tilde{\gamma}_L}{\tilde{\gamma}_L + \gamma_P} x_L,$$

where $\tilde{\gamma}_L \equiv \frac{\gamma_L}{1+\kappa}$. The larger are transaction costs (measured by κ), the less successful is the lobby in moving policy in its direction.

Expression 3.11 does not pin down the equilibrium contribution, which depends on details of the bargaining process such as the order in which offers are made and the players' discount factors. To motivate the analysis of multiple lobbies in the following section, consider the following bargaining environment. The lobby offers a **contribution function** $C(x)$ that promises a particular contribution $C \geq 0$ for every policy $x \in \Re$ that the politician could adopt. After $C(x)$ is offered, the politician chooses policy, and contributions are paid according to $C(x)$. (The assumption that promises are credible can be motivated by reputational concerns.)

We can think of the lobby as providing the politician with a "menu," where next to each policy is the price the lobby promises to pay. The lobby's problem is to choose a menu to maximize its utility, given that the politician optimally chooses x according to Equation 3.8. The key to solving this problem is to note that the lobby is indifferent among all contribution functions that induce the same outcome. Thus, the lobby's

---

[4] A positive affine transformation $v(u)$ takes the form $v = au + b$, where $a > 0$ and $b \in \Re$.

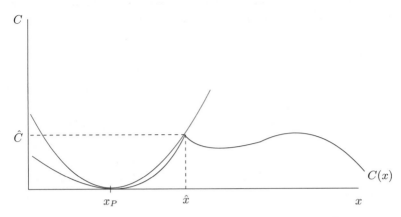

Figure 3.3. A contribution function that implements $(\hat{x}, \hat{C})$.

problem reduces to a) choosing some $(\hat{x}, \hat{C})$ to maximize its utility, given the constraint that the politician be willing to adopt $(\hat{x}, \hat{C})$ rather than walking away from the lobby's offer, and b) finding a contribution function that implements $(\hat{x}, \hat{C})$.

We have already shown how to solve the first part of this problem. The lobby chooses $\hat{x}$ from Expression 3.11, and the contribution $\hat{C}$ satisfies the constraint in the lobby's maximization problem (3.10) with equality. Given that the politician can guarantee herself a payoff of zero by walking away from the lobby's offer and implementing her most-preferred policy x_P, the politician's **reservation utility** is $\bar{u}_P = 0$, so that $\hat{C} = \gamma_P (\hat{x} - x_P)^2$.

All that remains is to find a contribution function that implements $(\hat{x}, \hat{C})$. Figure 3.3 illustrates one such function. As drawn, the politician is indifferent between $\hat{x}$, for which she receives $C(\hat{x}) = \hat{C}$, and x_P, for which she receives $C(x_P) = 0$. All other points on the contribution function leave the politician worse off than $(\hat{x}, \hat{C})$, as they lie below the indifference curve through that point. Thus, the politician (weakly) prefers to choose $\hat{x}$.

More generally, any contribution function implements $(\hat{x}, \hat{C})$ if it passes through $(\hat{x}, \hat{C})$ and nowhere lies above the politician's indifference curve through this point. Thus, with one lobby, the shape of the contribution function is unimportant as long as it satisfies this property.

As we show in the following section, however, the shape of contribution functions is important with multiple lobbies. We preview that discussion by considering two plausible restrictions on the shape that such functions may take in equilibrium.

First, we may require that the contribution function be differentiable in x for all $C(x) > 0$. In contrast to the contribution function illustrated in Figure 3.3, any such function is necessarily tangent to the politician's indifference curve through $\left(\hat{x}, \hat{C}\right)$. But recall that $\left(\hat{x}, \hat{C}\right)$ was chosen precisely because it is the point of tangency between an indifference curve for the lobby and the indifference curve for the politician that passes through $(x_P, 0)$. Thus, the slope of a differentiable contribution function that implements $\left(\hat{x}, \hat{C}\right)$ is equal to the slope of the lobby's indifference curve through $\left(\hat{x}, \hat{C}\right)$ at that point, that is, equal to the lobby's **marginal rate of substitution** between policy and contributions:[5]

$$\frac{\partial C(x)}{\partial x}\bigg|_{x=\hat{x}} = -2\gamma_L \left(\hat{x} - x_L\right).$$

When $x = \hat{x}$, a marginal change in x (which may increase or decrease the lobby's policy payoff, depending on the direction of the change) leaves the lobby's utility unchanged, as the corresponding change in contribution (which, conversely, makes the lobby worse or better off) exactly compensates the lobby for the change in its policy payoff. For this reason, we say that differentiable contribution functions are **locally compensating**.

Second, we may require that the contribution function be **compensating**, meaning that changes in $C(x)$ fully reflect changes in the lobby's policy payoff for all x (not just for marginal changes around $\hat{x}$, as with a locally compensating function), wherever contributions are positive.[6] In contrast to locally compensating contribution functions, there is only one compensating contribution function for a given $\left(\hat{x}, \hat{C}\right)$; Figure 3.4 shows the shape this function must take. Intuitively, if the politician knows the lobby's preferences, then it is plausible that she expects to

---

[5] The formula for an indifference curve in (x, C)-space is given by $u(x, C) = \bar{u}$, where the particular curve is defined by utility level $\bar{u}$. The slope of this curve—the marginal rate of substitution—can be found by differentiating this equation implicitly with respect to x: $u_x + u_C \frac{\partial C}{\partial x} = 0$, where u_x and u_C denote partial derivatives with respect to u and C, respectively. Rearranging terms gives $\frac{\partial C}{\partial x} = -\frac{u_x}{u_C}$. Substituting in the lobby's utility function gives the expression in the equation.

[6] Bernheim and Whinston (1986) refer to such compensation functions as "truthful," as they reflect the lobby's "true" valuation of x.

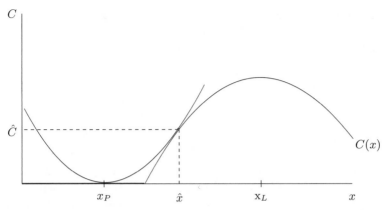

Figure 3.4. A compensating contribution function that implements $\left(\hat{x}, \hat{C}\right)$.

receive a smaller contribution the worse off the lobby will be as a result of her policy choice (i.e., the lobby is "compensated" for the change in policy). Thus, wherever contributions are positive, the contribution function is identical to the lobby's indifference curve passing through $\left(\hat{x}, \hat{C}\right)$.

3.5 *Menu Auctions*

We now extend the model of the previous section to consider influence by multiple lobbies, indexed by j. Lobby j has preferences represented by

$$u_j = -\gamma_j \left(x - x_j\right)^2 - C^j,$$

where C^j is a contribution to the politician by lobby j. The lobbies simultaneously and independently offer contribution functions, where $C^j\left(x\right)$ denotes the "menu" offered by lobby j, following which the politician chooses x and collects $\sum_j C^j\left(x\right)$.

Bernheim and Whinston (1986) showed how such **menu auctions** can be analyzed in a general setting. Grossman and Helpman (1994) were the first to apply the menu-auction framework to a particular lobbying environment, and today the term "Grossman-Helpman model" is typically applied to any lobbying model that takes the form of a menu auction.

Equilibrium requires that each lobby's contribution function be a best response to every other lobby's contribution function and that the politician choose policy optimally, given the contribution functions offered by the lobbies. As in the case with one lobby, this problem can be simplified by noting that for any lobby j, choosing an optimal contribution function reduces to a) choosing some $\left(\hat{x}^j, \hat{C}^j\right)$ to maximize the lobby's utility, given the constraint that the politician be willing to accept $\left(\hat{x}^j, \hat{C}^j\right)$ rather than walking away from the lobby's offer, and b) finding a contribution function that implements $\left(\hat{x}^j, \hat{C}^j\right)$. The key difference is that "walking away" no longer implies that the politician forsakes any contribution and chooses her most-preferred policy x_P. Rather, if the politician rejects lobby j's offer, she chooses the policy that maximizes her utility given the contribution functions named by all other lobbies.

Consider, for example, the case of two lobbies. Taking lobby 2's contribution function $C^2(x)$ as given, lobby 1 chooses $\left(\hat{x}^1, \hat{C}^1\right)$ to solve

$$\max_{x,C} \ -\gamma_1 (x - x_1)^2 - C$$
$$\text{s.t.} \ -\gamma_P (x - x_P)^2 + C + C^2(x) \geq \bar{u}_{P2},$$

where $\bar{u}_{P2}$ is the politician's utility from the best possible choice of x, given that she accepts contributions only from lobby 2. In other words, the politician must (weakly) prefer implementing $\hat{x}^1$ and receiving $\hat{C}^1$ and $C^2(\hat{x}^1)$ (the latter being the contribution from lobby 2 when $\hat{x}_1$ is implemented) to choosing the best possible policy when lobbied only by lobby 2.

In equilibrium, each lobby j chooses the same $\hat{x}^j$, as otherwise at least one lobby expects the politician to do something that she will not. However, given the freedom each lobby has in designing a contribution function once it has chosen $\left(\hat{x}^j, \hat{C}^j\right)$, in general there are multiple qualitatively different equilibria of this game—that is, equilibria with different policies and contributions. To restrict the set of equilibria, we follow the discussion in the previous section and assume that contribution functions take a particular shape.

We begin by restricting attention to equilibria in which contribution functions are locally compensating (i.e., differentiable). Then, given the preferences assumed here, the outcome is jointly efficient among the politician and both lobbies (i.e., none of the actors can be made better off without making at least one of the others worse off). To see this, note that in equilibrium the politician solves

$$\max_x \, - \gamma_P \left(x - x_P\right)^2 + \sum_j C^j\left(x\right),$$

where $C^j\left(x\right)$ is the contribution function named by lobby j. The first-order condition for this problem is

$$-2\gamma_p\left(\hat{x} - x_P\right) + \sum_j \frac{\partial C^j\left(x\right)}{\partial x}\Big|_{x=\hat{x}} = 0,$$

where we use $\hat{x}$ to reflect the fact that, in equilibrium, the politician implements the policy chosen in common by both lobbies. But, as discussed in the previous section, with differentiable contribution functions,

$$\frac{\partial C^j\left(x\right)}{\partial x}\Big|_{x=\hat{x}} = -2\gamma_j\left(\hat{x} - x_j\right),$$

which is the marginal rate of substitution between policy and contributions for lobby j at $\left(\hat{x}, \hat{C}^j\right)$. Substituting this into the first-order condition and simplifying gives

$$-\gamma_p\left(\hat{x} - x_P\right) - \sum_j \gamma_j\left(\hat{x} - x_j\right) = 0,$$

which is the necessary and sufficient condition for $\hat{x}$ to maximize the joint utility of the politician and both lobbies:

$$\hat{x} = \arg\max_x \, - \gamma_P\left(x - x_P\right)^2 - \sum_j \gamma_j\left(x - x_j\right)^2.$$

The result that equilibrium policy is jointly efficient when contribution functions are differentiable is sensitive to assumptions about the politician's and lobbies' preferences, though as Bernheim and Whinston (1986) show, joint efficiency is guaranteed with *compensating* contribution functions. In addition, when contribution functions are compensating, we can pin down the equilibrium contributions.

To illustrate, return to the case with two lobbies. In equilibrium, each lobby chooses the optimal policy-contribution pair, given the contribution function chosen by the other lobby. Let $\hat{x}$ denote the policy chosen in equilibrium, and let $\tilde{x}^j$ be the policy chosen when the politician takes into account only lobby j's contribution function $C^j\left(x\right)$. Then lobby 1's equilibrium contribution is given by

$$-\gamma_P\left(\hat{x} - x_P\right)^2 + \hat{C}^1 + C^2\left(\hat{x}\right) = -\gamma_P\left(\tilde{x}^2 - x_P\right)^2 + C^2\left(\tilde{x}^2\right).$$

The expression on the left-hand side of the equation is the politician's utility in equilibrium. Given that lobby 1 would never offer more than necessary to induce the politician to implement $\hat{x}$, this must equal the utility the politician could receive by ignoring lobby 1 and instead choosing policy based solely on lobby 2's offer, which is given on the right-hand side of the equation. Solving for $\hat{C}^1$ gives

$$\hat{C}^1 = \left[-\gamma_P \left(\tilde{x}^2 - x_P \right)^2 + \gamma_P \left(\hat{x} - x_P \right)^2 \right] + \left[C^2 \left(\tilde{x}^2 \right) - C^2 \left(\hat{x} \right) \right]. \quad (3.12)$$

Lobby 1's equilibrium contribution is equal to the difference in the politician's policy payoff from implementing $\tilde{x}^2$ rather than $\hat{x}$, plus the difference in the contribution provided by lobby 2 if $\tilde{x}^2$ is implemented rather than $\hat{x}$. Intuitively, to leave the politician indifferent between implementing $\hat{x}$ and implementing $\tilde{x}^2$, lobby 1 must compensate the politician for any gain forfeited—policy or contributions—by not implementing $\tilde{x}^2$.

When contribution functions are compensating, then $C^2 \left(\tilde{x}^2 \right) - C^2 \left(\hat{x} \right)$ can be derived from the condition that lobby 2's contribution function leave it indifferent between $\tilde{x}^2$ and $\hat{x}$:

$$-\gamma_2 \left(\tilde{x}^2 - x_2 \right)^2 - C^2 \left(\tilde{x}^2 \right) = -\gamma_2 \left(\hat{x} - x_2 \right)^2 - C^2 \left(\hat{x} \right).[7]$$

Rearranging,

$$C^2 \left(\tilde{x}^2 \right) - C^2 \left(\hat{x} \right) = -\gamma_2 \left(\tilde{x}^2 - x_2 \right)^2 + \gamma_2 \left(\hat{x} - x_2 \right)^2. \quad (3.13)$$

Substituting Equation 3.13 into Equation 3.12 gives

$$\hat{C}^1 = \gamma_P \left[- \left(\tilde{x}^2 - x_P \right)^2 + \left(\hat{x} - x_P \right)^2 \right] + \gamma_2 \left[- \left(\tilde{x}^2 - x_2 \right)^2 + \left(\hat{x} - x_2 \right)^2 \right].$$

This expression says that the equilibrium contribution by lobby 1 compensates both the politician and lobby 2 for implementing $\hat{x}$ rather than $\tilde{x}^2$. Intuitively, when contribution functions are compensating, each lobby fully internalizes the effect its presence has on the utility of every other lobby, as well as on the politician.

To derive a closed-form solution for $\hat{C}^1$ in terms of parameters of the model, it remains only to know $\tilde{x}^2$, the policy the politician would implement if she ignored lobby 1's offer and chose policy based on lobby 2's contribution function and her policy preferences. Intuitively, this is the policy that is jointly efficient between the politician and lobby 2,

---

[7] To ease notation, we assume that parameter values are such that the constraint $C_2 \left(\tilde{x}^2 \right) \geq 0$ does not bind. Informally, this is guaranteed by a weak conflict of interest among lobbies, in the sense that $\tilde{x}^2$ is not a bad outcome for lobby 2, relative to $\hat{x}$. Gehlbach et al. (2010) provide a formalization of this assumption in a general setting.

that is,

$$\tilde{x}^2 = \frac{\gamma_P}{\gamma_P + \gamma_2} x_P + \frac{\gamma_2}{\gamma_P + \gamma_2} x_2.$$

To verify that this is the case, observe that $\tilde{x}^2$ is the x that maximizes the politician's utility when she ignores lobby 1's offer:

$$\max_x \; -\gamma_P (x - x_P)^2 + C^2(x). \tag{3.14}$$

Solving for $C^2(x)$ from Equation 3.13 (where here we use generic policy x rather than the particular policy $\tilde{x}^2$) and substituting into Expression 3.14 gives

$$\max_x \; -\gamma_P (x - x_P)^2 + C^2(\hat{x}) - \gamma_2 (x - x_2)^2 + \gamma_2 (\hat{x} - x_2)^2.$$

Rewriting this in terms of expressions that depend only on x gives

$$\max_x \; -\gamma_P (x - x_P)^2 - \gamma_2 (x - x_2)^2,$$

which is the problem that solves for the policy that is jointly efficient between the politician and lobby 2.

Exercises

3.1   Consider the model of Section 3.1, where $\pi(C_A, C_B)$ is given by Equation 3.4 and $\alpha \in \left[0, \frac{1}{\gamma}\right)$. There is a mixed-strategy Nash equilibrium of this game in which:

- Party A plays $C_A = 0$ with probability $\gamma\alpha$ and mixes according to the uniform distribution on $\left[0, \frac{1}{\gamma} - \alpha\right]$ with probability $1 - \gamma\alpha$.
- Party B plays $C_B = 0$ with probability $\gamma\alpha$ and mixes according to the uniform distribution on $\left(\alpha, \frac{1}{\gamma}\right]$ with probability $1 - \gamma\alpha$.

Verify this as follows:

(a) Show that party A's expected utility is the same for all $C_A \in \left[0, \frac{1}{\gamma} - \alpha\right]$, given party B's strategy.

(b) Show that party B's expected utility is the same for all $C_B \in \{0\} \cup \left(\alpha, \frac{1}{\gamma}\right]$, given party A's strategy.

(c) Show that party A does not strictly prefer to deviate to some $C_A > \frac{1}{\gamma} - \alpha$, given party B's strategy.

(d) Show that party B does not strictly prefer to deviate to some $C_B \notin \{0\} \cup \left(\alpha, \frac{1}{\gamma}\right]$, given party A's strategy.

Which party spends more in expectation? Which earns positive rents? Interpret your results.

3.2 Consider the model of Section 3.1, where $\pi(C_A, C_B)$ is given by Equation 3.4, though now assume that parties differ in their cost of raising campaign funds, with the cost to party P given by $\gamma_P C_P$. Without loss of generality, assume that $\gamma_A \leq \gamma_B$.

Restrict attention to the case where $\alpha = 0$. There is a mixed-strategy Nash equilibrium of this game in which:

- Party A mixes according to the uniform distribution on $\left[0, \frac{1}{\gamma_B}\right]$.
- Party B plays $C_B = 0$ with probability $1 - \frac{\gamma_A}{\gamma_B}$ and mixes according to the uniform distribution on $\left[0, \frac{1}{\gamma_B}\right]$ with probability $\frac{\gamma_A}{\gamma_B}$.

Verify that this is an equilibrium as follows:

(a) Show that party A's expected utility is the same for all $C_A \in \left[0, \frac{1}{\gamma_B}\right]$, given party B's strategy.
(b) Show that party B's expected utility is the same for all $C_B \in \left[0, \frac{1}{\gamma_B}\right]$, given party A's strategy.
(c) Show that party A does not strictly prefer to deviate to some $C_A > \frac{1}{\gamma_B}$, given party B's strategy.
(d) Show that party B does not strictly prefer to deviate to some $C_B > \frac{1}{\gamma_B}$, given party A's strategy.

Which party spends more in expectation? Which earns positive rents? Interpret your results.

3.3 Generalize the model of Section 3.2 to an arbitrary number of organized and unorganized groups, where G is the set of all groups, $L \subseteq G$ is the subset of groups that are organized, and $\sum_{g \in G} \alpha_g = 1$. Let C_{gA} and C_{gB} be campaign spending by group g in support of parties A and B, respectively, with total spending $C_A = \sum_{g \in L} C_{gA}$ and $C_B = \sum_{g \in L} C_{gB}$.

(a) Derive the optimal contribution for every organized group $g \in L$, given $\mathbf{x}_A$ and $\mathbf{x}_B$.
(b) Write down the probability that party A wins as a function only of $\mathbf{x}_A$ and $\mathbf{x}_B$.
(c) Write down the expression giving the optimal policy for each

party. What is the optimal policy if all groups are organized? If no groups are organized?

3.4 Consider the model of informative campaign finance in Section 3.3. Derive the condition for existence of a pooling equilibrium, in which neither type advertises, as follows:

(a) Derive the probability that the good type wins in equilibrium.
(b) Derive the probability that the good type wins if she deviates to advertising.
(c) What condition must hold for there to exist a pooling equilibrium? Interpret your result.

3.5 Consider the following variant on the model of informative campaign finance in Section 3.3. As before, there are two strategic actors: an incumbent and a voter, though now there is uncertainty about the challenger's type rather than the incumbent's. In particular, the voter believes the incumbent to be "good" with certainty, whereas the voter's prior belief is that the challenger is "good" with probability q and "bad" with probability $1 - q$, where as before the marginal benefit to the voter of electing a good type is $\theta > 0$. The incumbent has verifiable information about the challenger's type (e.g., because of opposition research) and may communicate that the challenger is "bad," if this is the case, through advertising. As before, the voter suffers a cost of $\phi > 0$ if the incumbent advertises and is elected. All other elements of the game are identical to the model in Section 3.3.

Solve for the condition on parameters such that there is a separating equilibrium in which the incumbent advertises if the challenger is bad. How do your results differ qualitatively, if at all, from the case examined in Section 3.3 in which the incumbent has verifiable information about her own type?

3.6 Consider the following environment. There is a continuum of rich (r) citizens of mass $\alpha \in \left(0, \frac{1}{2}\right)$, each of whom has pre-tax income equal to one. In addition, there is a continuum of poor (p) citizens of mass $1 - \alpha$, each of whom has pre-tax income equal to zero. At issue is the tax rate $\tau \in [0, 1]$ assessed on the incomes of the rich: when the tax rate is τ, any rich citizen has post-tax income of

$$1 - \tau,$$

whereas any poor citizen has post-tax income of

$$\frac{\alpha\left(\tau - \tau^2\right)}{1 - \alpha}.$$

This may be derived as follows: a) there is a deadweight loss from taxation that comes out of the government budget constraint equal to proportion τ of all tax revenue, b) tax revenue net of the deadweight loss is divided equally among the poor.

The following problems explore political conflict between rich and poor in this environment using three alternative models of policy choice:

(a) Hotelling-Downs: There are two political parties $P = A, B$, each of which is office-seeking. Each party P announces a tax rate $\tau_P \in [0, 1]$. Citizens vote for the party whose announced tax rate maximizes their post-tax income. What is the tax rate chosen by each party in equilibrium?

(b) Campaign finance: There are two political parties $P = A, B$, each of which is office-seeking. Each party P announces a tax rate $\tau_P \in [0, 1]$. Citizens vote as in the model of Section 3.2, where $u_g(\tau)$ is post-tax income for citizens in group $g \in \{p, r\}$. The rich are organized, whereas the poor are not. What is the tax rate chosen by each party in equilibrium? What are the contributions C_A and C_B chosen by the lobby in equilibrium?

(c) Lobbying: There is an elected politician who represents the poor but who chooses the tax rate $\tau \in [0, 1]$ under the influence of a single lobby representing the rich. In particular, the politician maximizes a weighted average of the aggregate post-tax income of all poor citizens and any contribution paid by the lobby:

$$\gamma\left[(1 - \alpha)\left(\frac{\alpha\left(\tau - \tau^2\right)}{1 - \alpha}\right)\right] + C.$$

The parameter $\gamma > 0$ measures the degree to which the politician values the welfare of poor citizens versus contributions by the rich. The lobby maximizes the aggregate post-tax income of all rich citizens, net of any contribution paid to the politician:

$$\alpha\left(1 - \tau\right) - C.$$

What is the tax rate chosen by the politician in equilibrium? What is the contribution C paid by the lobby in equilibrium?

(d) Interpret your results. How does the tax rate chosen in equilibrium in each of the three models compare to the utilitarian optimum?

3.7 Consider a model of influence by two lobbies, $j = 1, 2$, where each lobby is interested in maximizing the size of the transfer T_j that it receives from the government. Assume that there is a political opportunity cost of these transfers equal to $\gamma(T_1 + T_2)$, with $\gamma > 0$, so that the politician maximizes

$$u_P = -\gamma(T_1 + T_2) + (C_1 + C_2).$$

Each lobby j has preferences represented by

$$u_j = \ln(T_j) - C_j,$$

so that there is a decreasing marginal benefit to transfers.

(a) Restrict attention to equilibria in which contribution functions are locally compensating. Find the equilibrium policy as a function only of parameters of the model.

(b) Now restrict attention to equilibria in which contribution functions are compensating. Find the equilibrium contributions as a function only of parameters of the model.

3.8 Consider the following environment. There are two business sectors, $s = A, B$, each of which relies upon investment capital that is distributed by a politician (P). Let K_s be the investment capital provided to sector s, assume that the politician must allocate all available capital, and normalize total available capital to one. Thus, $K_A + K_B = 1$.

Sector A is organized and may lobby the politician for investment capital through the promise of contributions; Sector B is not. The total profit for sector s, denoted π_s, is defined by available investment capital and (for sector A) any contribution C paid to the politician:

$$\pi_A = \ln K_A - C,$$
$$\pi_B = \ln K_B.$$

Sector A maximizes π_A when lobbying the politician.

Beyond organization, the two sectors differ in externalities from their production. Sector A is populated by firms that produce some "social bad" (e.g., pollution), whereas sector B is populated by firms that produce some "social good" (e.g., education). The politician values these externalities, as well as any contribution C from sector A, with preferences represented by

$$u_P = -\alpha K_A + \gamma K_B + C,$$

where $\alpha, \gamma > 0$ and $\alpha + \gamma > 1$.

(a) Derive the equilibrium allocation of investment capital that results from the lobbying game between sector A and the politician. (Use the constraint $K_A + K_B = 1$ to express u_P in terms of K_A, then solve for the K_A that is jointly efficient between sector A and the politician.)

(b) Derive the allocation of investment capital optimal to the politician if she walks away from Sector A's offer. What is the politician's utility in this case? Use this to derive the equilibrium contribution from sector A to the politician.

(c) Which sector receives more investment capital in equilibrium? Interpret your result.

Now suppose that both sectors are organized. How do your results change as compared to the case with only one organized sector?

3.9   This problem follows Besley and Coate (2001) in extending the citizen-candidate model of Section 1.4.3 to incorporate lobbying as in Section 3.5. Assume a finite set of citizens who vote strategically and are potentially candidates for office. There is no exogenous benefit from holding office, but the election winner may earn an endogenous rent by "selling" policy. In particular, following the election, two lobbies $j = 1, 2$ simultaneously and independently name a contribution function $C^j(x)$ that promises a particular contribution $C \geq 0$ for every policy $x \in \Re$ that could be chosen by the election winner. Lobby 1 has preferences represented by

$$u_j = -\gamma (x - 1)^2 - C^1,$$

where $\gamma > 0$ and C^1 is the contribution paid by lobby 1 to the election winner. Similarly, lobby 2 has preferences represented by

$$u_2 = -\gamma (x + 1)^2 - C^2.$$

Finally, any citizen i incurs a cost of entry δ, receives a payoff of $-(x - x_i)^2$ if x is implemented by the election winner, and receives an additional payoff equal to the contributions paid by the lobbies if elected. Conditional on winning (the cost of entry having been sunk), any election winner i thus has preferences represented by

$$u_i = -(x - x_i)^2 + C^1 + C^2.$$

Assume a unique median most-preferred policy $x_m = 0$, which implies that the lobbies are polarized, relative to the median citizen. In what follows, restrict attention to equilibria in which contribution functions are compensating and citizens play weakly undominated voting strategies. Further, for simplicity, restrict attention to equilibria in which citizens abstain from voting if all candidates are expected to implement the same policy.

(a) Derive the policy outcome when a citizen with most-preferred policy x_i has been elected, that is, derive the equilibrium policy in the lobbying game where a citizen with ideal point x_i is the policy maker.

(b) Derive the contributions paid by each lobby to the election winner to induce this outcome.

(c) What type of citizen (i.e., what x_i) would voters with median ideal point $x_m = 0$ most prefer be elected, given their expectation that the election winner will be lobbied?

(d) Denoting the type identified in part (c) by $\bar{x}_i$, derive the policy payoff and endogenous rent to any citizen with ideal point $\bar{x}_i$ who wins office.

(e) Assume that there is an arbitrarily large number of citizens with most-preferred policy $\bar{x}_i$. Further, assume that δ is small enough that there is no one-candidate equilibrium. Denoting by R the endogenous rent from holding office derived in part (d), derive the condition for existence of an equilibrium with N identical candidates with ideal point $\bar{x}_i$. In other words, for what values of δ is there an equilibrium with N such candidates? (In constructing this equilibrium, assume that if—off the equilibrium path—any citizen j with ideal point $x_j \neq \bar{x}_i$ enters against these N candidates, then citizens play voting strategies such that a majority who prefer election of a candidate with ideal point $\bar{x}_i$ pool their votes behind one of the N identical candidates.)

4

Veto Players

All of the models we have considered so far implicitly assume a single policy maker. However, in many political environments policy can be changed only with the agreement of multiple actors. Such actors—those with the ability to block a change from the status quo—are known as **veto players**. Veto players might derive their power from a country's constitution, as when the constitution dictates that policy cannot be changed without the agreement of the parliament and the president. Alternatively, they might arise endogenously through the political process. Parties that join a governing coalition, for example, typically acquire a veto over policy change.

A political system can be characterized by the number, preferences, and proposal power of its veto players. This characterization, suggests Tsebelis (2002), is more informative than traditional labels such as "parliamentary system" or "presidential system," which may group together countries with fundamentally different configurations of veto players or obscure important similarities across seemingly different systems. Knowing the attributes of veto players within a system, we can predict the likelihood of change from the status quo.

In general, veto players theory suggests that policy stability should be greater when the number of veto players is large and when the preferences of those players are divergent. This basic result can be derived in a social choice framework, where the dynamic structure of decision making is ignored. More specific predictions about policy choice require that we know the sequence of decisions within a political system, that is, which veto player is the **agenda setter** and which react to proposals made by that player. These predictions are best derived in a game-theoretic framework.

Following this initial discussion, we turn to models in which veto players are identified with "pivotal" legislative actors who are necessarily included in any winning coalition. We show how such institutional details as supermajority requirements and gatekeeping power can easily be analyzed using the tools developed in earlier sections of this chapter. We also discuss a model of portfolio allocation, where partial veto power arises from the fact that parties cannot be forced to accept ministries against their will.

Finally, we depart from the standard emphasis on conflict among veto players to focus instead on conflict between veto players and special interests. We demonstrate that the presence of multiple veto players may weaken the ability of special interests to lobby for policies that they prefer to the status quo but that veto players do not.

4.1 Policy Stability

To explore the impact of veto players on policy stability, we focus for simplicity on the case of one-dimensional policy. Tsebelis (2002) shows how the framework can be generalized to multiple dimensions. Thus, the policy space is the real number line, with generic policy x. Let $\bar{x}$ denote the status quo policy. There is a finite set of veto players, indexed $i = A, B, \ldots$. Any veto player i has Euclidean preferences over x, with ideal point x_i.

We are interested in the relationship between policy stability and the configuration of veto players. To explore this relationship, we ask two questions:

(i) For a given status quo and configuration of veto players, which policies $x \neq \bar{x}$ are weakly preferred to $\bar{x}$ by *all* veto players? The set of such policies is the **winset** of $\bar{x}$, or $W(\bar{x})$.[1]

(ii) For a given configuration of veto players, which policies have the property that there is no other policy preferred by all veto players? The set of such policies is the **core**, that is, the core is the set of all policies x such that $W(x) = \emptyset$.

Loosely speaking, we can associate greater stability with smaller winsets (fewer policies that can defeat a particular status quo) and larger cores

---

[1] An alternative definition of the winset $W(x)$ is the set of policies that are *strictly* preferred to x. The definition here simplifies the game-theoretic analysis in the following section, as in equilibria in which the status quo is overturned, some veto players might be indifferent between the adopted policy and the status quo.

(more status quo policies that are invulnerable to change). As we will show, the addition of veto players a) weakly decreases the size of the winset for any status quo $\bar{x}$, and b) weakly increases the size of the core. (Technically, the winset and core are defined with respect to a particular preference-aggregation rule. Here, we refer to the unanimity winset and unanimity core. In this and the following two sections we use the terms "winset" and "core" for simplicity.)

To begin, consider the case of a single veto player with ideal point x_A. Because A has Euclidean preferences, she weakly prefers all policies that are at least as close to x_A as is $\bar{x}$. Thus, if $\bar{x} < x_A$, the winset of $\bar{x}$ is $W(\bar{x}) = (\bar{x}, x_A + (x_A - \bar{x})]$, whereas if $\bar{x} > x_A$, the winset of $\bar{x}$ is $W(\bar{x}) = [x_A - (\bar{x} - x_A), \bar{x})$. Clearly, the core is $\{x_A\}$: the only status quo policy that A would not want to change is her own ideal point.

Now consider adding a second veto player B, with $x_B > x_A$. How does the size of the winset change for a given status quo $\bar{x}$? To answer this, we explore the following five mutually exclusive and exhaustive cases:

- $\bar{x} < x_A$: As before, A weakly prefers all $x \in (\bar{x}, x_A + (x_A - \bar{x})]$ to $\bar{x}$. In contrast, B weakly prefers all $x \in (\bar{x}, x_B + (x_B - \bar{x})]$ to $\bar{x}$. The winset of x is the intersection of these two sets, that is, the policies that both A and B weakly prefer to $\bar{x}$. Because $x_B > x_A$, $W(\bar{x}) = (\bar{x}, x_A + (x_A - \bar{x})]$, that is, the winset is the same as when A is the only veto player.

- $\bar{x} = x_A$: As before, there is no policy that A prefers to x_A. The set of policies that both players weakly prefer to x_A must therefore be empty, so $W(\bar{x}) = \emptyset$. Thus, the winset is identical to that when A is the only veto player.

- $x_A < \bar{x} < x_B$: The set of policies that A weakly prefers to $\bar{x}$ is $[x_A - (\bar{x} - x_A), \bar{x})$, whereas the set of policies that B weakly prefers to $\bar{x}$ is $(\bar{x}, x_B + (x_B - \bar{x})]$. As there is no intersection of these two sets, $W(\bar{x}) = \emptyset$. In contrast, when A is the only veto player, the winset for positions of the status quo in this interval is not empty.

- $\bar{x} = x_B$: There is no policy that B weakly prefers to x_B, so $W(\bar{x}) = \emptyset$. Again, this contrasts with the case when A is the only veto player.

- $\bar{x} > x_B$: The set of policies that A weakly prefers to $\bar{x}$ is $[x_A - (\bar{x} - x_A), \bar{x})$, whereas the set of policies that B weakly prefers to $\bar{x}$ is $[x_B - (\bar{x} - x_B), \bar{x})$. Given that $x_B > x_A$, $W(\bar{x}) = [x_B - (\bar{x} - x_B), \bar{x})$, that is, the winset is smaller than when A is the only veto player.

Thus, for every possible status quo, the addition of a second veto player either reduces the size of the winset or leaves it unchanged.

How does the core change with the addition of a second veto player? From this analysis, we see that the winset is empty for all status quo policies in the interval $[x_A, x_B]$. Thus, the core is all positions in $[x_A, x_B]$, in contrast to the case where A is the only veto player, where the core is $\{x_A\}$. Intuitively, a change from any position between x_A and x_B makes at least one veto player worse off. (Because of this property, the unanimity core is sometimes referred to as the **Pareto set**.) Consequently, at least one player would veto any move from a status quo in this interval.

What if the second veto player has the same preferences as the first, that is, $x_A = x_B$? Then both the winset of any status quo policy and the core remain unchanged from the case with a single veto player. When, as here, a veto player is added whose ideal point is in the core of the ideal points of the existing veto players, we say that the new veto player is **absorbed**.

More generally, the winset of any status quo policy becomes (weakly) larger and the core becomes (weakly) smaller as x_B converges to x_A. Thus, policy stability—in the sense of small winsets and large cores— is diminished when the preferences of veto players are closely aligned. Intuitively, a veto over policy change is consequential only if some other player would not exercise the same veto. For this reason, empirical study of veto players often distinguishes between veto players from the same political party and those from different parties (e.g., Henisz, 2000; Beck et al., 2001).

The preceding discussion adopts the simplifying assumption that the location of the status quo policy is exogenous. Keefer and Stasavage (2003) demonstrate that the status quo (in their setting, the default inflation rate) may result from the decisions of private actors, in anticipation of actions taken by politicians. When this is the case, multiple veto players can act as a constraint on policy making ex post, so that promises made ex ante (e.g., not to inflate) are more credible.

4.2 Agenda Setting

The analysis just presented shows what policies *might* replace the status quo, but it does not pin down the actual policy chosen. Here, we assume that one of the players is the agenda setter, who may propose a change from the status quo. This policy change is adopted if all of the remaining veto players agree; otherwise, the status quo persists.

With one veto player, the sole veto player is the agenda setter, who always adopts her ideal point. With more than one veto player, the agenda setter knows that only policies weakly preferred to the status quo by the other veto players can be adopted. In any subgame-perfect Nash equilibrium, the policy adopted must therefore be among those most preferred by the agenda setter from the union of the winset of the status quo and the status quo itself, that is, $W(\bar{x}) \cup \{\bar{x}\}$. To see this, note that any policy within this set could be adopted, so the agenda setter would never choose a policy other than one among those she most preferred, and that at least one veto player (perhaps the agenda setter) would veto a policy outside of this set.[2]

To explore the implications of this result, consider the example in the previous section, where a second veto player B has been added, with $x_B > x_A$; we assume that A retains agenda-setting power. How does this change the equilibrium policy from that chosen when A is the sole veto player? As before, there are five cases to consider:

- $\bar{x} < x_A$: $W(\bar{x}) = (\bar{x}, x_A + (x_A - \bar{x})]$. Of all positions in $W(\bar{x}) \cup \{\bar{x}\}$, the agenda setter most prefers x_A, her ideal point.
- $\bar{x} = x_A$: $W(\bar{x}) = \emptyset$, so $W(\bar{x}) \cup \{\bar{x}\} = \{x_A\}$. The equilibrium policy is the status quo, which in this case is x_A.
- $x_A < \bar{x} < x_B$: $W(\bar{x}) = \emptyset$, so $W(\bar{x}) \cup \{\bar{x}\} = \{\bar{x}\}$. The equilibrium policy is the status quo.
- $\bar{x} = x_B$: $W(\bar{x}) = \emptyset$, so $W(\bar{x}) \cup \{\bar{x}\} = \{\bar{x}\}$. The equilibrium policy is the status quo, which in this case is x_B.
- $\bar{x} > x_B$: $W(\bar{x}) = [x_B - (\bar{x} - x_B), \bar{x})$, so $W(\bar{x}) \cup \{\bar{x}\} = [x_B - (\bar{x} - x_B), \bar{x}]$. Of these positions, the agenda setter most prefers $\max[x_B - (\bar{x} - x_B), x_A]$. In other words, if $\bar{x}$ is close to x_B, A must settle for a position between x_A and x_B, whereas if $\bar{x}$ is far from x_B, A can achieve her ideal point.

Figure 4.1 illustrates equilibrium policy as a function of the status quo $\bar{x}$ when A is the agenda setter. For $\bar{x} < x_A$ or $\bar{x} > x_B + (x_B - x_A)$, equilibrium policy is the same as when A is the only veto player. However,

---

[2] Note that there may be more than one subgame-perfect Nash equilibrium associated with a given policy outcome. For example, if the agenda setter most prefers the status quo $\bar{x}$, she could propose either $\bar{x}$ or a policy that she knows some other veto player will reject.

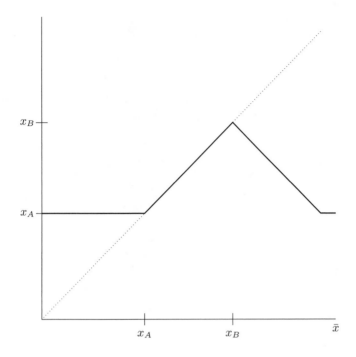

Figure 4.1. Equilibrium policy with two veto players when A is the agenda setter.

for intermediate positions of the status quo, equilibrium policy is closer to the status quo than when A is the only veto player.

This analysis seems to corroborate the finding of the previous section that policy stability is never smaller, and is sometimes larger, with the addition of a veto player. However, this assumes that A retains agenda-setting power when B is added as a veto player, which is a very strong assumption. A constitutional change that adds a new veto player, for example, might grant that actor agenda-setting power in certain policy arenas. What if instead B becomes the agenda setter? To explore this possibility, consider each of the five cases explored earlier:

- $\bar{x} < x_A$: $W(\bar{x}) = (\bar{x}, x_A + (x_A - \bar{x})]$. Of all positions in $W(\bar{x}) \cup \{\bar{x}\}$, the agenda setter (in this case B) most prefers $\min[x_A + (x_A - \bar{x}), x_B]$. As in the earlier case where $\bar{x} > x_B$, the agenda setter can achieve her ideal point when the status quo is far from the core, and other-

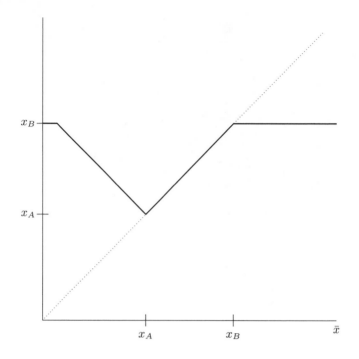

Figure 4.2. Equilibrium policy with two veto players when B is the agenda setter.

wise must settle for a position between the two veto players' ideal points.

- $\bar{x} = x_A$: $W(\bar{x}) = \emptyset$, so $W(\bar{x}) \cup \{\bar{x}\} = \{x_A\}$. The equilibrium policy is the status quo, which in this case is x_A.
- $x_A < \bar{x} < x_B$: $W(\bar{x}) = \emptyset$, so $W(\bar{x}) \cup \{\bar{x}\} = \{\bar{x}\}$. The equilibrium policy is the status quo.
- $\bar{x} = x_B$: $W(\bar{x}) = \emptyset$, so $W(\bar{x}) \cup \{\bar{x}\} = \{\bar{x}\}$. The equilibrium policy is the status quo, which in this case is x_B.
- $\bar{x} > x_B$: $W(\bar{x}) = [x_B - (\bar{x} - x_B), \bar{x})$, so $W(\bar{x}) \cup \{\bar{x}\} = [x_B - (\bar{x} - x_B), \bar{x}]$. The equilibrium policy is x_B.

Figure 4.2 illustrates equilibrium policy as a function of $\bar{x}$ when B is the agenda setter. In contrast to the case where A is the agenda setter, equilibrium policy is now x_B rather than x_A for extreme positions of the status quo. Moreover, for $\bar{x} < x_A$, equilibrium policy is *further* from the status quo than when A is the only veto player. The addition of a veto player may therefore make policy change more likely if the marginal veto player acquires agenda-setting power and prefers that policy move further in some direction than does the existing veto player.

The preceding discussion assumes that the agenda setter makes a take-it-or-leave-it offer, which is then subject to an up-or-down vote by the other veto player. In fact, as Primo (2002) shows, the equilibrium policy is the same when the agenda setter can respond to any veto with a new offer, regardless of whether bargaining takes place over a finite or infinite time horizon. More consequential is the assumption that the agenda setter knows the other veto player's preferences with certainty, which implies that vetoes never occur in equilibrium. When that is not the case, then the agenda setter must weigh the increased benefit of a more aggressive offer, in the event that it is accepted, against the increased probability that such an offer is rejected. Moreover, repetition now creates scope for reputation building, as a veto may cause the agenda setter to update her beliefs about what offers will be accepted; see, for example, McCarty (1997) and Cameron (2000). In addition, the party with the power to veto the agenda setter's offer may have an incentive to declare what offers she would be willing to accept. Matthews (1989) examines such a "cheap talk" model.

4.3 Pivots

As conceptualized in the previous two sections, veto players are those actors whose agreement is both necessary and sufficient to move policy from the status quo. A related set of models helps us to understand who these actors are. Focusing on policy making in legislatures, the theory of **pivots** (Krehbiel, 1998; see also Brady and Volden, 1998) identifies "pivotal" legislators whose agreement is both necessary and sufficient for a bill to become law. The authority of these legislators derives from certain aspects of legislative procedure, such as whether a supermajority is needed to conduct normal business or to override a presidential veto. Models in this literature address the conditions for **gridlock**, which is precisely what we call "policy stability" elsewhere in this chapter, as well as the size of coalitions that coalesce around particular bills. In addition, because agenda-setting power may arise from control of the legislative process through key committee assignments, these models speak to the power of the majority party (Cox and McCubbins, 2005).

We begin by examining pivots under majority rule. We then extend the model to incorporate supermajority considerations.

4.3.1 Majority Rule

Consider a legislature of N legislators, each of whom has Euclidean preferences over policy $x \in \Re$. For simplicity, we assume that N is odd and that legislators have unique ideal points. Order the legislators by their ideal points $1, \ldots, m, \ldots N$, where m is median legislator, and let x_i denote the ideal point of an arbitrary legislator i. As before, $\bar{x}$ denotes the status quo policy.

Under majority rule, the median legislator is pivotal: her agreement is both necessary and sufficient to move policy from the status quo. Clearly, the acquiescence of the median legislator is necessary, as a majority cannot be assembled in support of some $x' \neq \bar{x}$ without her support. Further, her support is sufficient, because if she (weakly) prefers some alternative x' over the status quo $\bar{x}$, then so do enough other legislators to form a majority. To see this, assume without loss of generality that $\bar{x} < x_m$. Given Euclidean preferences, the median legislator prefers any $x' \in (\bar{x}, 2x_m - \bar{x}]$ to $\bar{x}$, as x' is (weakly) closer to her ideal point. For any legislator $i > m$, any point in this interval is also closer to i's ideal point, and so preferred given Euclidean preferences. Thus, there is almost never gridlock (policy stability) under majority rule: so long as $\bar{x} \neq x_m$, there is a set of alternatives to the status quo that can garner the support of a majority. In the language of Section 4.1, the core is the single point $\{x_m\}$. Further, if we assume that amendments may be freely offered to any proposal on the floor, then policy necessarily converges to x_m.

In many settings, a proposal to alter the status quo is initiated by an agenda setter—committee or party leader—who presents a take-it-or-leave-it offer to the full legislature. This is the central insight of Romer and Rosenthal (1978), who show that the agenda setter can take advantage of her monopoly power to force an outcome different from that preferred by the median individual.[3] Formally, the agenda setter is a second veto player, as both her agreement and that of the median legis-

---

[3] Building on the insight of Niskanen (1971), who suggests that bureaucracies seek to maximize their budgets, Romer and Rosenthal illustrate their argument by assuming that an expenditure-maximizing committee proposes a budget to the residents of some jurisdiction, who then vote up or down on the proposal in a referendum. The logic travels easily to the legislative setting. For variants of the Romer-Rosenthal model in which voters are imperfectly informed about some feature of the political environment, see Banks (1990) and Lupia (1992).

lator is required for some proposal to be approved. Applying the analysis in Section 4.2, the agenda setter chooses her most-preferred point in $W(\bar{x}) \cup \{\bar{x}\}$, where $W(\bar{x})$ is the winset of $\bar{x}$. With the exception of the case where $\bar{x}$ is equal to x_m, the equilibrium policy is skewed in the direction of the agenda setter's ideal point.

In a legislative setting, the Romer-Rosenthal model implicitly assumes a **closed rule**, in which the proposal forwarded to the full legislature for consideration may not be amended. In this setting, the **gridlock interval**—the set of status quo policies such that no change is possible—is the set of all policies between x_m and the ideal point of the agenda setter, inclusive (i.e., the core). Any point outside of this interval is jointly inefficient: both the median legislator and the agenda setter would benefit by moving policy to a point in the core.[4] With a closed rule, the agenda setter would propose such a bill, and it would pass.

In contrast, when proposals are considered under an **open rule**, where any proposal on the floor is open to amendment, the equilibrium outcome may be inefficient. To see this, assume a sequential-move game between an agenda setter and the full legislature. Following the approach in Denzau and Mackay (1983), the agenda setter has **gatekeeping power**, deciding whether to initiate consideration of a change to the status quo by choosing a point $x' \in \Re$. If $x' = \bar{x}$, the game ends; implicitly, no bill has been forwarded to the floor for consideration. In contrast, if $x' \neq \bar{x}$, then the full legislature considers the bill, where amendments may be freely offered to any proposal on the floor.

Given that the agenda setter has proposed some $x' \neq \bar{x}$, the equilibrium outcome is that under majority rule. Thus, the agenda setter has a choice: a) maintain the status quo $\bar{x}$ by exercising her gatekeeping power, or b) adopt *some* proposal $x' \neq \bar{x}$ (it does not matter which), resulting in x_m. Clearly, the agenda setter would never propose some $x' \neq \bar{x}$ if the status quo $\bar{x}$ is closer to her ideal point than is x_m. But as Figure 4.3, where we denote the agenda setter by C ("committee"), illustrates, this implies that the gridlock interval includes policies that are inefficient: for all $\bar{x} \in (x_C - (x_m - x_C), x_C)$, there is no policy change, even though both the agenda setter and median legislator would be better off if policy moved to x_C. Essentially, a commitment problem prevents Pareto-improving changes from being implemented: when proposals are considered under an open rule, the full legislature cannot commit to not adopting x_m (Crombez, Groseclose, and Krehbiel, 2006).

---

[4] We define efficiency with respect to the two veto players. Obviously, some other legislators might be worse off.

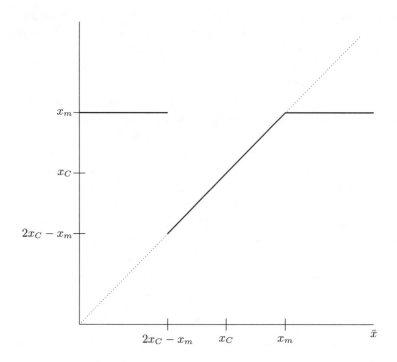

Figure 4.3. Equilibrium policy with an agenda-setting committee (C) that has gatekeeping power.

4.3.2 Supermajorities

In many institutional environments, a supermajority may be necessary to adopt certain changes to the status quo. For example, of the 184 countries surveyed by the Comparative Constitutions Project (Elkins, Ginsburg, and Melton, 2009), 61 allow vetoes to be overridden by a supermajority (typically two-thirds). Further, as illustrated by the cloture rule in the U.S. Senate, legislative chambers may require a supermajority to conduct normal business.

To analyze the role of supermajorities, we extend the previous discussion to identify the set of veto players in any legislative setting. To do so, we exploit a feature of Euclidean preferences: if some legislator i (weakly) prefers an alternative x' to the status quo $\bar{x}$, then so do either a) all legislators to her left (if $x' < \bar{x}$), or b) all legislators to her right (if $x' > \bar{x}$).[5] (This is simply a generalization of the argument with respect

---

[5] This statement holds more generally if preferences satisfy the **single-crossing**

to x_m in the previous section: with Euclidean preferences, all legislators with ideal points to one side of $\frac{x'+\bar{x}}{2}$ support one of the two alternatives, whereas all to the other side support the other.) Consequently, any $x' \neq \bar{x}$ that has the support of at least one legislator is supported by either a **left coalition** or a **right coalition**, where a left coalition includes legislator 1 and the right coalition includes legislator N. We identify the set of pivotal (i.e., veto) players by finding the smallest such coalitions such that a proposal can pass.

To illustrate, consider again the case of majority rule. The smallest left coalition that can pass a proposal is $\{1, \ldots, m\}$, that is, the median legislator and all legislators to her left. Similarly, the minimum winning right coalition is $\{m, \ldots, N\}$. The sole veto player is thus the median legislator m. If she supports a proposal, then so do all legislators to her left or right. If she does not, then the proposal does not have a majority.

Now consider the case of a legislature that can pass a proposal with a simple majority but that requires a supermajority to override a presidential veto. Assume that the president (P) also has Euclidean preferences over policy, with ideal point $x_P < x_m$. Then, as with majority rule, the smallest left coalition that can pass a proposal is $\{1, \ldots, m\}$. Any bill $x' < \bar{x}$ that has the support of this coalition will be signed by the president, given that the president's ideal point lies to the left of x_m.

Identifying the minimum winning right coalition is a bit trickier. To begin, define the **veto pivot** v as the legislator whose inclusion in a right coalition just guarantees that a presidential veto of some bill can be overridden. Formally, if V votes are necessary to overcome a presidential veto, then $v = N - V + 1$. For example, if the legislature has ninety-nine members, sixty-six of whom must vote for a proposal in order to overcome a presidential veto, then $v = 34$. Assume further that $x_P < x_v$, so that the president is more "extremist" than is the veto pivot; Figure 4.4 depicts the arrangement of the ideal points. Then the smallest right coalition that can pass a bill is $\{v, \ldots, N\}$. Any alternative $x' > \bar{x}$ that has the support of the veto pivot (and thus all legislators to her right) but not the president will be vetoed by the president, but that veto will be overridden.

As Figure 4.4 illustrates, $v < m$, so the minimum winning left coalition

---

property of Gans and Smart (1996). In contrast, single-peakedness is not sufficient for this statement to hold (and not necessary, as preferences may satisfy single-crossing but not single-peakedness). To see this, consider two legislators, $i = 1, 2$, and assume $\bar{x} < x_1 < x_2 < x'$. Then it is possible to construct preferences (e.g., in which legislator 2's utility drops away sharply on the right) such that legislator 1 prefers x' to $\bar{x}$ but legislator 2 does not.

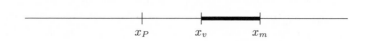

Figure 4.4. The configuration of ideal points in the example featuring a veto pivot. The core is marked with a thick black line.

includes both v and m. Similarly, the minimum winning right coalition includes these two legislators. Thus, any minimum winning coalition necessarily includes both v and m. Moreover, the support of both v and m is sufficient. If both prefer some alternative to the status quo, then so do all legislators to their left or right, which by construction is sufficient for a bill to pass.

The median legislator and veto pivot are veto players. Following the analysis in Section 4.1, the core is $[x_v, x_m]$. Any alternative to a status quo in this interval cannot garner the support of either a left or right coalition sufficient to pass. Intuitively, the opportunity for gridlock is greater when presidential vetoes and overrides are taken into account than is the case with majority rule.

Now extend the example to assume that any proposal requires a supermajority to pass, but that this supermajority is smaller than that required to override a veto. For concreteness, consider the U.S. Senate, where the filibuster rule necessitates a three-fifths majority on most matters, but the Constitution mandates a two-thirds majority to override a presidential veto. Given $x_P < x_v$, this institutional feature does not change the composition of the minimum winning right coalition, as that already includes more than three-fifths of the members. The minimum winning left coalition, however, is now $\{1, \ldots, f\}$, where $f > m$ is the **filibuster pivot**, whose inclusion guarantees a three-fifths majority. Now the veto players are v and f, and the core is $[x_v, x_f]$.

Our discussion of veto and filibuster pivots has thus far ignored the identity of the agenda setter. Indeed, in some legislative settings, it may be reasonable to assume that the agenda setter's ideal point is absorbed by that of the other veto (i.e., pivotal) players. For example, if the agenda setter is the median legislator, then she is necessarily included in both the minimum winning left and right coalitions. Even when that is the case, however, the equilibrium policy may depend on where in the core the agenda setter's ideal point lies.

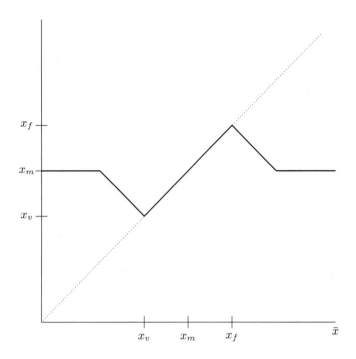

Figure 4.5. Equilibrium policy in the example featuring a veto pivot, filibuster pivot, and agenda-setting committee.

To illustrate, continue to assume that $x_v < x_m < x_f$, and assume
that the agenda setter's proposal is considered under a closed rule. As
demonstrated in Section 4.2, the equilibrium policy is the position most
preferred by the agenda setter in $W(\bar{x}) \cup \{\bar{x}\}$, where $W(\bar{x})$ is the winset
of the status quo. Relabeling A as v and B as f, Figures 4.1 and 4.2
plot the equilibrium policy against $\bar{x}$ when the agenda setter is the veto
pivot v and filibuster pivot f, respectively.

Now consider the equilibrium outcome when the agenda setter is the
median legislator. Figure 4.5 depicts the equilibrium policy as a function
of the status quo. For many values of the status quo, the equilibrium
policy is more centrist than when agenda-setting power is held by the
veto pivot or filibuster pivot. Thus, the preferences of the agenda setter
can influence the policy outcome even when that actor's ideal point is
absorbed by those of the other veto players.

4.4 Portfolio Allocation

Our discussion thus far has relied upon a common definition of veto players as actors with the ability to block any change from the status quo. Thus defined, the agreement of all veto players is both necessary and sufficient for some change in policy to be adopted.

In this section, we relax this definition of veto players to consider actors with the ability to block *some* changes from the status quo. The substantive focus of our discussion is government formation in parliamentary systems, a topic that we take up again in Chapter 6. Following Austen-Smith and Banks (1990) and Laver and Shepsle (1990, 1996), we assume that a government comprises a set of ministers, each of whom has responsibility for some policy dimension. Each ministry is assigned to a single party, which then has complete freedom to choose policy along that dimension. The assumption that parties have complete autonomy over the ministries they control captures the idea that policy is made in parliamentary systems by ministers rather than by parliament. Parliament has the power to call a **vote of no confidence**, however, so a government survives only if all possible majority coalitions view the existing allocation of portfolios as better than the available alternatives.

Critically, we assume that no party can be forced to accept a ministry against its will. This assumption gives existing government members a measure of veto power over changes to the status quo. Although they cannot prevent the formation of a government that excludes them, they are able to block a reshuffling of portfolios that leaves them in possession of at least one ministry. As we will see, this power has the effect of increasing government stability, just as (full) veto power typically increases policy stability. It also raises the possibility of a **minority government**, in which ministries are allocated to parties that collectively possess a minority of seats in the parliament.

To make this discussion concrete, consider a two-dimensional policy space $\Re^2$ with generic policy $\mathbf{x}$. Each policy dimension is the responsibility of a particular ministry (e.g., finance or foreign affairs), which must be assigned to exactly one party. Thus, no more than two parties can participate in the government.

There are three parties, $i = 1, 2, 3$. We abstract from issues of preference heterogeneity and discipline within parties, assuming that each party is a unitary actor with Euclidean preferences over policy, where $\mathbf{x}_i$ denotes party i's ideal point. As in the one-dimensional case, a party with Euclidean preferences prefers positions that are closer to its ideal

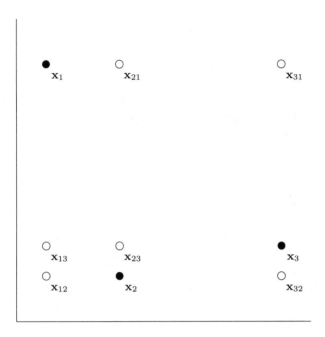

Figure 4.6. The configuration of ideal points (filled circles) and other implementable policies (open circles) in the discussion of portfolio allocation.

point (in Euclidean-distance terms) to those further away. Thus, a party with Euclidean preferences has circular indifference curves centered on its ideal point.

In particular, Euclidean preferences imply that a party's preferences are separable across the two dimensions, so that its most-preferred policy on one dimension is unaffected by the policy chosen on the other dimension. Consequently, a party in control of a ministry always chooses the same policy along the dimension controlled by that ministry, regardless of which party has been given control of the other ministry.

Figure 4.6 depicts the parties' ideal points and the policy outcomes associated with potential governments. Each party's ideal point (depicted by a filled circle) is one possible outcome: if assigned both ministries, then the party chooses its most-preferred policy on each dimension. We denote other possible outcomes (depicted by open circles) by $\mathbf{x}_{ij}$, where i and j denote the party assigned the ministry responsible for the first and second policy dimension, respectively.

The assignment of portfolios to parties dramatically restricts the set of implementable policies. In and of itself, this can increase the stability of governments, as there may be no implementable policy that is preferred to the status quo by a parliamentary majority. In particular, there may be stable status quo policies even when there is no Condorcet winner, an idea that originates with Shepsle (1979), who focused on the division of labor among legislative committees rather than among ministers. A status quo that is stable because institutions restrict the set of available alternatives, rather than because actors' preferences are restricted in some way, is known as a **structure-induced equilibrium** (see also Shepsle and Weingast, 1981b).

To see this, assume that no party has a majority of seats in parliament, so that any government can be overthrown by any two parties acting in concert. Consider the case where the status quo is x_{23}, a government in which party 2 has been given the first ministry and party 3 the second. By inspection, there is no other *implementable* policy that is preferred by at least two parties, although there are infinitely many points in $\Re^2$ that are preferred to x_{23} by at least two parties. Party 1, for example, prefers both x_{13} and x_{21} to x_{23}, but these points are farther from both party 2's and party 3's ideal points than is x_{23}. Thus, x_{23} is an element of the **portfolio core**: the set of implementable policies x such that there is no other implementable policy y preferred to x by parties that constitute a parliamentary majority.

In contrast, party 2's ideal point, x_2, is not in the portfolio core: both party 1 and party 3 prefer x_{23} to x_2. But if the status quo is x_2, party 2 would veto any move to x_{23}. Intuitively, party 2 would never agree to a redistribution of portfolios such that it lost one ministry while retaining the other. We say that x_2 is an element of the **restricted portfolio core**: the set of implementable policies x such that there is no other implementable policy y that is both a) preferred to x by parties that constitute a parliamentary majority, and b) preferred to x by any party that participates in y.

Thus, x_2 also represents a stable government, albeit one that could not have come into existence given the current allocation of seats in the parliament. What might be the origins of this minority government? One plausible scenario is that party 2 previously held a parliamentary majority, allowing it to form a government on its own. Having subsequently lost its majority, party 2 hangs onto power because of its ability to veto any alternative government acceptable to both party 1 and party 3. Laver and Shepsle (1996) refer to a party with this power—able to veto any government preferred by a majority to the government where that party controls all ministries—as a **strong party**.

The assumption that cabinet ministers have complete autonomy to choose policy in parliamentary systems (subject to retaining a majority in parliament) can be motivated on various grounds, not least of which is that the administrative machinery of the state is in the hands of the government. In certain environments, however, parliament may possess the power to pass any policy of its choosing, regardless of who controls the relevant ministry. Even so, the government (if not some particular minister) may set the terms of debate through its anticipated use of a **vote of confidence**, whereby the prime minister ties a policy proposal to the survival of the government. Exercise 4.6 considers this institutional feature.

4.5 Veto Players and Special Interests

The previous sections focus on policy conflict among veto players. Here we address instead policy conflict between veto players and special interests. Our modeling approach follows Gehlbach and Malesky (2010), who utilize the bargaining framework presented in Section 3.4 to show that it is easier for special interests to obtain preferential treatment when veto players are few in number. This result builds upon Max Weber's insight that "[t]he monocratic chief is more open to personal influence and is more easily swayed, thus making it more readily possible to influence the administration of justice and other governmental activity in favor of ... powerful interests" (Weber, 1978, pp. 283-284).

For concreteness, assume that policy takes one of two values, $x \in \{0, 1\}$, where the status quo $\bar{x} = 0$. There are one or more veto players, indexed by $i = 1, \ldots, N$, where $i = 1$ is the agenda setter and the other veto players are "ratifiers." There is a single lobby (L), which may provide contributions to any and all veto players in an attempt to influence policy.

Veto players have preferences represented by

$$u_i = \omega_x + C^i(x_i), \tag{4.1}$$

where ω_x is the payoff (the same for all veto players) when policy x is implemented, and $C^i(x_i) \geq 0$ is the contribution, defined in the following discussion, provided by the organized group to veto player i in return for choosing policy x_i (which may differ from the policy x that is ultimately implemented). Similarly, the lobby has preferences represented by

$$u_L = \varphi_x - \sum C^i(x_i). \tag{4.2}$$

Normalize $w_0 = \varphi_0 = 0$, define $w \equiv w_1$ and $\varphi \equiv \varphi_1$, and assume that $w < 0 < \varphi$. Thus, veto players most prefer $x = 0$, whereas the lobby most prefers $x = 1$.

Policy is chosen as follows. The organized group presents a contribution function $C^1(x_1)$ to the agenda setter, who then chooses $x_1 \in \{0, 1\}$ to maximize utility as in Equation 4.1. If the agenda setter is the only veto player or if $x_1 = 0$, then x_1 is implemented. Otherwise, the organized group presents $C^2(x_2)$ to the second veto player (the first ratifier), who chooses $x_2 \in \{0, 1\}$ to maximize utility as in Equation 4.1. The process continues until $j = J$ or some veto player j chooses $x_j = 0$, whichever comes first. This captures the idea that any departure from the status quo $\bar{x} = 0$ must be initiated by the agenda setter, that any such change must be approved by all ratifiers, and that the organized group can lobby each veto player.

When there is a single veto player, then, as in Section 3.4, equilibrium policy maximizes the joint payoff of the veto player and the lobby:

$$\max_x w_x + \varphi_x.$$

Thus, the equilibrium policy $x^* = 0$ if $w + \varphi < 0$, whereas $x^* = 1$ if $w + \varphi > 0$. The lobby provides no contribution to the veto player if $x^* = 0$, as the veto player most prefers that policy. In contrast, if $x^* = 1$, then the lobby compensates the veto player for the reduction in her policy payoff by providing a contribution of $-w$. From this, we can derive the equilibrium utility for the lobby as

$$u_L(x^*) = 0 \text{ if } x^* = 0, \tag{4.3}$$
$$= w + \varphi \text{ if } x^* = 1.$$

Now consider the case of two veto players. The outcome of the "ratification game" that follows $x_1 = 1$ is exactly analogous to that with a single veto player, with the lobby's payoff in this subgame (i.e., ignoring any contributions paid to the agenda setter) given by Equation 4.3. But then the total cost of inducing $x_1 = 1$, given that the proposal is subsequently ratified, is $-2w$: both the agenda setter and the ratifier must be compensated for adopting a policy other than that which they most prefer. Consequently, the condition for $x^* = 1$ is $2w + \varphi > 0$, which is more stringent than that with one veto player, given that $w < 0$.

Clearly, this analysis extends to an arbitrary number of veto players N, so that the condition for $x^* = 1$ is $N\omega + \varphi > 0$. Thus, if veto players are sufficiently numerous, the cost to the lobby of inducing its most-preferred policy is not worth the resulting benefit. The presence of multiple veto players reduces the power of special interests to lobby for policies that only they prefer.

It is worth emphasizing that the veto players in the example just presented have identical preferences. Although the model can easily be generalized to allow for heterogeneous preferences, it is interesting to note the difference in analysis from Section 4.1. When veto players cannot be lobbied, then the number of veto players with identical preferences is irrelevant; all that matters is the configuration of veto players' ideal points. In contrast, the presence of multiple veto players with identical preferences can discourage certain policies from being implemented if there is policy conflict between veto players and special interests. Exercise 4.7 demonstrates one implication of this result: when organized interests prefer "partial reform" over "full reform" (as suggested, for example, by Hellman, 1998), then full reform may be more likely when veto players are numerous.

Exercises

4.1 Consider the model of Sections 4.1 and 4.2, and assume three veto players A, B, C, with ideal points $x_A < x_C < x_B$.

(a) For all possible locations of the status quo, find the winset for this configuration of veto players. How, if at all, does this differ from the case where only A and B are veto players?

(b) What is the core for this configuration of veto players? How, if at all, does this differ from the case where only A and B are veto players?

(c) Suppose C is the agenda setter. A and B must both agree to any change proposed by C; otherwise policy remains at the status quo $\bar{x}$. For all possible locations of the status quo, find the equilibrium policy.

Now repeat your analysis, assuming that $x_C < x_A < x_B$.

4.2 Recall the Romer-Rosenthal model of Section 4.3.1, where an agenda setter proposes an alternative to the status quo, following which all members of the legislature vote up or down on the alternative under a closed rule. The following example, which is based on Dewan and Spirling (2011), demonstrates that members of an opposition party can be strictly better off if they all vote against the alternative, even if some members prefer the alternative to the status quo.

Assume a legislature of five members, indexed by i, where legislators 1, 2, and 4 belong to the majority party and legislators 3 and 5 belong to the opposition party. Legislators have Euclidean preferences over policy $x \in \Re$, with ideal points as shown in the following figure, which also indicates the position of the status quo $\bar{x}$. As depicted, $x_3 - x_2 = \bar{x} - x_3$, and $x_4 - x_3 = 2(\bar{x} - x_4)$.

Legislator 2 (the median majority member) has agenda-setting power.

(a) What is the equilibrium policy when any legislator votes for the alternative if and only if she prefers it to the status quo?

(b) What is the equilibrium policy when any member of the majority party votes for the alternative if and only if she prefers it to the status quo, whereas members of the opposition vote against the alternative, regardless of whether they prefer it to the status quo?

(c) Why are members of the opposition better off voting in unison against the agenda setter's proposal?

(d) Provide a configuration of ideal points and the status quo such that members of the opposition are better off voting sincerely on the agenda setter's proposal.

4.3 Consider the model of pivots in Section 4.3. Assume that an agenda-setting committee makes a proposal to the full legislature, which then votes up or down on the proposal (i.e., the rule is closed). A simple majority is needed to pass, but a bill that passes may be vetoed by the president. A supermajority is needed to override the veto. The configuration of ideal points of the median legislator (m), committee (C), president (P), and veto pivot (v) is as follows:

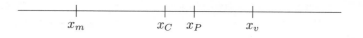

As depicted, $x_C - x_m > x_P - x_C$.

(a) What is the smallest left coalition that can pass a bill? (It may be useful to think of the president as a legislator who may be included in this coalition.)

(b) What is the smallest right coalition that can pass a bill?

(c) Who are the veto players?

(d) What is the core (i.e., gridlock interval, given a closed rule)?

(e) What is the equilibrium outcome as a function of the status quo?

4.4 Consider the model of portfolio allocation in Section 4.4. Referring to Figure 4.6, which is drawn to scale, complete the analysis as follows:

(a) What is the portfolio core?

(b) What is the restricted portfolio core?

4.5 Consider the model of portfolio allocation in Section 4.4. Assume that there are two parties, $i = 1, 2$, with Euclidean preferences over $\mathbf{x} \in \Re^2$. The set of implementable policies is $\{\mathbf{x}_1, \mathbf{x}_2, \mathbf{x}_{12}, \mathbf{x}_{21}\}$, where $\mathbf{x}_i$ denotes party i's ideal point and $\mathbf{x}_{ij}$ represents the policy outcome when the first policy dimension is assigned to party i and the second to party j. Assume that party 1 controls a majority of seats in the parliament.

(a) What is the portfolio core?

(b) What is the restricted portfolio core?

4.6 This exercise presents a simple version of Huber's (1996) model of the confidence-vote procedure in parliamentary systems. For simplicity, assume that there are two actors: a prime minister (P) and a legislator (L) who represents the prime minister's legislative majority. The policy space is the real number line, with generic policy x and status quo $\bar{x}$. Each actor $i = P, L$ receives a payoff equal to $-|x - x_i|$ from whatever policy x is implemented. In addition, as described in the following discussion, the prime minister and legislator may bear a cost from actions that result in a loss of political capital or the fall of the government.

The timing of events is as follows:

- The legislator proposes a policy $y \in \Re$.
- The prime minister chooses to accept the legislator's proposal y or to call a vote of confidence in the government. If the prime minister accepts the proposal, then y is implemented, whereas

if she calls a vote of confidence in the government, then she proposes a particular policy $z \in \Re$ that is attached to the vote. Calling a vote of confidence costs the prime minister e, where $e \geq 0$ is a parameter of the model.

- If a vote of confidence has been called, the legislator chooses to accept the prime minister's proposal z or to censure the government. If she accepts, then z is implemented, whereas if she censures the government, then the status quo $\bar{x}$ is implemented. Censuring the government costs the prime minister c_P and the legislator c_L, where $c_P, c_L \geq 0$ are parameters of the model.

For concreteness, let $\bar{x} = 0$, $x_L = 1$, $x_P = 3$, $e = \frac{1}{4}$, and $c_P = c_L = \frac{1}{2}$. Find the policy implemented in equilibrium by backward induction, as follows:

(a) What is the set of proposals that the legislator prefers to censuring the government?
(b) What is the optimal proposal for the prime minister, given that she calls a vote of confidence in the government?
(c) What is the set of proposals that the prime minister prefers to calling a vote of confidence in the government?
(d) What is the optimal proposal by the legislator?
(e) Now assume that the status quo $\bar{x} = 2$. What policy is implemented in equilibrium? What does your answer say about the impact of the confidence-vote procedure on policy stability?

4.7 Consider the model of veto players and special interests in Section 4.5, but now assume that policy $x \in \{0, 1, 2\}$, where $x = 0$ is the status quo, $x = 1$ is "partial reform," and $x = 2$ is "full reform." As before, veto players and the lobby have preferences over policy and contributions defined by Equations 4.1 and 4.2. Let $\omega_0 = \varphi_0 = 0$, and assume that $\omega_1 < 0 < \omega_2$ and $\varphi_2 < 0 < \varphi_1$. Thus, veto players prefer full reform to the status quo to partial reform, whereas the lobby has the inverse preference ordering.

Policy is chosen in a process analogous to that in Section 4.5, but now the agenda setter chooses $x_1 \in \{0, 1, 2\}$, whereas any ratifier $i > 1$ chooses $x_i \in \{0, x_1\}$. Thus, ratifiers may either veto a proposal, resulting in maintenance of the status quo ($x = 0$), or ratify it.

(a) Consider first the case of one veto player. What conditions must hold for partial reform to be implemented? For full reform to be implemented?

(b) Now consider the case of two veto players. What conditions must hold for partial reform to be implemented? For full reform to be implemented?

(c) How are the likelihood of partial and full reform affected by the number of veto players?

5

Delegation

In this chapter, we continue to consider environments with multiple policy makers, though the emphasis is different from that in Chapter 4. Rather than assuming that the agreement of all actors is necessary to change policy, the models here assume a single **principal**, which may either act on its own or delegate policy authority to an **agent**. In political science, the principal is typically a legislature, whereas the agent is either a bureaucratic agency or a committee with expertise in some policy arena.

From the legislature's perspective, delegating policy authority involves a trade-off. On the one hand, the agent's expertise implies that it can choose a policy better suited to the state of the world. Even with substantial staff resources, the typical member of a legislature may be poorly equipped to respond to fast-changing technological or economic conditions. On the other hand, the preferences of the legislature and the agent may not be perfectly aligned. When the agent is a bureaucratic agency, we say that this creates the possibility of **bureaucratic drift**—that is, the possibility that the ultimate policy outcome may be different from that desired by the legislature. Much of the literature explores the impact of various mechanisms and institutions on this trade-off.

We begin by presenting a simple spatial model of delegation, where for concreteness we refer to a relationship between a legislature and an agency. We then expand this baseline model in various ways. We consider the use of discretion limits as an instrument to prevent bureaucratic drift; we explore issues of legislative and bureaucratic capacity; and we examine the ways in which agency incentives can be structured by administrative procedures.

Following discussion of these topics, we explore agency decision making when the legislature can override the agency's decision. As we will see, when the legislature has override power, the agency's action reduces to a costless signal about the state of the world; the question is whether the agency transmits any information in equilibrium. This discussion leads us to the final topic of the chapter: delegation to an expert legislative committee, whose recommendation to the full legislature can be overridden, subject to the rules of legislative procedure.

5.1 Baseline Model

We consider a delegation environment with two players: a legislature (L) and an agency (A). Both the legislature and the agency have preferences over outcomes in $\Re$ (i.e., policy is one-dimensional), where x denotes any generic outcome. We assume that the legislature has preferences represented by the utility function $u_L(x) = -|x|$, which implies an ideal point of 0, whereas the agency has preferences represented by $u_A(x) = -|x - x_A|$, where x_A is the agency's ideal point. Without loss of generality, we assume that $x_A > 0$.

At the beginning of the game, the legislature chooses whether to delegate policy authority to the agency. Following this, a random shock $\omega \in \Re$ is realized. To cleanly capture the idea that the agency has specific expertise, we assume that the shock is observed by the agency but not by the legislature. Finally, whoever has policy authority—the legislature or the agency, depending on whether policy authority has been delegated—chooses a policy $p \in \Re$.

The outcome x is jointly determined by the policy p and a random shock ω. For simplicity, we assume that $x = p + \omega$, which is a special case of what Bendor and Meirowitz (2004) term **perfect shock absorption**.[1] Intuitively, because the agency knows ω, it can absorb the shock and achieve its ideal point by choosing the policy $p = x_A - \omega$. For concreteness, we further assume that the shock takes one of two values, $\omega \in \{-\epsilon, \epsilon\}$, where $\epsilon > 0$ and either shock is equally likely; Exercise 5.1 explores an alternative distributional assumption.

To examine the delegation decision, we begin by deriving the legislature's expected utility when it does not delegate. Because the distribution of ω is symmetric, the legislature cannot do better than by choosing

---

[1] Callander (2008b) considers more general functional forms, such that the legislature cannot infer the mapping from policy to outcome merely by observing a single policy-outcome pair. The ability to invert the mapping is irrelevant in the simple setting explored in this section, where the legislature has no ability to override the agency's choice.

its ideal point, $p = 0$. (In fact, given the assumption of absolute-value preferences, any $p \in [-\epsilon, \epsilon]$ is a best response.) This implies an expected utility of $-\epsilon$: whatever the realization of ω, the final outcome x will be ϵ away from the legislature's ideal point. Thus, the legislature bears a cost from not knowing with certainty how the policy it chooses will map onto the outcome. That cost is greater when policy uncertainty is large (i.e., for large ϵ).

Now consider choice of policy by the agency when the legislature delegates. Given the assumption of perfect shock absorption, the agency chooses $p = x_A - \omega$, which guarantees its ideal point. The legislature's expected utility from delegation is therefore $-x_A$: whatever the realization of the random shock, the outcome is x_A away from the legislature's ideal point of 0.

The decision to delegate therefore reduces to a comparison of ϵ and x_A. If $\epsilon > x_A$, then it is more important to take advantage of the agency's expertise, and the legislature delegates. In contrast, if $\epsilon < x_A$, then the cost of bureaucratic drift dominates, and the legislature chooses not to delegate.

This simple model illustrates an important insight: if the legislature has a choice of agencies to which it can delegate, then it prefers the agency whose preferences are most similar to its own.[2] This **ally principle** (Bendor, Glazer, and Hammond, 2001) can be seen in Figure 5.1, which depicts the legislature's expected utility for different values of x_A. Conditional on delegating, the legislature is strictly better off with an agency with ideal point closer to 0 (i.e., to the legislature's ideal point). As we will demonstrate later, the ally principle may not hold in other settings.

The exposition here follows Bendor and Meirowitz (2004) in deemphasizing the role of quadratic (i.e., risk-averse) utility functions, which have been used in some of the other seminal papers cited in this chapter. As Bendor and Meirowitz show, Euclidean preferences are sufficient to derive many of the key results in the literature. To see that risk aversion plays no role in the baseline model, assume that the legislature and agency have preferences represented by the functions $u_L = -x^2$ and $u_A = -(x - x_A)^2$, respectively; all other elements of the model are unchanged. Then, as before, the legislature chooses $p = 0$ if it does not delegate, for an expected utility of $-\epsilon^2$ (with risk-averse preferences, this

---

[2] An alternative perspective is that the legislature might allocate the same task to multiple agencies for the sake of redundancy, though if agencies behave strategically, this can lead to collective-action problems; see Ting (2003).

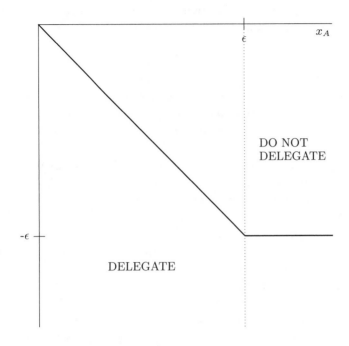

Figure 5.1. Expected utility for the legislature in the baseline model of delegation to agencies.

is the unique best response). In contrast, when the legislature delegates, the agency chooses $p = x_A - \omega$, given the assumption of perfect shock absorption, for an expected payoff to the legislature of $-(x_A)^2$. It is therefore optimal to delegate if $-(x_A)^2 > -\epsilon^2$, or $\epsilon > x_A$.

5.2 Discretion Limits

The baseline model just presented assumes that delegation is an all-or-nothing proposition. Conditional on delegating, this seems to imply that bureaucratic drift can be substantial. As Epstein and O'Halloran (1994, 1999) demonstrate, however, bureaucratic drift can be attenuated by limiting the discretion of bureaucratic agencies. A clear example of such limited discretion is the instruction of the United States Congress in 1975 that the National Highway and Traffic Safety Administration "set corporate average fuel economy standards somewhere between 20 and 27.5 miles per gallon" (Epstein and O'Halloran, 1994, p. 701). Such limits help the legislature to balance the trade-off between bureaucratic expertise and bureaucratic drift.

To examine the implications of limited discretion, consider the following variant of the baseline model of Section 5.1. As before, the legislature chooses to delegate or not. If it chooses to delegate, then it further chooses an interval $[l, r]$ within which the policy chosen by the agency can fall. Finally, if the agency has been given authority to choose policy, it chooses p, given the constraint $p \in [l, r]$.[3]

From the agency's perspective, the effect of limited discretion is to reduce its ability to absorb the random shock ω. When would the legislature want to impose this limit? The key observation is that bureaucratic drift pulls policy to the right, relative to what the legislature would choose if it knew ω, given that $x_A > 0$. Thus, in equilibrium, the constraint $p \geq l$ cannot be binding. In contrast, the constraint $p \leq r$ can be used to limit bureaucratic drift.

In particular, by choosing $r = \epsilon$, the legislature can achieve its ideal point when $\omega = -\epsilon$, while accepting an outcome to the right of its ideal point when $\omega = \epsilon$. It is straightforward to see that no other r can provide a higher payoff to the legislature: any $r > \epsilon$ does less to combat bureaucratic drift, whereas any $r < \epsilon$ results in a lower payoff when $\omega = -\epsilon$ that at best would be exactly compensated by a larger payoff when $\omega = \epsilon$.

Thus, *if* the legislature delegates policy authority to the agency, a best response for the legislature is to name the discretion limit $(-\infty, \epsilon]$. This produces an outcome of $x = 0$ when $\omega = -\epsilon$ and an outcome of either $x = x_A$ or $x = 2\epsilon$ when $\omega = \epsilon$, depending on whether the agency's optimal policy in that case, $p = x_A - \epsilon$, is less than or greater than $r = \epsilon$, respectively. Given that positive and negative shocks are equally likely, this provides the legislature with an expected payoff of $-\frac{x_A}{2}$ if $x_A < 2\epsilon$ and $-\epsilon$ if $x_A > 2\epsilon$. Alternatively, it could choose not to delegate, which as shown in Section 5.1 gives an expected payoff of $-\epsilon$. The agency therefore strictly prefers to delegate with limited discretion if and only if $x_A < 2\epsilon$.

To understand the consequences of limited discretion, recall that in the baseline model, delegation is optimal if $x_A < \epsilon$. Thus, the legislature

---

[3] We follow the literature in assuming a distinct delegation decision, but in the environment here the legislature could equivalently choose $l = r = 0$, resulting in an equilibrium policy of 0. As already shown, this is the optimal policy when the legislature does not delegate.

delegates authority to the agency for a wider range of parameter values when it can impose limits on the ability of the agency to absorb shocks. Put differently, the legislature is more willing to tolerate an agency whose preferences are divergent from its own when it can write limits into the agency's statutory authority.

The discussion here identifies the optimal mechanism from the set of mechanisms that take a particular form. In particular, we have restricted attention to **action restrictions**, which specify that the agency can adopt some policies but not others. An alternative type of mechanism is a **menu law**, which specifies a policy $p(\omega)$ and contribution $C(\omega)$ for each value of the random shock ω, where the agency is to implement $p(\omega)$ in return for a transfer of $C(\omega)$ from the legislature to the agency. As Gailmard (2009) discusses, the legislature can never do worse by offering a menu law.[4] Implementing such a mechanism, however, requires that the legislature be able to credibly commit to providing the promised contributions, and in the typical institutional setting there is no third party to enforce damages in the event the legislature breaks its promise. In contrast, action restrictions simply require that the agency credibly commit to not choosing some policy that has been statutorily forbidden. Although there probably are settings in which even this is impossible, action restrictions arguably ask less in terms of commitment power than do menu laws.

5.3 Legislative Capacity

The formalization in Section 5.2 assumes that the legislature can costlessly impose limits on the discretion of the bureaucratic agency. In practice, imposing discretion limits comes at a cost, as the legislature must draft and pass detailed legislation to prevent bureaucratic drift. The less professionalized the legislature, the more costly this will be. In the United States, for example, there is enormous variation in staff resources and floor time across state legislatures. Similar variation can be observed across national legislatures.

Following Huber and Shipan (2002), we can explore this argument by assuming that the legislature bears a direct cost of limiting discretion that is decreasing in its capacity. To focus ideas, assume that if the legislature chooses to delegate, it imposes a discretion limit d, such that

---

[4] This follows from the equivalence of menu laws and direct mechanisms and application of the revelation principle (Myerson, 1979).

$p \leq d$: as discussed earlier, the legislature would never prefer to impose a binding lower bound on the policy that the agency can adopt, given that $x_A > 0$. Further, assume that the cost to the legislature of imposing d is a convex function of the distance between d and the policy that the agency prefers to adopt in the event of a negative shock, which is $x_A + \epsilon$. For concreteness, let this cost be equal to $\frac{\alpha}{4}[(x_A + \epsilon) - d]^2$, where $\alpha > \frac{1}{x_A}$. The parameter α measures the legislature's capacity: the smaller is α, the less costly it is to impose discretion limits, and so the greater is the legislature's capacity. Finally, assume that $x_A < 2\epsilon$, which is the condition for delegation in the model of the previous section.

To find the optimal level of discretion d^* when the legislature chooses to delegate, we begin by assuming that $d^* \in (\epsilon, x_A + \epsilon)$—that is, that the agency is granted discretion to choose some policy between what the legislature most prefers in the event of a negative shock ($p = \epsilon$) and what the agency most prefers in that eventuality ($p = x_A + \epsilon$). We will show shortly that the condition on parameters guarantees this. Then the legislature's expected utility from the discretion level d is

$$\max_d \; -\frac{1}{2}(d - \epsilon) - \frac{1}{2}x_A - \frac{\alpha}{4}[(x_A + \epsilon) - d]^2. \qquad (5.1)$$

The first term in this expression is the payoff from the event $\omega = -\epsilon$, when the agency chooses $p = d$, weighted by the probability of that event ($\frac{1}{2}$). Although the agency would prefer to choose a higher p when the shock is negative, the discretion limit $p \leq d$ does not allow this. The second term is the legislature's probability-weighted payoff when $\omega = \epsilon$: as shown earlier, the agency chooses $p = x_A - \epsilon$, for an outcome of $x = x_A$. Finally, the third term is the cost to the legislature of imposing d.

Expression 5.1 is a concave problem, so the first-order condition is sufficient for a solution. Differentiating by d and setting the derivative equal to zero gives

$$-\frac{1}{2} + \frac{\alpha}{2}[(x_A + \epsilon) - d^*] = 0.$$

Rearranging gives

$$d^* = x_A + \epsilon - \frac{1}{\alpha}. \qquad (5.2)$$

As preliminarily assumed, $d^* \in (\epsilon, x_A + \epsilon)$, given the assumption $\alpha > \frac{1}{x_A}$.

Examining Equation 5.1, we see that the legislature places greater limits on the agency's discretion—the optimal d is lower—when the parameter α is small. In other words, bureaucratic drift is decreasing in the legislature's capacity. To see how this affects the decision of the legislature to delegate, we can substitute d^* from Equation 5.2 into the maximand of Expression 5.1 to derive the legislature's expected payoff from delegating:

$$-\frac{1}{2}\left[\left(x_A + \epsilon - \frac{1}{\alpha}\right) - \epsilon\right] - \frac{1}{2}x_A - \frac{\alpha}{4}\left[(x_A + \epsilon) - \left(x_A + \epsilon - \frac{1}{\alpha}\right)\right]^2 =$$
$$-x_A + \frac{1}{4\alpha}.$$

In contrast, as shown in Section 5.1, the legislature's expected payoff from not delegating is $-\epsilon$. The legislature therefore chooses to delegate when $-x_A + \frac{1}{4\alpha} > -\epsilon$, or

$$x_A < \epsilon + \frac{1}{4\alpha}. \tag{5.3}$$

By inspection, the right-hand side of Condition 5.3 is large when α is small. Intuitively, the legislature is more likely to delegate when it has greater capacity to prevent bureaucratic drift. Conversely, as α approaches infinity, so that imposing discretion limits becomes prohibitively costly, the condition for delegation becomes $x_A < \epsilon$, as in the baseline model without discretion limits.

5.4 Bureaucratic Capacity

The previous discussion assumes that bureaucracies are able to implement any policy consistent with the statutory authority they have been granted, and that they are fully informed about the consequences of any policy that they choose. In many institutional environments, this assumption is incorrect. There is enormous variation across countries in both the size and structure of bureaucracies. In the early 1990s, for example, employment in government administration in the typical OECD country was over twice as large as that in the average Latin American or post-communist country, and over three times as large as that in the typical African country (Schiavo-Campo, de Tommaso, and Mukherjee, 1997; see also Brym and Gimpelson, 2004). With respect to structure, developing countries differ considerably in the extent to which they approximate the Weberian ideal type of meritocratic recruitment and internal promotion (Rauch and Evans, 2000). These differences are potentially consequential for bureaucratic performance. As Brown, Earle, and Gehlbach (2009) show in a study of regional governance in Russia, the ability of governments to provide public goods that are complementary to private economic activity is positively related to the size of the public administration. Similarly, economic growth is greater in countries with bureaucratic structures that are more "Weberian" (Evans and Rauch, 1999).

To consider the impact of bureaucratic capacity on the delegation decision, we first explore a simplified version of the model in Huber and McCarty (2004). We make two modifications to the baseline model of Section 5.1. First, we assume that the agency implements its policy choice with noise. In particular, when the agency chooses p, the actual policy implemented is $p + \zeta$, where ζ is a random variable that takes one of two values, $\zeta \in \{-\mu, \mu\}$, with $\mu > 0$ and either realization equally likely. The parameter μ thus measures bureaucratic capacity: the larger is μ, the lower is capacity. Second, we assume that the legislature and the agency have risk-averse preferences represented by the quadratic utility functions $u_L = -x^2$ and $u_A = -(x - x_A)^2$, respectively, where as before $x_A > 0$.

We begin by deriving the legislature's expected payoff when it does not delegate. As before, the best policy choice is $p = 0$, resulting in the outcomes $x = -\epsilon$ and $x = \epsilon$, each with probability one-half. Given the assumption of a quadratic loss function, the legislature's expected payoff from not delegating is $-\epsilon^2$.

In contrast, when the legislature delegates policy authority to the agency, the agency chooses p to maximize its expected utility, having observed the value of the random shock ω. When $\omega = -\epsilon$, the agency's problem is

$$\max_p -\frac{1}{2}\left[(p - \mu - \epsilon) - x_A\right]^2 - \frac{1}{2}\left[(p + \mu - \epsilon) - x_A\right]^2.$$

The assumption that noise in the implementation process is distributed symmetrically around the intended policy p implies that the optimal choice sets $p = x_A + \epsilon$, as in the baseline model. Similarly, when $\omega = \epsilon$, the optimal choice sets $p = x_A - \epsilon$. In either case, the final outcome is $x = x_A + \mu$ with probability one-half and $x = x_A - \mu$ with probability one-half. The legislature's expected utility from delegating is therefore

$$-\frac{1}{2}(x_A - \mu)^2 - \frac{1}{2}(x_A + \mu)^2 = -(x_A)^2 - \mu^2. \tag{5.4}$$

The first term on the right-hand side of the equality represents the legislature's loss from the expected outcome, whereas the second is the variance of the outcome. This **mean-variance property** is a convenient feature of quadratic utility functions.

Comparing Expression 5.4 to the legislature's expected utility from not delegating $\left(-\epsilon^2\right)$, we see that the legislature chooses to delegate if $\epsilon^2 > (x_A)^2 + \mu^2$. This condition has an intuitive interpretation. As $\mu \to 0$, so that the agency is able to implement the policy of its choice without noise, the condition reduces to $\epsilon > x_A$, which is precisely the condition in the baseline model for the legislature to prefer delegation. As μ increases, delegation becomes relatively less attractive: any bureaucratic advantage in expertise is outweighed by poor implementation of policy.

An alternative interpretation of bureaucratic capacity is that the agency has the expertise necessary to choose a policy suited to the state of the world. Clearly, if the agency cannot observe the random shock ω, then there is no incentive for the legislature to delegate policy authority, as it would incur the cost of bureaucratic drift without the benefit of adjustment to ω.

To explore this interpretation, we follow Bendor and Meirowitz (2004) in assuming that with probability π the agency receives a perfectly informative signal of the random shock ω, whereas with probability $1 - \pi$ the agency receives a completely uninformative signal. If the agency is uninformed, then it chooses $p = x_A$, resulting in the outcomes $x = x_A - \epsilon$ and $x = x_A + \epsilon$, each with probability one-half. We continue to assume that both the legislature and the agency have quadratic utility functions.

Under this interpretation, the legislature's expected utility from delegating is

$$-\pi \left(x_A\right)^2 - (1 - \pi) \left[\frac{1}{2} \left(x_A - \epsilon\right)^2 + \frac{1}{2} \left(x_A + \epsilon\right)^2\right],$$

where the first term is the policy loss when the agency receives an informative signal, weighted by the probability of that signal, whereas the second term is the probability-weighted expected policy loss when the agency receives an uninformative signal. Simplifying gives

$$- \left(x_A\right)^2 - (1 - \pi) \epsilon^2.$$

The legislature chooses to delegate when this expected payoff is greater than that from not delegating, $-\epsilon^2$, which after simplifying gives

$$\pi \epsilon^2 > \left(x_A\right)^2. \tag{5.5}$$

When $\pi = 1$, this reduces to the familiar condition $\epsilon > x_A$. As π

declines—that is, as the agency has less capacity to observe the value of the random shock—the condition is less likely to hold. Intuitively, the legislature will only delegate authority to an agency with sufficiently large capacity to adjust to the random shock.

A natural question is when the agency would choose to invest in expertise, as captured by π. To explore this, we modify this model to assume that after the legislature moves but before realization of the random shock ω, the agency endogenously chooses π. Capacity-building is costly, so the agency chooses to invest in π if and only if it has been delegated policy authority by the legislature.[5] For concreteness, we assume that this cost equals $\frac{\kappa}{2}\pi^2$, where $\kappa > \epsilon^2$.

The agency's optimal choice of π when it has been delegated policy authority solves

$$\max_{\pi} \ - \pi \left(x_A - x_A \right)^2 -$$

$$(1 - \pi) \left[\frac{1}{2} \left[(x_A - \epsilon) - x_A \right]^2 + \frac{1}{2} \left[(x_A + \epsilon) - x_A \right]^2 \right] - \frac{\kappa}{2}\pi^2,$$

where the first and second terms are the probability-weighted policy loss to the agency when it receives an informative and uninformative signal, respectively, and the third term is the cost of acquiring expertise. Simplifying gives

$$\max_{\pi} \ - (1 - \pi) \epsilon^2 - \frac{\kappa}{2}\pi^2.$$

This is a concave problem, so the first-order condition is sufficient for a solution:

$$\pi^* = \frac{\epsilon^2}{\kappa}. \tag{5.6}$$

Intuitively, the agency acquires less expertise when the cost of doing so (κ) is large. In addition, the agency invests in greater capacity when there is more policy uncertainty, as measured by the parameter ϵ.

To examine the implications of endogenous agency expertise for the delegation decision, we can substitute π^* from Equation 5.6 into Condition 5.5. Doing so gives the following condition for the legislature to delegate policy authority to the agency:

$$\epsilon^2 > \sqrt{\kappa} \, (x_A). \tag{5.7}$$

---

[5] This captures in stark form the argument that agency independence creates an incentive for the agency to acquire information; see, e.g., Bawn (1995), Aghion and Tirole (1997), and Gailmard and Patty (2007). Exercise 5.3 further explores this idea.

As in the baseline model, the incentive to delegate is greater when policy uncertainty is large, relative to the potential for bureaucratic drift (i.e., when ϵ is large relative to x_A). This incentive, however, is muted to the extent that acquiring expertise is costly to the agency—that is, when κ is large.

Condition 5.7 suggests a possible failure of the ally principle discussed earlier. If there is a choice of agencies to which the legislature can delegate authority, then all other things being equal, the legislature prefers to delegate to the agency whose preferences are closest to its own. All other things, however, may not be equal. In particular, the agency with ideal point closest to zero may find it comparatively costly to acquire expertise. In this case, the legislature may prefer to sacrifice greater bureaucratic drift for the sake of increased capacity to adjust policy to changing circumstances.

5.5 Administrative Procedures

The baseline model and its various extensions considered earlier assume that, up to any statutory limits on the agency's discretion, the agency can costlessly pursue any policy. This creates the possibility of bureaucratic drift. In principle, the legislature could monitor the agency to ensure that it pursues *outcomes* that are consistent with the legislature's intent, but this is costly: by assumption, the agency has an advantage in expertise. Moreover, the legislative coalition that delegated policy authority may subsequently lose power. This **coalitional drift** (Horn and Shepsle, 1989) can eliminate the legislature's incentive to monitor the agency's performance, even when that is technically feasible. Finally, even when monitoring is costless and the legislative coalition remains unchanged, conflicts of interest within the coalition may make it difficult to combat bureaucratic drift.

McCubbins, Noll, and Weingast (1987, 1989) suggest an alternative means of combating bureaucratic drift: designing administrative procedures that limit the agency's freedom to maneuver. This can take various forms, two of which we explore here. First, administrative procedures can decentralize monitoring to actors with a strong stake in policy outcomes. Second, administrative procedures can increase **decision costs**—for example, by requiring that cost-benefit analysis be undertaken prior to implementing policy (Boardman et al., 2010).[6]

[6] An additional perspective is provided by Ting (2002), who shows that the legisla-

We first consider the role of administrative procedures in decentralizing monitoring to actors with a stake in the policy outcome. The general idea is that the legislature can empower constituent groups to examine bureaucratic decisions, to obtain information about how decisions were made, and to seek redress. Rather than having to implement a costly, centralized "police patrol" strategy, the legislature can thereby rely on citizens to pull the "fire alarm" when agency actions deviate from legislative intent (McCubbins and Schwartz, 1984).[7] Further, administrative procedures can "stack the deck" (e.g., through assignment of burden of proof) in favor of constituent groups whose preferences are closely aligned with those of the enacting coalition (McCubbins et al., 1987, 1989). In addition to ensuring that fire alarms will be pulled when the enacting coalition would want them to be, this can protect policy against subsequent coalitional drift.

Modeling these arguments (more generally, any argument about monitoring of agency decisions, whether by constituent groups or other actors) is sensitive to assumptions about what happens if the agency is caught choosing a policy that leads to an outcome that differs from legislative intent. Depending on the institutional setting, it is possible that some status quo policy is implemented, that control over policy returns to the legislature, that the agency pays a fine, and so forth.[8] Given these considerations, we do not attempt a general presentation here. In the next section we consider what happens when control over policy returns to the legislature.

To consider the role of decision costs, we adopt the simple approach of Spiller and Tiller (1997), assuming that the agency incurs a cost c if it implements some policy different from the status quo $\bar{p}$.[9] Both c and $\bar{p}$ are endogenous: in choosing to delegate policy authority to the agency, the legislature names a pair $(c, \bar{p})$. All other elements of the game are identical to those in the baseline model of Section 5.1. To focus on

---

ture can reduce bureaucratic drift through the strategic allocation of tasks across agencies.

[7] Of course, citizens may have an incentive to falsely report that the agency has deviated. Lupia and McCubbins (1994) show that this is less likely when citizens' preferences are aligned with the legislature's and when there is a cost to misrepresentation.

[8] Compare, for example, Huber and Shipan (2002) and Bendor and Meirowitz (2004, Section 4a).

[9] In principle, both the legislature and the agency may bear an exogenous cost of moving policy from the status quo, as in Gerber, Lupia, and McCubbins (2004). The discussion here addresses costs that can be manipulated by the legislature.

the role of administrative procedures, we assume $\epsilon > x_A$, which is the condition for delegation in the baseline model.

We begin by considering the agency's choice to implement some policy $p \neq \bar{p}$ or retain the status quo $\bar{p}$, taking as given the legislature's choice $(c, \bar{p})$. As shown in Section 5.1, if the agency chooses some $p \neq \bar{p}$, it implements $p = x_A - \omega$, resulting in an outcome $x = p + \omega$ equal to its ideal point. Given the cost c, this results in a payoff to the agency of $-c$. In contrast, the agency's payoff if it retains the status quo is $-|(\bar{p} + \omega) - x_A|$. The agency therefore retains the status quo if

$$c > |(\bar{p} + \omega) - x_A|. \tag{5.8}$$

Condition 5.8 demonstrates that the agency's choice may depend on the realization of the random shock ω. In general, there are three possibilities:

(i) The agency retains the status quo $\bar{p}$, regardless of the realization of ω.
(ii) The agency chooses $p = x_A - \omega$, regardless of the realization of ω.
(iii) The agency retains the status quo $\bar{p}$ for one realization of ω and chooses $p = x_A - \omega$ for the other.

In choosing the optimal pair $(c, \bar{p})$, the legislature anticipates these possible outcomes. Among all $(c, \bar{p})$ that result in the agency's retaining the status quo, regardless of realization of ω, the legislature's maximum expected payoff is $-\epsilon$: the agency does not adjust to the random shock, so the legislature cannot do worse than by setting $\bar{p} = 0$. Similarly, among all $(c, \bar{p})$ that result in the agency's choosing $p = x_A - \omega$, regardless of the realization of ω, the legislature's expected payoff is $-x_A$. The legislature, however, can do better than either $-\epsilon$ or $-x_A$ by naming some $(c, \bar{p})$ such that the agency retains the status quo for one realization of ω and chooses $p = x_A - \omega$ for the other.

In particular, by naming some $c \in (x_A, 2\epsilon - x_A)$ and $\bar{p} = \epsilon$, the legislature achieves its ideal point when $\omega = -\epsilon$, while incurring a policy loss of x_A when $\omega = \epsilon$, for an expected payoff of $-\frac{x_A}{2}$. Given the three possible outcomes just enumerated, and the assumption that $\epsilon > x_A$, the legislature can do no better.

To see that the agency behaves in a manner that produces these outcomes, consider in turn each of the possible realizations of ω. When $\omega = -\epsilon$, Condition 5.8 reduces to $c > x_A$, which holds, given that $c \in (x_A, 2\epsilon - x_A)$. Thus, in the event of a negative shock, the agency retains the status quo, resulting in an outcome equal to the legislature's ideal point $(x = \bar{p} + \omega = 0)$. In contrast, when $\omega = \epsilon$, the condition for the agency to retain the status quo (5.8) simplifies to

$$c > 2\epsilon - x_A,$$

which does not hold, given that administrative procedures have been chosen such that $c \in (x_A, 2\epsilon - x_A)$. Thus, the agency implements $p = x_A - \omega$, for a policy outcome of $x = x_A$.

In the particular environment here, the legislature's expected utility from a decision-cost strategy is the same as that from imposing discretion limits, as in Section 5.2. In each case, the legislature is able to get its ideal point when the random shock is negative. Intuitively, both discretion limits and decision costs discourage the agency from overcompensating (from the legislature's perspective) when the shock is negative.

5.6 Legislative Override

The preceding discussion has assumed that the legislature has no ability to override the decision made by the agency. Here we relax this assumption in order to consider legislative action after the agency has made a policy decision. The key point is that the agency's decision may reveal information about the value of the random shock, which the legislature can then use to move policy to its ideal point. Anticipating this, the agency may therefore fail to adjust policy to the random shock, leaving the legislature no better off than if it had not delegated in the first place.[10]

To consider this argument, assume that policy authority has been delegated to the agency. As before, the agency observes the value of the random shock ω, following which it chooses a policy in $\Re$. To distinguish the agency's choice from the legislature's, we denote by p_A the policy chosen by the agency. Following the agency's move, the legislature chooses a policy $p_L \in \Re$, having observed p_A but not the realization of ω. Implicitly, if $p_L \neq p_A$, the legislature has overridden the agency's choice. The final outcome $x = p_L + \omega$. As in Section 5.4, we assume that the legislature and the agency have risk-averse preferences represented by the quadratic utility functions $u_L = -x^2$ and $u_A = -(x - x_A)^2$, respectively.

---

[10] Calvert, McCubbins, and Weingast (1989) present a model in which the legislature and executive can veto but not amend agency decisions. Conceptually, this is close to the model of delegation to committees under a closed rule, considered in the following section.

Absent the possibility of legislative override, the agency would choose $p_A = x_A - \omega$, for an outcome of $x = x_A$ and an expected payoff to the legislature of $-(x_A)^2$. The question is whether the agency similarly conditions its choice on the value of the random shock when the legislature can override its decision. Formally, the model has the structure of a signaling game; we therefore ask whether there exists a separating equilibrium in which the agency chooses a different policy when $\omega = -\epsilon$ than it does when $\omega = \epsilon$. To focus the discussion, we refer in what follows to the strategy $p_A = x_A - \omega$, though any separation (e.g., $p_A = 0$ if $\omega = -\epsilon$, $p_A = 1$ if $\omega = \epsilon$) has the same strategic implications.

To check for the existence of such an equilibrium, we begin by noting that when the agency chooses distinct policies, depending on the realization of ω—that is, when it separates—the legislature fully updates its beliefs about the value of the random shock. Thus, when the agency chooses $p_A = x_A + \epsilon$, the legislature infers that $\omega = -\epsilon$ and responds by choosing $p_L = \epsilon$, resulting in an outcome equal to the legislature's ideal point, $x = 0$. Similarly, when $p_A = x_A - \epsilon$, the legislature subsequently overrides the agency's choice and chooses $p_L = -\epsilon$. In either case, the agency's expected payoff is $-(x_A)^2$.

A necessary condition for existence of this equilibrium is that the agency have no incentive to deviate to $p_A = x_A + \epsilon$ when $\omega = \epsilon$. Were it to do so, the legislature would incorrectly infer that $\omega = -\epsilon$, choosing $p_L = \epsilon$ and producing the outcome $x = 2\epsilon$. Thus, for the agency to have no incentive to deviate in this manner when $\omega = \epsilon$, the following condition must hold:

$$-(x_A)^2 \geq -(2\epsilon - x_A)^2.$$

Simplifying gives $\epsilon \geq x_A$. Thus, there is no separating equilibrium when $\epsilon < x_A$. (As in any game with costless signaling, there always exists a pooling equilibrium in which no information is transmitted.) Interestingly, this is precisely the same condition as in the baseline model for the legislature to prefer not to delegate policy authority. The logic, however, is quite different. In the baseline model, the legislature prefers not to delegate policy authority to an agency with very different preferences, as the cost of bureaucratic drift outweighs any advantage in policy expertise. In the model with legislative override, delegation to an agency with very different preferences eliminates the value of agency expertise, as the agency has an incentive to misreport the value of the random shock (through choice of p_A) in order to receive a better policy outcome.

We have yet to show that a separating equilibrium exists when $\epsilon \geq x_A$.

To do so, we first observe that the agency has no incentive to deviate to $p_A = x_A - \epsilon$ when $\omega = -\epsilon$. Were it to do so, the legislature would incorrectly infer that $\omega = \epsilon$, choosing $p_L = -\epsilon$. But this results in the outcome $x = -2\epsilon$, which is even worse for the agency than the legislature's ideal point. Second, we must verify that for either value of the random shock ω, the agency has no incentive to deviate to any other policy $p_A \neq \{x_A - \epsilon, x_A + \epsilon\}$. As these values of p_A are off the equilibrium path, beliefs for the legislature are not pinned down by the agency's strategy. We therefore specify that the legislature infers that $\omega = \epsilon$ for any p_A off the equilibrium path. As just shown, this implies that the legislature chooses $p_L = -\epsilon$, for an outcome of $x = -\epsilon + \omega$. At best, from the agency's perspective, the final outcome is $x = 0$, implying that the agency has no incentive to deviate for either value of ω.

5.7 Delegation to Committees and Legislative Procedure

The previous section shows that when the legislature has the ability to override the agency's decision, the agency reveals its private information only if its preferences are not too divergent from those of the legislature. The same argument applies if we think of the agent not as a bureaucratic agency but as a legislative committee. Conceptually, delegation to an agency with costless legislative override is identical to delegation to a committee and consideration of the subsequent report under an **open rule**—that is, a rule giving the full legislature the authority to amend any proposal made by the committee. Gilligan and Krehbiel (1987) consider such an environment, comparing it to a **closed rule**, where the full legislature must vote up or down on the committee's proposal.

To explore information transmission by committees under a closed rule, we modify the model of the previous section so that, following any proposal p by the agent (here, committee), the legislature chooses to accept or reject. If the proposal is rejected, a status quo policy $\bar{p}$ is implemented. We assume that $\bar{p} = 0$, which is the legislature's preferred policy under no information. For consistency with the previous discussion, we retain the notation A to describe the agent.[11]

As in the previous section, we look for a separating equilibrium, in

---

[11] Gilligan and Krehbiel's model builds on Crawford and Sobel (1982), which assumes that the random shock is continuously distributed. The presentation here follows McCarty and Meirowitz (2007, pp. 227–232).

which the committee conditions its policy choice on the realized value of the random shock. To derive the optimal such choice, we must consider which policies the legislature would accept for each value of the random shock, given that it fully updates its beliefs in equilibrium. The legislature accepts any proposal p such that

$$- (p + \omega)^2 \geq - (\bar{p} + \omega)^2 .$$

Given the assumption $\bar{p} = 0$, which implies that the expression on the right side of the inequality is $-\epsilon^2$ for either value of ω, the condition simplifies to

$$(p + \omega)^2 \leq \epsilon^2.$$

Taking the square root of each side gives the following two inequalities:

$$p + \omega \leq \epsilon,$$
$$p + \omega \geq -\epsilon.$$

Thus, when the legislature infers that $\omega = -\epsilon$, it approves any proposal $p \in [0, 2\epsilon]$, whereas when the legislature infers that $\omega = \epsilon$, it approves any proposal $p \in [-2\epsilon, 0]$.

It immediately follows that the committee can achieve any outcome between $-\epsilon$ and ϵ when conditioning on the shock, given that $x = p + \omega$. If $\epsilon \geq x_A$, the committee can therefore implement its ideal point by proposing $p = x_A + \epsilon$ when $\omega = -\epsilon$ and $p = x_A - \epsilon$ when $\omega = \epsilon$. (Clearly, there is no incentive to deviate from either proposal, so this equilibrium can be supported by a range of beliefs off the equilibrium path.) This differs from the case with an open rule, where, as shown earlier, the legislature achieves *its* ideal point ($x = 0$) in a separating equilibrium under the same condition ($\epsilon \geq x_A$).

As shown in the previous section, there is no separating equilibrium under an open rule if $\epsilon < x_A$. The closed rule is more forgiving. In particular, if $\epsilon < x_A \leq 2\epsilon$, then there exists a separating equilibrium in which the equilibrium outcome is $x = \epsilon$. To achieve this, the committee proposes $p = 2\epsilon$ when $\omega = -\epsilon$ and $p = 0$ when $\omega = \epsilon$. Clearly, the committee has no incentive to deviate when $\omega = -\epsilon$, as it is already proposing the maximum policy that the legislature would ever accept. In contrast, when $\omega = \epsilon$, the committee might have an incentive to deviate if the legislature inferred from this that $\omega = -\epsilon$, in which case the legislature would be willing to support a larger policy. To limit the incentive for the committee to deviate, we therefore specify beliefs off the equilibrium path such that the legislature infers that $\omega = \epsilon$ for any

Table 5.1. *Existence of Separating Equilibria under Alternative Rules*

	Open Rule	**Closed Rule**
$x_A \leq \epsilon$	Exists SE w/ $x^* = 0$	Exists SE w/ $x^* = x_A$
$\epsilon < x_A \leq 2\epsilon$	No SE	Exists SE w/ $x^* = \epsilon$
$x_A > 2\epsilon$	No SE	No SE

$p \neq \{0, 2\epsilon\}$. This implies that it rejects any proposal $p > 0$ that is off the equilibrium path, resulting in the status quo policy $\bar{p} = 0$ and $x = \epsilon$, which is the same as the equilibrium outcome. Thus, the only potentially profitable deviation is to $p = 2\epsilon$, which the legislature would accept, believing that $\omega = -\epsilon$. For this not to be profitable to the committee, the following condition must hold:

$$ -\left[(0 + \epsilon) - x_A\right]^2 \geq -\left[(2\epsilon + \epsilon) - x_A\right]^2, $$

where the expression on the left is the equilibrium payoff and the expression on the right is the payoff from the best possible deviation when $\omega = \epsilon$. Simplifying gives $x_A \leq 2\epsilon$.

Summarizing, the closed rule provides for information transmission by the committee in environments under which the open rule does not. In and of itself, however, this does not ensure that the legislature prefers a closed to an open rule. To see this, consider Table 5.1, which summarizes the effect of legislative procedure in different regions of the parameter space. Clearly, if $x_A \leq \epsilon$, then the legislature prefers delegation under an open rule to that under a closed rule, so long as the actors play a separating equilibrium in each.

Consider, then, the case where $\epsilon < x_A \leq 2\epsilon$. In the absence of a separating equilibrium, the committee transmits no information, so the legislature must choose policy ignorantly. As shown in Section 5.1, the legislature prefers $p = 0$ when it has no information about the value of the random shock, which it can obtain under an open rule by choosing $p_L = 0$. This produces an expected payoff of $-\epsilon^2$, which is precisely the legislature's expected payoff under a closed rule with information transmission. Thus, the legislature is indifferent between an open and a closed rule when $\epsilon < x_A \leq 2\epsilon$.

Finally, when $x_A > 2\epsilon$, there exists no separating equilibrium under either an open or a closed rule, so the legislature chooses ignorantly in either case. In the event of a closed rule, the legislature can achieve its preferred policy (but not outcome) by rejecting whatever proposal is made by the committee, as by assumption the status quo $\bar{p} = 0$. Either rule therefore produces an expected policy loss of ϵ^2, so again the committee is indifferent.

At least in the United States, however, closed rather than open rules seem to be the norm. Why should this be the case? Gilligan and Krehbiel (1987) suggest that closed rules create incentives for committees to acquire policy expertise. As shown here, the presence of a closed rule creates a rent for the committee: the final outcome is closer to its ideal point. If we endogenize the committee's expertise, as in Section 5.4, then the committee may have greater incentive under a closed rule to invest in its ability to identify the value of the random shock. This, in turn, increases the value of the committee to the legislature, justifying the choice of a closed-rule procedure. Exercise 5.5 considers this argument.[12]

This informational rationale for a closed rule contrasts with earlier, distributive theories of restrictive amendment procedures (Shepsle, 1978; Shepsle and Weingast, 1987; Weingast and Marshall, 1988). Each perspective grants that restrictive rules provide rents to committee members, but they differ in the rationale for those rents. Distributive theories posit that legislatures essentially function as cartels, with members protecting each others' rents through committee assignments and legislative procedures. In contrast, the informational theory presented here suggests that, from the perspective of the full legislature, rents are a necessary evil to encourage committees to develop the expertise on which the legislature depends.

Exercises

5.1 Consider the baseline model of Section 5.1, with the following modification. The random shock ω is distributed uniformly on the interval $[-\gamma, \gamma]$, where $\gamma > x_A$. All other elements of the model are the same as before.

    (a) What policy will the legislature choose if it does not delegate? What is the legislature's expected utility in this case?

    (b) What policy will the agency choose if it is delegated policy authority? What is the legislature's expected utility in this case?

---

[12] For discussion, see Krishna and Morgan (2001), who consider efficiency under alternative amendment procedures for both homogeneous and heterogeneous committees.

(c) Derive the condition for the legislature to delegate policy authority to the agency.

5.2   This exercise follows Huber and Shipan (2002) and Volden (2002) in modeling separation of powers in a delegation setting. Consider the following variant of the model in Section 5.1. There are two players: a legislature (L) and an executive (E), with preferences over outcomes represented by the utility functions $u_L(x) = -x^2$ and $u_E(x) = -(x - x_E)^2$, respectively. The executive plays two roles: it has control over bureaucratic implementation if authority is delegated by the legislature (i.e., it plays the role of the agency in the baseline model), and it has the ability to veto any proposal made by the legislature prior to realization of the random shock. The timing of events is as follows: 1) the legislature proposes to delegate authority or proposes a policy p; 2) the executive accepts or rejects the legislature's proposal; 3) the random shock ω is realized; 4) if the executive accepts the legislature's proposal (to delegate or to implement p), the game proceeds as in Section 5.1, whereas if the executive rejects the legislature's proposal, an exogenous status quo policy $\bar{p}$ is implemented. For simplicity, restrict attention to the case where $0 < \bar{p} < x_E$.

(a) Would the executive veto a proposal by the legislature to delegate policy authority? Why or why not?

(b) Now consider a proposal by the legislature to implement some policy p, without delegation. From the legislature's perspective, what is the best p that will not be vetoed by the executive?

(c) When would the legislature delegate authority in equilibrium? Interpret your result.

5.3   This exercise, which builds on Sections 5.2 and 5.4, presents a′ simple one-period version of the model in Gailmard and Patty (2007) in order to show that greater discretion can encourage the development of bureaucratic expertise. (The full version of the Gailmard-Patty model explores the interaction between discretion and personnel systems.) The game proceeds as follows. The legislature initially decides whether to delegate policy authority to the agency. If it delegates, it imposes a discretion limit $d \in (\epsilon, x_A + \epsilon)$, such that the policy p chosen by the agency must satisfy $p \leq d$. (The endpoints of this interval represent the policies most preferred by the legislature and the agency, respectively, when $\omega = -\epsilon$.) Following this, the agency decides whether to invest in expertise at a fixed cost κ. The random shock ω is then realized. This is observed by the agency if it has invested in expertise, and it is unobserved otherwise. Finally, the agency chooses a policy $p \leq d$. To focus on the interesting case, we assume that $\epsilon > \kappa$ and $2(\epsilon - \kappa) < x_A < 2\epsilon$. As in Section 5.2, the legislature and the agency have preferences represented by the utility functions $u_L(x) = -|x|$ and $u_A(x) = -|x - x_A|$, respectively.

(a) What policy does the agency choose if it has not invested in expertise, given the discretion limit d? What is its expected utility in this case?

(b) For each value of ω, what policy does the agency choose if it has invested in expertise, given the discretion limit d? From the perspective of the investment decision (i.e., before realization of the random shock ω), what is its expected utility in this case?

(c) Find the d that leaves the agency just indifferent between investing in expertise and not investing. From the legislature's perspective, this is the optimal d, given that it delegates policy authority to the agency.

(d) Derive the condition for the legislature to prefer delegation by comparing the expected payoff from delegating, given that d is chosen optimally to induce investment in agency expertise, and from not delegating. (Delegation without subsequent investment in expertise can never be better than retaining policy authority, given that the agency's and the legislature's preferences are not perfectly aligned.) Interpret your result.

5.4 This problem, which is based on Stephenson (2007), explores the impact of decision costs on the incentive to acquire bureaucratic expertise. Policy takes one of two values, $x \in \{0, 1\}$, where $x = 0$ is the status quo. We assume that the legislature and the agency have identical policy preferences. In particular, each actor receives a payoff of y if $x = 0$ and a random payoff of b if $x = 1$, where $b = 1$ with probability β and $b = 0$ with probability $1 - \beta$. We assume that $0 < y < \beta$.

The game proceeds as follows. The legislature initially decides on a decision cost $c \in (0, 1 - y)$, which is the cost borne by the agency if it chooses $x = 1$ (i.e., if it deviates from the status quo).

The agency then chooses an investment in expertise π, the cost of which is $\frac{\pi^2}{2}$. Following this, with probability π the agency receives a perfectly informative signal of b, whereas with probability $1 - \pi$ it receives a completely uninformative signal. Finally, the agency chooses $x \in \{0, 1\}$.

(a) Assume first that the legislature has chosen some $c < \beta - y$.

    (1) Derive the optimal policy for the agency when it receives a perfectly informative signal that $b = 1$.

    (2) Derive the optimal policy for the agency when it receives a perfectly informative signal that $b = 0$.

    (3) Derive the optimal policy for the agency when it receives an uninformative signal of b.

    (4) Solve for the agency's optimal level of expertise π. How does this value depend on c?

(b) Now assume that the legislature has chosen some $c > \beta - y$.

    (1) Derive the optimal policy for the agency when it receives a perfectly informative signal that $b = 1$.

    (2) Derive the optimal policy for the agency when it receives a perfectly informative signal that $b = 0$.

    (3) Derive the optimal policy for the agency when it receives an uninformative signal of b.

    (4) Solve for the agency's optimal level of expertise π. How does this value depend on c?

(c) What is the optimal decision cost from the legislature's perspective? (Does the legislature want π to be high or low?)

5.5   The following variant of the model in Section 5.7 explores the argument in Gilligan and Krehbiel (1987) that restrictive amendment procedures can encourage the development of expertise by legislative committees. At the beginning of the game, the full legislature chooses to consider the committee's proposal under an open or closed rule; assume that this commitment is binding. Following this, the committee decides whether to invest in expertise at a fixed cost κ. The committee observes the value of the random shock ω if and only if it has invested in expertise, following which it makes a proposal to the full legislature. Finally, the legislature considers the committee's proposal under an open or closed rule, given its earlier choice. Assume that the actors play the separating equilibria in Table 5.1, where they exist. Further, until stated otherwise, assume that $x_A \leq \epsilon$.

(a) Consider first the committee's decision when the legislature has committed to an open rule. What is the committee's expected payoff if it invests in expertise? If it does not?

(b) Now consider the committee's decision when the legislature has committed to a closed rule. What is the committee's expected payoff if it invests in expertise? If it does not?

(c) How does the condition for the committee to invest in expertise under an open rule compare to that under a closed rule?

(d) Derive the condition on parameters for the legislature to prefer a closed over an open rule. Interpret your result.

(e) Now assume that $x_A > \epsilon$. Would the legislature ever prefer a closed over an open rule? Why or why not?

6

Coalitions

Many of the models we have considered in previous chapters focus implicitly on the construction of coalitions in support of particular policies. In models of electoral competition, for example, parties or candidates seek the support of majority coalitions among the electorate. In contrast, in models of veto players, an agenda setter endeavors to assemble a unanimity coalition among political actors with the power to block change from the status quo.

In this chapter, the focus on coalitions is explicit. We consider coalition formation both in small groups, such as legislatures and committees, and in polities. Regardless of the setting, there is typically a privileged actor—agenda setter, incumbent, and so forth—who has the first opportunity to form a winning coalition. The models differ with regard to what occurs if coalition formation is unsuccessful: an exogenous default policy is implemented; agenda-setting power passes to another actor; or a challenger (to the incumbent) takes office.

We begin with a canonical model of legislative bargaining due to Baron and Ferejohn (1989) and its generalization to other policy environments. We then consider a related model that explores the impact of institutional features on the cohesion of legislative coalitions. We next turn attention to an alternative model of coalition formation that illustrates government formation in a parliamentary system. In each of these models, a minimum winning coalition is typically formed in equilibrium; we subsequently examine two alternative explanations for the supermajorities often observed in practice. Finally, we ask how coalition choice in polities depends on two features of the institutional environment: the size of the "selectorate" that decides whether to retain the incumbent and the size of the winning coalition necessary to retain power.

6.1 Legislative Bargaining

Baron and Ferejohn's (1989) model of policy bargaining in groups builds on Rubinstein's (1982) seminal model of two-player bargaining. Following Baron and Ferejohn, we refer to *legislative* bargaining, though the model may apply as well to decision making in committees, courts, and other small groups.

The Baron-Ferejohn model examines a particular policy problem: the distribution of a resource among members of a legislature governed by majority rule. Social choice theory tells us that there is no Condorcet winner in this environment if there are at least three legislators. Nonetheless, as in the Rubinstein model, bargaining always ends after one round, and with some restrictions on the set of equilibria, we can state what any legislator expects to receive from the bargaining process.

We begin our analysis of bargaining over distributions with a legislative "ultimatum" game, in which one member is chosen as agenda setter to make a take-it-or-leave-it offer to the rest of the legislature. We subsequently extend the model to two periods and then to an infinite-horizon setting. For each version of the model we ask two questions: what is the nature of the policy that emerges in equilibrium, and what share of the resource does each legislator expect to receive from the bargaining process?

The redistributive policy environment in the Baron-Ferejohn model is important but special. We therefore conclude this section with a discussion of Banks and Duggan's (2000, 2006a) generalization of the Baron-Ferejohn model to Euclidean policy.

6.1.1 A Legislative Ultimatum Game

Consider a legislature of $N \geq 3$ members who bargain over the distribution of an infinitely divisible resource. Assume N to be odd and index legislators by $i = 1, 2, \ldots, N$. At the beginning of the game, one of these legislators is chosen as agenda setter, with the probability that legislator i is chosen denoted by p_i, where p_i is exogenous and $\sum_i p_i = 1$. Let the vector of such probabilities be given by $\mathbf{p} = (p_1, \ldots, p_N)$. Differences in p_i could arise from differences in seniority, from whether a member belongs to a minority or majority party, or from other factors.

Whoever is chosen offers a distribution $\mathbf{x} = (x_1, \ldots, x_N)$ of the resource, where $\sum_i x_i = 1$. All legislators then vote to approve or reject $\mathbf{x}$, where $\mathbf{x}$ is adopted if more than $\frac{N}{2}$ members vote to approve. We assume that legislators play weakly undominated voting strategies, which, as discussed in Section 1.4.1, implies that they vote sincerely over the two choices. If the proposal is accepted, each legislator receives a payoff equal to the share of the resource received. If it is defeated, a default policy with payoffs $\bar{\mathbf{x}} = (\bar{x}_1, \ldots, \bar{x}_N)$ is implemented, where $\sum_i \bar{x}_i < 1$. The total resource to be divided is therefore greater if an agreement is reached than if it is not. We denote by V_i the expected payoff in equilibrium for legislator i.

What distribution will the legislator chosen as agenda setter propose? Because only a majority is necessary for approval, the agenda setter need not surrender any more than necessary to secure that majority. She therefore assembles a **minimum winning coalition** in the cheapest possible way, offering $x_i = \bar{x}_i$ to those legislators with the lowest $\bar{x}_i$ until she has a majority, and keeping the remainder for herself. (It is a best response for those in the coalition to vote for this proposal because they are indifferent between its passing and failing, whereas it is not a best response for the agenda setter to offer any more to coalition members because she could always do better by offering a bit less.)

The analysis is especially straightforward when all legislators have the same default payoff. Consider, for example, the case where $\bar{x}_i = 0$ for all legislators i. Then whoever is chosen as agenda setter is indifferent among all possible coalitions, and she always retains the entire pool of resources for herself. If we further assume that legislators have the same probability of being named agenda setter, that is, $p_i = \frac{1}{N}$ for all i, then the expected payoff for any member i is $V_i = \frac{1}{N}(1) = \frac{1}{N}$.

Consider, in contrast, an environment in which there are three legislators with default payoffs $\bar{\mathbf{x}} = (.1, .2, .1)$ and probabilities of being chosen agenda setter $\mathbf{p} = (.4, .4, .2)$. If legislator 1 is chosen as agenda setter, she brings legislator 3 into the coalition, as $\bar{x}_3 = .1 < .2 = \bar{x}_2$, implying a policy choice of $\mathbf{x} = (.9, 0, .1)$. In contrast, legislator 2 is indifferent between forming a coalition with legislator 1 (implying $\mathbf{x} = (.1, .9, 0)$), and forming one with legislator 3 (implying $\mathbf{x} = (0, .9, .1)$). Finally, if legislator 3 is chosen to be agenda setter, she forms a coalition with legislator 1 and offers $\mathbf{x} = (.1, 0, .9)$. If we assume that legislator 2 chooses between the two optimal coalitions with equal probability (i.e., plays a mixed strategy in which $(.1, .9, 0)$ and $(0, .9, .1)$ are each chosen with probability one-half), then the expected payoffs in equilibrium are

$$V_1 = p_1\,(.9) + p_2 \left[\frac{1}{2}\,(.1) + \frac{1}{2}\,(0)\right] + p_3\,(.1) = .4,$$

$$V_2 = p_1\,(0) + p_2 \left[\frac{1}{2}\,(.9) + \frac{1}{2}\,(.9)\right] + p_3\,(0) = .36,$$

$$V_3 = p_1\,(.1) + p_2 \left[\frac{1}{2}\,(0) + \frac{1}{2}\,(.1)\right] + p_3\,(.9) = .24.$$

Thus, when we drop the assumption of identical legislators, the expected payoff to any legislator in equilibrium is a potentially complicated function of the characteristics of all members ($\mathbf{p}$ and $\mathbf{\bar{x}}$).

6.1.2 A Two-period Model of Legislative Bargaining

We now extend the bargaining model to two periods. Assume that if no proposal is adopted in the first period a new agenda setter (possibly the same as that chosen in the first period) is chosen at the beginning of the second period, again according to the probability vector $\mathbf{p}$. Further, to capture the idea that it is costly to drag out the bargaining process, assume that if the pool of resources is divided in period 2 rather than period 1, then payoffs are discounted according to the vector of discount factors $\Delta = (\delta_1, \ldots, \delta_N)$. One (admittedly liberal) interpretation of this assumption is that δ_i captures the probability that legislator i is reelected at the end of the current period, where if not reelected she is replaced by another member from the same constituency. Differences in δ_i could then reflect differences in the degree to which members of the legislature represent safe districts. If no policy has been approved by the end of the second period, legislators receive default payoffs $\mathbf{\bar{x}} = (\bar{x}_1, \ldots, \bar{x}_N)$. We denote by V_{it} the expected payoff in equilibrium for legislator i at the beginning of period t, conditional on bargaining not having been concluded by this point in the game: this is legislator i's **continuation payoff**.

The game is solved by backward induction. Consider, for example, the case where legislators are chosen to be agenda setter with equal probability ($p_i = \frac{1}{N}$), value the future equally ($\delta_i = \delta$), and receive the same default payoff $\bar{x}_i = 0$. Then, by the analysis in the previous section, if the game continues to period 2, whoever has been chosen to be agenda setter proposes that she keep everything for herself, and that proposal is adopted. Any legislator i's expected payoff at the beginning of period 2, given that bargaining did not conclude in period 1, is thus $V_{i2} = \frac{1}{N}$.

Anticipating this, whoever has been chosen agenda setter in period 1 understands that she must provide $\delta V_{i2} = \frac{\delta}{N}$ to $\frac{N-1}{2}$ other legislators in order to form a coalition, implying that she keeps $1 - \left(\frac{N-1}{2}\right)\frac{\delta}{N}$ for herself. The agenda setter therefore retains more than half of the resource to be divided:

$$1 - \left(\frac{N-1}{2}\right)\frac{\delta}{N} > \frac{1}{2}.$$

This advantage derives from the fact that voting is by majority rule, so that the "share" of the excluded minority can be appropriated by the agenda setter. The more that other legislatures discount the future (i.e., the smaller is the discount factor δ), the greater is this advantage.

What share of the resource to be divided can a legislator expect to receive in equilibrium? Clearly, the answer depends on the nature of coalitions formed in period 1, as any coalition with $\frac{N-1}{2}$ other members is a best response for whoever is chosen agenda setter. However, if we restrict attention to the equilibrium in which all legislators are chosen as coalition partners with equal probability, then the expected payoff in equilibrium at the beginning of the game for any legislator i is

$$V_{i1} = \frac{1}{N}\left[1 - \left(\frac{N-1}{2}\right)\frac{\delta}{N}\right] + \frac{N-1}{N}\left(\frac{1}{2}\right)\frac{\delta}{N} = \frac{1}{N},$$

where the $\frac{1}{2}$ in the second term is the probability of being included in any other legislator's coalition. Thus, the expected payoff at the start of the game is the same as in the legislative ultimatum game. Clearly, this logic extends to an arbitrary number of periods, so that the expected payoff to each legislator is the same regardless of the number of periods.

This result—that the value of the bargaining process to a player is independent of the length of the process—contrasts sharply with the outcome of the (finite-horizon) Rubinstein bargaining model on which the Baron-Ferejohn model is based. What accounts for this difference? The Rubinstein model is a model of alternating offers: a proposer who fails to make an offer that is accepted is replaced as agenda setter in the following period. In contrast, in the Baron-Ferejohn model the probability of being named agenda setter is independent of the previous play of the game. Consequently, when legislators are identical, the expected payoff is the same at the beginning of each period.

Now consider a three-member legislature with $\mathbf{p} = (.4, .4, .2)$, $\Delta = (.25, .5, .5)$, and $\bar{x}_i = 0$ for all legislators i. As with the previous example, any legislator chosen to be agenda setter in period 2 retains the entire resource for herself. The expected payoff in equilibrium for any legislator

i at the start of period 2, conditional on bargaining having continued to that period, is thus $V_{i2} = p_i$. Any member i therefore votes for a proposal x_i in period 1 only if $x_i \geq \delta_i p_i$. But this is then the same problem as the legislative ultimatum game with default payoffs $\bar{\mathbf{x}} = (.1, .2, .1)$ analyzed in the last section. The lesson is that we can sometimes think of the default payoffs in a one-shot game as the (discounted) continuation values in a game with a longer horizon.

6.1.3 An Infinite-horizon Model of Legislative Bargaining

We now consider an infinite-horizon version of the Baron-Ferejohn model, where bargaining always continues to the next period if an offer is rejected. Given the assumption that the recognition probabilities are independent of the previous play of the game, the game is stationary: the terminal histories and players' preferences over them do not vary from period to period. It may therefore seem reasonable to restrict attention to **stationary strategies**, where in any period a legislator makes the same proposal if chosen as agenda setter and applies the same decision rule when deciding whether to accept a proposal, regardless of the previous history of play. In the Rubinstein bargaining model, a restriction to stationary strategies is without loss of generality: the unique subgame-perfect Nash equilibrium is in fact stationary. In the Baron-Ferejohn model, however, there are multiple, qualitatively different equilibria, and many outcomes are ruled out by focusing only on **stationary equilibria**—that is, equilibria in which actors play stationary strategies.

In particular, in the spirit of the folk theorem from repeated games, *any* allocation $\mathbf{x}$ is possible in some subgame-perfect Nash equilibrium of the infinite-horizon legislative bargaining game if players are sufficiently patient. Such an outcome can be supported by strategies in which a) any agenda setter proposes $\mathbf{x}$ and that proposal is passed, and b) if any agenda setter deviates by proposing something other than $\mathbf{x}$, then that proposal is defeated and the agenda setter in the next period proposes an allocation, which passes, that leaves the deviator out of the coalition (and if that agenda setter deviates, then the agenda setter in the next period ...).

This is an abundance-of-riches result, perhaps unsatisfying from an empirical perspective but characteristic of many infinite-horizon games. The restriction to stationary strategies can sharpen the model's predictions. One justification for this restriction is the earlier interpretation of

δ_i as the probability that a legislator is reelected. If legislators are "replaced" over the course of the game, then it may be more difficult for the legislator in any given period to condition her actions on the outcome of the game in previous periods. That said, it should be stressed that restriction to stationary equilibria rules out norms of legislative behavior that depend on the expectation of rewards or punishment based on previous play of the game.

To illustrate the sharp predictions that can follow from a restriction to stationary equilibria, consider again the case where there are N identical legislators, each of whom receives a payoff of zero in any period in which there is not an agreement. Because strategies are stationary, we drop the time subscript and denote the expected payoff in equilibrium to legislator i at the beginning of any period, conditional on bargaining having advanced that far, by V_i. It is therefore optimal for member i to vote for a proposal if and only if $x_i \geq \delta V_i$. Note that V_i must be the same for all legislators i: if V_i were higher for some legislator, then she would never be chosen to be in a coalition, which in turn would imply that V_i is lower rather than higher for that member. Thus, we can denote by V the common expected payoff at the beginning of any period. Assuming that legislators are chosen at random to be included in any coalition, we can therefore derive V as

$$V = \frac{1}{N}\left[1 - \left(\frac{N-1}{2}\right)\delta V\right] + \frac{N-1}{N}\left(\frac{1}{2}\right)\delta V = \frac{1}{N}.$$

which is the same as in the finite-horizon model with identical legislators. This in turn implies that the offer made in the infinite-horizon model takes the same form as in the finite-horizon model, in any period but the last: $\frac{N-1}{2}$ legislators are offered $\frac{\delta}{N}$, and the agenda setter retains $1 - \left(\frac{N-1}{2}\right)\frac{\delta}{N}$ for herself.

In fact, we can say more: for a given infinite-horizon legislative bargaining model, where the legislators are not necessarily identical, any stationary equilibrium has the same vector of expected payoffs (possibly different for different legislators), a result due to Eraslan (2002). In the case of identical legislators considered here, for example, legislators might be assigned to coalitions by other than an equal-probability rule, but the expected payoff for any legislator at the beginning of any period would still be $\frac{1}{N}$. To see this, assume $N = 3$, and let q_{ij} be the probability in some stationary equilibrium that legislator i, if chosen as the agenda setter, chooses legislator j to be in her coalition. Then the expected payoff at the beginning of any period for legislator 1 can be written as

$$V = \frac{1}{3}(1 - \delta V) + \frac{1}{3}q_{21}\delta V + \frac{1}{3}q_{31}\delta V. \tag{6.1}$$

Similarly, the expected payoff for legislators 2 and 3 can be written as

$$V = \frac{1}{3}(1 - \delta V) + \frac{1}{3}q_{12}\delta V + \frac{1}{3}q_{32}\delta V,$$

$$V = \frac{1}{3}(1 - \delta V) + \frac{1}{3}q_{13}\delta V + \frac{1}{3}q_{23}\delta V.$$

These three equations imply

$$q_{21} + q_{31} = q_{12} + q_{32} = q_{13} + q_{23},$$

which can be simplified further by noting that $q_{13} = 1 - q_{12}$, $q_{21} = 1 - q_{23}$, and $q_{32} = 1 - q_{31}$ (because probabilities sum to one). Thus,

$$1 - q_{23} + q_{31} = q_{12} + 1 - q_{31} = 1 - q_{12} + q_{23}.$$

Finally, a bit of substitution gives $q_{12} = q_{23} = q_{31}$, which implies $q_{13} = q_{21} = q_{32}$.

Focusing on legislator 1, we can therefore rewrite Equation 6.1 as

$$V = \frac{1}{3}(1 - \delta V) + \frac{1}{3}q_{21}\delta V + \frac{1}{3}q_{23}\delta V$$

$$= \frac{1}{3}(1 - \delta V) + \frac{1}{3}\delta V = \frac{1}{3},$$

where in the first line we use $q_{31} = q_{23}$, as just derived, and in the second line we use $q_{21} + q_{23} = 1$. Thus, for example, there is a stationary equilibrium with $q_{12} = q_{23} = q_{31} = 0$ and $q_{13} = q_{21} = q_{32} = 1$, from which the expected payoff for legislator 1 can be derived as

$$V = \frac{1}{3}(1 - \delta V) + \frac{1}{3}(1)\delta V + \frac{1}{3}(0)\delta V = \frac{1}{3}.$$

6.1.4 Legislative Bargaining in the Spatial Model

The Baron-Ferejohn model follows Rubinstein (1982) in assuming that the policy over which actors bargain is the division of some resource. This precludes consideration of many important policy environments, including those in which actors have **satiable preferences**—that is, in which actors most prefer policies that do not lie at the boundary of the policy space. An example is social policy, where legislators' ideal points may lie somewhere between the left-most and right-most position.

Banks and Duggan (2000, 2006a) generalize the Baron-Ferejohn model to Euclidean policy, with the Baron-Ferejohn model as a special case.[1] The key difference between Banks and Duggan (2000) and Banks and Duggan (2006a) is that the former assumes that all legislators weakly prefer any policy $\mathbf{x} \in \mathbf{X}$ to the status quo; the latter imposes no such restriction.

To illustrate this approach, assume as before that there are N legislators, with N odd, and restrict attention to the case where each legislator has an identical probability $\left(\frac{1}{N}\right)$ of being named agenda setter. If chosen, the legislator proposes a policy $x \in \Re$; thus, policy is one-dimensional. If some proposal x is accepted, then any legislator i receives a payoff u_i in that and *all subsequent periods* of

$$- \left(x - x_i \right)^2,$$

where we assume a common discount factor $\delta < 1$. Legislators have distinct ideal points x_i, with median ideal point x_m. A status quo policy $\bar{x}$ prevails until a proposal is accepted, with an analogous payoff in each period for any legislator i.

The assumption of quadratic policy loss ensures that there is a unique **no-delay stationary equilibrium** (Cho and Duggan, 2003), that is, an equilibrium in which any legislator i, whenever chosen to be agenda setter, makes the same offer (possibly different from that of other legislators); any legislator i adopts the same decision rule whenever deciding to vote for an offer; and only offers that would be accepted by a majority are made in equilibrium (so that bargaining ends in the first period). Further, as Banks and Duggan (2006b) show, when utility is quadratic we can simplify the analysis by noting that if the median legislator weakly prefers some offer over a continuation of the bargaining process, then so do a majority of legislators, and vice versa (a generalization of Black's Median Voter Theorem [Black, 1948] to voting over lotteries over policies).

In this equilibrium, the median legislator is decisive—she effectively decides whether a proposal is accepted or rejected—but proposals other than the median ideal point may be made in equilibrium. In particular, if the status quo $\bar{x}$ is sufficiently close to the median x_m or legislators are sufficiently patient, then any legislator with ideal point to the left

---

[1] Formally, the policy space in the Baron-Ferejohn model is a simplex of dimension $N - 1$, where N is the number of legislators. Banks and Duggan allow for utility functions sufficiently general to capture the assumption that legislators' payoffs are equal to the share of the resource received.

of x_m proposes $x_m - \lambda$, where $\lambda \geq 0$ is a variable for which we will solve; any legislator to the right of x_m proposes $x_m + \lambda$; and the median legislator proposes x_m. Any legislator i, in turn, votes for any proposal that provides an expected payoff of at least

$$u_i\left(\bar{x}\right) + \frac{\delta}{1-\delta}\left(\frac{1}{N}\right)\sum_j u_i\left(x^j\right), \qquad (6.2)$$

where x^j is the proposal made by legislator j whenever she is chosen to be agenda setter. By construction, the second term in Expression 6.2 is precisely δV_i, where V_i is the continuation payoff to legislator i in a no-delay stationary equilibrium. Thus, any legislator votes for a proposal if the expected payoff from doing so is at least as large as the expected payoff from receiving the status quo payoff for one more period and then receiving a perpetual payoff from whatever policy is proposed and accepted in the following period.

It remains only to find the λ such that the median legislator prefers to accept a proposal by any other legislator to rejecting the proposal and continuing on to the next period. The discounted payoff from accepting any such proposal is

$$-\frac{\lambda^2}{1-\delta}. \qquad (6.3)$$

As specified, any legislator to the left or right of the median legislator proposes a policy λ to the left or right, respectively, of x_m; the median legislator's payoff from this policy $\left(-\lambda^2\right)$ is received in perpetuity. In contrast, as given by Expression 6.2, the expected payoff to the median legislator from rejecting this proposal is

$$-\left(\bar{x} - x_m\right)^2 - \frac{\delta}{1-\delta}\left[\left(\frac{1}{N}\right)0 + \left(\frac{N-1}{N}\right)\lambda^2\right]. \qquad (6.4)$$

The first term is the payoff from the status quo policy in the current period. The second is the continuation payoff, discounted by δ: with probability $\frac{1}{N}$, the median legislator is chosen to be agenda setter in the next period, in which case she implements her ideal point, whereas with probability $\frac{N-1}{N}$, the median legislator accepts a proposal λ to the left or right of her ideal point.

It is optimal for the median legislator to accept any proposal made by a legislator to her left or right if Expression 6.3 is at least as large as

Expression 6.4. Simplifying gives

$$\lambda \leq \sqrt{\frac{N\left(1-\delta\right)\left(\bar{x}-x_m\right)^2}{N-\delta\left(N-1\right)}}. \tag{6.5}$$

Condition 6.5 puts a bound on what legislators to the left or right of the median can propose and have accepted. So long as the status quo $\bar{x}$ is close to the median ideal point x_m or the discount factor δ is close to one, the condition holds with equality: any legislator to the left or right of the median prefers that λ be as large as possible.

In particular, as the status quo $\bar{x}$ approaches the median x_m or as legislators become perfectly patient ($\delta \to 1$), the set of proposals made in equilibrium collapses on the status quo. This illustrates a general property of no-delay stationary equilibria in the Banks-Duggan model: the equilibrium proposals are continuous in parameters of the model. One implication of this result is that the qualitative predictions of various models that are special cases of the Banks-Duggan model are robust to small perturbations in their parameters. For example, the Romer-Rosenthal model of Section 4.3 assumes that bargaining does not continue past the first round—formally, that the discount factor $\delta = 0$—and that one legislator is certain to be chosen as agenda setter. Continuity implies that the equilibrium proposal is similar to that in the Romer-Rosenthal model if legislators place a small weight on the future or if some legislator other than the agenda setter has a small probability of being recognized.

6.2 Cohesion

In our discussion of the Baron-Ferejohn model and its generalization by Banks and Duggan, we focused on how the process of coalition formation determines the policy chosen by a legislature or similar body. We now take up a related question: to what extent do coalitions formed on one vote carry over to another? We address this topic—the cohesion of legislative coalitions—using a model by Diermeier and Feddersen (1998).

Diermeier and Feddersen distinguish between a **ruling coalition**, a legislative majority whose members serve as agenda setters, and a **policy coalition**, which is the set of members who vote to approve any particular bill. The central insight of the Diermeier-Feddersen model is that cohesion is greater with a **vote of confidence** procedure, where failure to approve some proposal results in dissolution of the government. As in Huber's model of the confidence vote (see Exercise 4.6), members of the ruling coalition are willing to accept a less attractive offer from the agenda setter for the sake of remaining in power. This makes it more likely that members of the ruling coalition are chosen to be in any particular policy coalition, which increases cohesion across legislative votes.

We adapt the Baron-Ferejohn model of the previous section as follows. To explore cohesion across multiple votes, assume that members vote in each period on the distribution of a *new* infinitely divisible resource, rather than deciding once and for all on the distribution of a single resource. We examine a two-period model; Diermeier and Feddersen generalize to an arbitrary finite horizon. At the beginning of each period, one legislator from the ruling coalition (on which more to follow) is chosen to be agenda setter using an equal-probability rule. The agenda setter then makes an ultimatum offer $\mathbf{x} = (x_1, \ldots, x_N)$ to the N legislators, where $\sum x_i = 1$. Voting is by majority rule. If the proposal fails, then a default distribution $\bar{\mathbf{x}}$ is implemented, where $\bar{x}_i = \frac{1}{N}$ for any legislator i. We assume no discounting.

We compare two institutional environments: one where the ruling coalition always survives to the second period, and one where the ruling coalition dissolves if a majority votes against the proposal under consideration in the first period. The second environment represents a parliamentary system with a confidence-vote procedure. If the ruling coalition dissolves, we assume that the default policy $\bar{\mathbf{x}}$ is implemented in the second period (i.e., no agenda setter is chosen or vote taken). In both environments, we assume that the agenda setter forms a policy coalition at random from among those that provide the highest payoff.

Consider first the case where the ruling coalition always survives to the second period, that is, where there is no confidence vote. For concreteness, assume that $N = 3$, where legislators 1 and 2 belong to the ruling coalition. By assumption, in each period, legislators 1 and 2 are each chosen to be agenda setter with probability one-half. By the logic of Section 6.1.1, whoever is chosen to be agenda setter chooses one of the other legislators to be in her policy coalition, offering that player one-third of the resource (the default payoff) and keeping the remainder for herself. For legislators 1 and 2, the expected payoff in each period is therefore

$$\frac{1}{2}\left(\frac{2}{3}\right) + \frac{1}{2}\left[\frac{1}{2}\left(\frac{1}{3}\right) + \frac{1}{2}(0)\right] = \frac{5}{12},$$

where the first term on the left is the probability-weighted payoff from being chosen to be agenda setter, and the second term is the probability-weighted payoff from not being named agenda setter (in which case the legislator becomes a member of the policy coalition with probability one-half, given the assumption that agenda setters randomize over policy coalitions that provide the highest payoff). In contrast, the expected payoff in either period for legislator 3 is

$$\frac{1}{2}\left[\frac{1}{2}\left(\frac{1}{3}\right)+\frac{1}{2}(0)\right]+\frac{1}{2}\left[\frac{1}{2}\left(\frac{1}{3}\right)+\frac{1}{2}(0)\right]=\frac{1}{6},$$

as legislator 3 is never chosen to be agenda setter.

The cohesion of policy coalitions when there is no confidence vote can be derived as follows. Let $\{i,j\}$ represent the policy coalition that includes legislators i and j. In either period, the probability that the policy coalition is $\{1,2\}$ is

$$\frac{1}{2}\left(\frac{1}{2}\right)+\frac{1}{2}\left(\frac{1}{2}\right)=\frac{1}{2},$$

as 1) each member of the ruling coalition is chosen to be agenda setter with probability one-half, and 2) each member of the ruling coalition, if chosen to be agenda setter, chooses the other member of the ruling coalition to be in her policy coalition with probability one-half. Similarly, the probability in either period that the policy coalition is $\{1,3\}$ is

$$\frac{1}{2}\left(\frac{1}{2}\right)=\frac{1}{4},$$

as legislator 3 can never be chosen to be agenda setter; this is also the probability that the policy coalition is $\{2,3\}$. Given that coalition formation is independent across periods, the probability that the policy coalition is the same in *both* periods is therefore

$$\left(\frac{1}{2}\right)^2+\left(\frac{1}{4}\right)^2+\left(\frac{1}{4}\right)^2=\frac{3}{8}. \tag{6.6}$$

Consider now legislative cohesion under a confidence-vote procedure, where the survival of the ruling coalition to the second period is tied to the vote in the first period. We begin by analyzing policy choice in the second period. If the ruling coalition survives from the first period, then the outcome in the second period is identical to that with no vote of confidence, as already derived. In contrast, if the ruling coalition falls, then by assumption the resource is divided equally among the three legislators in the second period.

We now analyze coalition choice in the first period. Without loss of generality, assume that legislator 1 is chosen to be agenda setter. Legislator 2 accepts any offer such that her payoff x_2 satisfies

$$x_2 + \frac{5}{12} \geq \frac{1}{3} + \frac{1}{3},$$

where the expression on the left is the payoff if the proposal passes and the ruling coalition survives to the second period, and the expression on the right is the payoff if the proposal fails and the default allocation is implemented in both periods. Simplifying, we see that legislator 2 accepts any offer such that $x_2 \geq \frac{1}{4}$. In contrast, legislator 3 accepts any offer such that her payoff x_3 satisfies

$$x_3 + \frac{1}{6} \geq \frac{1}{3} + \frac{1}{3},$$

or $x_3 \geq \frac{1}{2}$.

Clearly, it is cheaper to include legislator 2 in the policy coalition— legislator 2 is willing to accept a smaller offer in the first period for the sake of having a chance to be agenda setter in the second. Similarly, if chosen to be agenda setter, legislator 2 always chooses legislator 1 to be in her policy coalition. Thus, the policy coalition is always $\{1, 2\}$ in period 1, whereas the policy coalition is $\{1, 2\}$ with probability one-half in period 2, as shown earlier. The policy coalition survives across the two periods with probability one-half, which is greater than the probability given by Equation 6.6. Legislative coalitions are more cohesive with a confidence vote than without.

6.3 Government Formation

We now consider an alternative model of coalition choice, based on Baron and Diermeier (2001), that represents policy choice in a parliamentary system. The central idea of the Baron-Diermeier model is that policy is chosen by government, which is a subset of the parties represented in parliament; bargaining over policy takes place within this **proto-coalition**. However, any government (and associated policy) must be supported by a majority in parliament. A key assumption is that there are officeholding benefits (e.g., jobs for party members) that can be freely redistributed among members of the government. Thus, in contrast to the model of portfolio allocation in Section 4.4, bargaining over policy is jointly efficient among coalition members.

To illustrate the Baron-Diermeier model, we consider a one-dimensional policy environment; Baron and Diermeier (2001) analyze a model with two policy dimensions. There are three parties in parliament, $i = 1, 2, 3$, none of which can form a majority on its own. Each party has quadratic preferences over policy $x \in [-1, 1]$, where party 1 most prefers $x = -1$; party 2, $x = 0$; and party 3, $x = 1$.[2] In addition, parties value office-holding benefits that can be freely redistributed among parties in the government; we assume that these are sufficient to allow for efficient bargaining. Letting x_i represent party i's ideal point and y_i the distribution of office holding benefits to party i, preferences for any party i are therefore represented by the function

$$u_i(x, y_i) = -(x - x_i)^2 + y_i.$$

The timing of events is as follows. One party is chosen to be the **formateur**, which chooses some subset of parties represented in parliament to form a government. Baron and Diermeier (2001) assume that the probability of being chosen formateur is proportional to a party's seat share;[3] later we will discuss the implications of this assumption. The government (proto-coalition) then bargains over policy and officeholding benefits. We focus on a bargaining environment in which the formateur makes a simultaneous take-it-or-leave-it offer to other members of the government, but other bargaining protocols could be considered. Following receipt of this offer, all parties in parliament express confidence or no confidence in the government. If the government receives the support of a majority, the agreed policy and distribution of officeholding benefits are implemented; otherwise a status quo policy $\bar{x}$ is implemented and no officeholding benefits are distributed. We assume that $\bar{x} \in (0, 1)$; the argument is symmetric for $\bar{x} \in (-1, 0)$.

The primary question the model addresses is how the policy outcome depends on the identity of the formateur. To the extent that formateurs are associated with distinct policy outcomes, this gives voters a clear choice between parties, so long as the probability that a party is chosen to be formateur is related to its vote share.

Consider, then, the outcome when party 1 is chosen to be formateur. In principle, party 1 can form a government with party 2, with party 3, or with both parties 2 and 3. Whatever the choice, the subsequent bargaining maximizes the joint utility of all parties in the government, with

---

[2] Similarly, Baron and Diermeier (2001) assume that parties have ideal points arranged symmetrically in two-dimensional space.

[3] For empirical support of this assumption, see Diermeier and Merlo (2004).

each coalition member given officeholding benefits such that it is just indifferent between accepting the proposal and rejecting it (see Section 3.4 for a similar bargaining environment with freely transferable utility). Any such government survives a no-confidence vote in parliament, given that two parties are sufficient for a majority.[4] In the discussion to follow, we denote by x^G the policy outcome for a given government G (e.g., x^{12} is the policy outcome when parties 1 and 2 are in the government).

In particular, if party 1 forms a government with party 2, the policy outcome is

$$x^{12} = \arg\max_{x} \; - [x - (-1)]^2 - (x - 0)^2 = -\frac{1}{2}.$$

Party 1 provides officeholding benefits y_2 to party 2 such that it is indifferent between this policy and the status quo $\bar{x}$:

$$- \left(x^{12} - 0\right)^2 + y_2 = - (\bar{x} - 0)^2 ,$$

that is, $y_2 = \frac{1}{4} - \bar{x}^2$. (Note that this value is negative—party 2 transfers officeholding benefits to party 1—for $\bar{x} > \frac{1}{2}$.) Party 1's utility from a government with party 2 is therefore

$$- \left[x^{12} - (-1)\right]^2 - y_2 = -\frac{1}{2} + \bar{x}^2. \tag{6.7}$$

In contrast, if party 1 forms a government with party 3, the policy outcome $x^{13} = 0$. The officeholding benefits y_3 for party 3 solve

$$- \left(x^{13} - 1\right)^2 + y_3 = - (\bar{x} - 1)^2 ,$$

that is, $y_3 = 1 - (\bar{x} - 1)^2$, so that party 1's utility from forming a government with party 3 is

$$- \left[x^{13} - (-1)\right]^2 - y_3 = -2 + (\bar{x} - 1)^2 .$$

Finally, if party 1 forms a government with both parties 2 and 3, $x^{123} = 0$, which is the same as x^{13} but also results in a transfer of officeholding benefits from party 2 to party 1 in return for implementing party 2's most-preferred policy rather than $\bar{x}$ (i.e., $y_2 = -\bar{x}^2$). Party 1's utility from a grand coalition with parties 2 and 3 is thus

$$-1 + 2\bar{x}\left(\bar{x} - 1\right), \tag{6.8}$$

which is greater than that from forming a government with party 3 alone.

---

[4] One can verify that a minority government would never emerge in equilibrium: a government of party 1 or 3 alone would not receive the support of the other two parties, whereas party 2 prefers forming a grand coalition of all three parties to governing alone.

Party 1 thus chooses between forming a government with party 2 alone and forming a government with both parties 2 and 3. Comparing Expressions 6.7 and 6.8, we see that for any $\bar{x} \in [0, 1]$, party 1 is better off forming a government with party 2 alone:[5]

$$-\frac{1}{2} + \bar{x}^2 > -1 + 2\bar{x}(\bar{x} - 1).$$

The logic is similar when party 3 is the formateur. Forming a government with parties 1 and 2 ($x^{123} = 0$) is preferable to forming a government with party 1 alone ($x^{13} = 0$), as utility can be extracted from party 2 for implementing its most-preferred policy. In particular, a grand coalition with parties 1 and 2 implies a transfer of officeholding benefits of $y_1 = 1 - (\bar{x} + 1)^2$ and $y_2 = -\bar{x}^2$, respectively. In contrast, a government with party 2 alone results in a policy outcome of $x^{23} = \frac{1}{2}$ and a transfer of officeholding benefits of $y_2 = \frac{1}{4} - \bar{x}^2$. Comparing the payoff to party 3 from these two outcomes, we see that party 3 prefers forming a government with party 2 alone when

$$-(0 - 1)^2 - \left[1 - (\bar{x} + 1)^2\right] - (-\bar{x}^2) < -\left(\frac{1}{2} - 1\right)^2 - \left(\frac{1}{4} - \bar{x}^2\right),$$

that is, when $\bar{x} < \frac{\sqrt{6} - 2}{2}$. In contrast, when $\bar{x} > \frac{\sqrt{6} - 2}{2}$, party 3 prefers to form a grand coalition.

Finally, consider government formation when party 2 is the formateur. A coalition with either party 1 or party 3 results in a policy loss of $-\frac{1}{4}$, but the formateur receives more officeholding benefits when forming a government with party 1: the necessary transfer to party 1,

$$y_1 = \frac{1}{4} - (\bar{x} + 1)^2,$$

is for all $\bar{x} > 0$ strictly less than the transfer to party 3,

$$y_3 = \frac{1}{4} - (\bar{x} - 1)^2.$$

In addition, one can verify that the payoff to party 2 from forming a government with party 1 is greater than that from a grand coalition of all three parties. Thus, the policy outcome when party 2 is the formateur is $x^{12} = -\frac{1}{2}$.

We can summarize this discussion as follows. Given a status quo of

---

[5] Observe also that party 1's utility from forming a government with party 2 alone is greater than party 1's utility from the status quo outcome of $\bar{x}$ and no officeholding benefits, which is $-(\bar{x} + 1)^2$. One can verify that the analogous statement holds for the other governments to be discussed.

$\bar{x} \in (0,1)$, if either party 1 or party 2 is the formateur, then the policy outcome is $x = -\frac{1}{2}$. In contrast, if party 3 is the formateur, then the policy outcome is $x = \frac{1}{2}$ if $x < \frac{\sqrt{6}-2}{2}$ and $x = 0$ if $x > \frac{\sqrt{6}-2}{2}$. Policy thus exhibits an anti-status quo bias: if the centrist party is chosen as formateur, it chooses a coalition partner to the opposite side of the default policy, whereas if the rightist party is chosen as formateur, equilibrium policy is inversely correlated with the position of the status quo. This reflects a key insight of the Baron-Diermeier model. The status quo policy does not affect the policy chosen by any particular government, but by determining the bargaining power of potential coalition partners—the farther is the status quo from a party's ideal point, the cheaper it is to bring that party into the government—it can influence which government is chosen by any particular formateur.

A key assumption of the Baron-Diermeier model is that there are sufficient officeholding benefits to allow for efficient bargaining over policy. Absent these benefits, bargaining within governments would follow a veto-players model, with the policy outcome related to the status quo for some coalitions. In the setting just described, for example, the policy outcome when party 1 is the formateur would be $-\bar{x}$: party 1 would form a government with party 2, following which party 1 would propose a policy that leaves party 2 just indifferent between accepting and rejecting the proposal.

The Baron-Diermeier model easily lends itself to richer environments in which coalition choice is preceded by an election. If the probability of being chosen formateur is proportional to seat share in parliament, then in elections with proportional representation, voters have an incentive to vote for parties based on the governments they would expect them to form.[6] In the example just given, voters with ideal points to the right of zero prefer to vote for party 3, even if their ideal points are closer to party 2's most-preferred position ($x = 0$) than to party 3's ($x = 1$). Intuitively, voters with these preferences prefer to elect party 3 as a counterbalance to party 1. The Baron-Diermeier model therefore illuminates strategic voting in proportional-representation systems, where misrepresentation of preferences may result from voters' understanding of the government formation process.

---

[6] Austen-Smith and Banks (1988) present an early model of strategic voting in anticipation of coalition choice.

6.4 Endogenous Supermajorities

The models considered thus far generally support Buchanan and Tullock's (1962) and Riker's (1962) contention that minimum winning coalitions are the likely outcome of any coalition-building process. We now turn to a pair of models that help to explain the supermajority coalitions often observed in practice. We consider first a model by Weingast (1979), who shows why a **norm of universalism** may emerge, whereby all members of a legislature support and benefit from distributive legislation. The puzzle of universalism is that the "pork barrel" policies funded by such bills are highly divisible—they may be targeted at individual members' districts—yet the cost of their provision typically falls on the entire electorate. Consequently, as shown especially by the Baron-Ferejohn model, a majority coalition is able to effectively expropriate members of the minority. The key insight of Weingast's model is that legislators may prefer universal coalitions ex ante, if they do not know whether they are likely to be in a majority coalition ex post.

To see this, we modify the legislative ultimatum game of Section 6.1.1 in the following way. Rather than assuming an exogenous budget, we assume that projects must be financed by taxes included in the same bill. Further, we assume that there are limits to how much can be spent in any particular district. In particular, each legislator i has a single available project that can be funded by the bill under consideration. The benefit of legislator i's project is b_i, whereas the cost is c_i. For simplicity, we assume that the benefit accrues entirely to member i, whereas the cost is borne equally by all members; Shepsle and Weingast (1981a) consider the more general case. Further, we assume that $b_i = b$ and $c_i = c$ for all i. Members have identical recognition probabilities. The status quo is for no projects to be funded. We assume $b > c$, which ensures that projects are funded in equilibrium, regardless of the norm in effect.

We begin by considering a norm of minimum winning coalitions (i.e., no supermajority norm). Unlike the Baron-Ferejohn model, no surplus is available to the agenda setter, given the assumptions that only readily available projects can be considered, that all such projects are of the same size, and that the tax burden must be shared equally. In equilibrium, whoever is named agenda setter chooses a minimum winning coalition of $\frac{N+1}{2}$ legislators (where N is the number of legislators, assumed to be odd), including herself, each of whom receives a benefit b from her funded project. The aggregate cost of these $\frac{N+1}{2}$ projects is shared equally by all N legislators, so the tax burden on each member is $\left(\frac{N+1}{2N}\right) c$. Given the assumption that $b > c$, which implies $b > \left(\frac{N+1}{2N}\right) c$, any member of the coalition prefers that the proposal pass, whereas any member outside it prefers that the proposal fail.

Following the discussion in Section 6.1, we restrict attention to the equilibrium in which any agenda setter chooses a coalition from among all possible winning coalitions according to an equal-probability rule. To derive the probability that a legislator becomes a member of a majority coalition and thus has her project funded, recall that the number of combinations (without replacement) of K distinct elements from a set of N objects is $\binom{N}{K} = \frac{N!}{K!(N-K)!}$. Define $M \equiv \frac{N+1}{2}$, the size of the minimum winning coalition. Then the number of minimum winning coalitions is $\binom{N}{M}$, whereas the number of minimum winning coalitions that exclude any member i is $\binom{N-1}{M}$. The probability of being included in some minimum winning coalition is thus

$$1 - \binom{N-1}{M} / \binom{N}{M} = 1 - \frac{\frac{(N-1)!}{M!(N-1-M)!}}{\frac{N!}{M!(N-M)!}} = 1 - \frac{N-M}{N} = \frac{N+1}{2N},$$

where the last equality uses the definition of M. Prior to the choice of agenda setter, the expected utility for any legislator is therefore

$$\left(\frac{N+1}{2N}\right) b - \left(\frac{N+1}{2N}\right) c,$$

where the first term is the probability-weighted benefit from having one's project included in the bill, and the second is the cost borne by all legislators. Simplifying gives $\left(\frac{N+1}{2N}\right)(b - c)$.

Now consider a legislative rule that requires the unanimous support of all members to pass any distributive legislation. Such a rule is best understood as an informal norm that is supported through unmodeled repeat play. Given that $b > c$ by assumption, whoever is named agenda setter proposes that all members' projects be financed, and this bill is passed. Any legislator's expected utility is therefore

$$b - c > \left(\frac{N+1}{2N}\right)(b - c).$$

Legislators are better off ex ante under a norm of universalism than when distributive bills are supported by a minimum winning coalition, which helps to explain why pork barrel legislation can attract the support of large coalitions.

Groseclose and Snyder (1996) provide an alternative explanation for supermajority coalitions. In their model, a "vote buyer"—any actor, such as a party leader or president, with the ability to offer something in return for a legislator's vote—assembles a larger-than-minimum winning coalition in order to reduce the cost of holding that coalition together. The basic logic is that small changes in the size of one's coalition may result in a large *relative* increase in the number of legislators that a competing vote buyer would need to pick off to prevent passage of a bill.

We assume a legislature of N members, where N is odd, with legislators indexed by i. Legislators vote over two alternatives, $x \in \{0, 1\}$. It is useful to think of $x = 0$ as the status quo and $x = 1$ as the bill under consideration. There are two vote buyers, A and B, who prefer the bill and the status quo, respectively. Let ω be the payoff to A from her most-preferred alternative ($x = 1$), let φ be the payoff to B from her most-preferred alternative ($x = 0$), and normalize to zero the payoff to both A and B from their least-preferred alternatives. Assume that $\omega > \left(\frac{N+1}{2}\right) \varphi$, which ensures that A is always able to pass the bill. The question is what A must pay to produce that outcome.

Vote buyer A moves first, offering $(T_{A1}, \ldots, T_{AN})$, where T_{Ai} is the transfer to legislator i in return for voting for $x = 1$. Having observed A's offer, vote buyer B then offers $(T_{B1}, \ldots, T_{BN})$, where T_{Bi} is the transfer to legislator i in return for voting for $x = 0$. We assume that legislators care only about transfers, not about policy per se, so that legislators vote for the alternative that provides the larger transfer. If a legislator has not been bribed, we assume that she votes for the status quo, whereas if she has been promised the same positive transfer by both A and B, we assume that she votes for the bill (e.g., because A made the first offer). Voting is by majority rule, so whichever alternative receives at least $\frac{N+1}{2}$ votes is the winner.

By assumption, any unbribed legislator votes for the status quo. Thus, A must bribe at least $\frac{N+1}{2}$ members for the bill to pass. Further, A must prevent B from picking off so many members of her coalition that she no longer has a majority.

Consider first the case where A builds a coalition of exactly $\frac{N+1}{2}$ members, that is, a minimum winning coalition. Vote buyer B can block the bill by picking off exactly one member of A's coalition. It is worth φ to B to do this, so she will block the bill unless $T_{Ai} \geq \varphi$ for each member i in A's coalition. Clearly, A would never spend more than necessary to pass the bill, so A offers a common $T_A = \varphi$ to $\frac{N+1}{2}$ legislators, and she offers nothing to the remainder. The total cost to A is $\left(\frac{N+1}{2}\right)\varphi$, which by assumption is less than the benefit to A of passing the bill.

Now consider the case where A builds a coalition of $\frac{N+3}{2}$ members, that is, one more than necessary. To block the bill, B must pick off two members of A's coalition. As before, the benefit to B of doing so is φ, so to pass the bill, A offers a common $T_A = \frac{\varphi}{2}$ to her coalition members. The total cost to A is therefore

$$\left(\frac{N+3}{2}\right)\frac{\varphi}{2} < \left(\frac{N+1}{2}\right)\varphi,$$

so that A prefers a supermajority of $\frac{N+3}{2}$ members to a minimum winning coalition. Intuitively, A needs only to expand her coalition by one member to double the number of legislators whom B must bribe to prevent passage of the bill.

Now consider the general case, where A forms a coalition of $\frac{N+1}{2} + m$ members, where m measures the size of the supermajority. To block the bill, B must pick off $m+1$ members. It is worth φ to do this, so A offers a common $T_A = \frac{\varphi}{m+1}$ to each member of her coalition to pass the bill. The total cost to A is

$$\left(\frac{N+1}{2} + m\right)\frac{\varphi}{m+1},$$

which is decreasing in m for all $N > 1$.

Thus, the equilibrium coalition is universal: A can minimize her cost by including all N legislators in her coalition. This strong result is driven by the assumption that voters care only about transfers, though some arguably weak assumptions guarantee that equilibrium coalitions are more than minimum winning when legislators also care about policy outcomes (Banks, 2000; Groseclose and Snyder, 2000). Exercise 6.6 provides a simple example where the equilibrium coalition is larger than minimum winning but less than universal.

6.5 Selectorates

We now consider a model of coalition choice in a polity rather than a legislature or committee. The material of this section grew out of a quest to explain the phenomenon of the democratic peace: the empirical finding that democracies do not fight each other. The argument, laid out in Bueno de Mesquita et al. (1999), is that democratic leaders must satisfy a broader coalition in order to remain in power, and so they are more likely to invest in the public good of fighting a war once one has started than to provide private goods that benefit only coalition members. This makes democracies unappealing targets, especially for other democracies that are similarly constrained.

The choice between public and private goods obviously extends beyond this international relations context, and so the same theoretical framework has been used to explain why some societies are more likely than others to produce policies that benefit the general public rather than narrow constituencies (e.g., Bueno de Mesquita et al., 2003).[7] The theory begins by classifying two groups of individuals that are important for political survival: the **selectorate** (Shirk, 1993), which is the set of individuals that chooses whether to retain an incumbent leader, and the **winning coalition**, which is some subset of the selectorate upon which the incumbent depends for survival.

Regimes vary according to the absolute and relative sizes of these two groups. Democracies, for example, have large selectorates (in most countries, close to the voting-age public), with something like a majority of the selectorate necessary to form a winning coalition. In contrast, in many authoritarian regimes the selectorate may be a narrow group of individuals (e.g., military officers), among which either a small or large proportion may constitute a winning coalition. A key idea is that the loyalty of members of the incumbent's coalition is greater when the winning coalition is small relative to the selectorate, as then promises by a challenger to include defectors in her governing coalition are less credible.

6.5.1 Political Competition

Political competition in the selectorate model is very similar to that in the Groseclose-Snyder vote-buying model. To illustrate, we begin by considering a simple one-period version of the model that abstracts from questions of loyalty and the provision of public goods. There is a finite population of N individuals, $S \leq N$ of which belong to the selectorate. An incumbent (I) and a challenger (C) each assemble coalitions from the selectorate. The challenger seizes power if the incumbent has the support of fewer than W members of the selectorate ("selectors"), where $W \leq \frac{S+1}{2}$ is a parameter of the model, and the challenger has the sup-

---

[7] For a model of bargaining over public and private goods in legislatures rather than (as here) in polities, see Volden and Wiseman (2007).

port of at least W members of the selectorate; otherwise the incumbent retains power. The parameter W is thus the size of the (minimum) winning coalition. Members of the population who do not belong to the selectorate are not strategic players; the role of the parameter N will be explained shortly.

The timing of events is as follows. The incumbent first proposes a vector of transfers $(T_{I1}, \ldots, T_{IS})$, where T_{Ii} is the transfer that selector i receives if the incumbent is retained. The challenger subsequently proposes a vector of transfers $(T_{C1}, \ldots, T_{CS})$ that is paid out if she seizes power from the incumbent. In each case, the sum of the proposed transfers cannot exceed tax revenue, which for simplicity we assume to be fixed and equal (i.e., proportional, after a normalization) to the size of the population N. In addition, we impose the constraint that $T_{Ii} = T_I$ for all $T_{Ii} > 0$, that is, the incumbent must offer the same transfer to all members of her coalition. Similarly, we require $T_{Ci} = T_C$ for all $T_{Ci} > 0$.

Members of the selectorate then "vote" for the incumbent or the challenger. We assume that competition is between members of the two coalitions, so that selector i votes if and only if $T_{Ii} > 0$ or $T_{Ci} > 0$. In particular, any such selector i supports the incumbent if $T_{Ii} \geq qT_{Ci}$, and otherwise supports the challenger. The parameter $q \in (0,1)$ is a measure of incumbency advantage: when q is small, members of the selectorate are willing to retain the incumbent even when the challenger promises considerably more. Later we will endogenize this advantage. Finally, the winner takes power, provides the promised transfers to all coalition members, and retains any tax revenue not paid out as transfers. Both the incumbent and the challenger maximize net tax revenue, the receipt of which is conditional on (re)election.

In contrast to the Groseclose-Snyder model, the incumbent has no incentive to assemble a larger-than-minimum winning coalition, as the challenger must assemble a coalition of W members (i.e., replacement requires a **constructive vote of no confidence**), regardless of the size of the incumbent's coalition.[8] In equilibrium, the incumbent therefore offers a common $T_I = \frac{qN}{W}$ to W members of the selectorate. As the challenger only has resources totaling N and must make the same offer to any member of her coalition, she cannot simultaneously offer $T_{Ci} > \frac{N}{W}$ to some member of the incumbent's coalition and build a coalition of size W. The incumbent earns a rent from her reelection, collecting unspent

---

[8] In principle, the incumbent could force the challenger to assemble a coalition of more than W selectors by choosing a coalition of at least $2W$ members, but this is more costly than forming a minimum winning coalition.

tax revenue totalling

$$N - W\left(\frac{qN}{W}\right) = (1-q)\,N.$$

6.5.2 The Loyalty Norm

We now extend the model of the previous section to an infinite-horizon setting, where in each period a challenger is randomly selected from a population of ex ante identical individuals. If the challenger wins, she becomes the incumbent in the following period, whereas if she loses, she permanently exits the game. Similarly, once defeated an incumbent may never again contest office. All players share a common discount factor δ.

We endogenize the incumbency advantage of the previous section as follows. Assume that the incumbent has a strict preference order defined over members of the selectorate. Selectors are otherwise identical, so that in forming a coalition (i.e., a set of selectors for whom proposed transfers are positive) with K members, the incumbent names the K selectors who are highest in her preference order. As in Bueno de Mesquita et al. (2002), these preferences can be motivated by assuming that selectors have arbitrarily small, heterogeneous **affinities** for the incumbent that define the cheapest possible coalition. We assume a common prior belief that all preference orders are equally probable.

The incumbent's preference over selectors is revealed when she first takes power (implicitly, at the start of the game for the first-period incumbent). Thus, selectors are uncertain about the identity of future governing coalitions if the incumbent is replaced, so that any coalition proposed by a challenger is fully credible only for one period. We can think of this as a stylized formalization of the idea that challengers might find that different supporters are needed to govern once in power.

Given that all preference orders are equally probable, any selector knows that the probability of being named to the winning coalition if the challenger takes power is $\frac{W}{S}$. Thus, the value of being a member of the challenger's coalition is

$$T_C + \delta\left[\frac{W}{S}V_I + \left(1 - \frac{W}{S}\right)V_O\right], \tag{6.9}$$

where V_I is the value of being in the (new) incumbent's coalition, and V_O is the value of being outside it.

Following the logic of the previous section, in equilibrium the challenger divides available tax revenue, assumed to be proportional to the size of the population N, among the members of her coalition. Thus, $T_C = \frac{N}{W}$. Further, the incumbent chooses transfers T_I such that the value of being in her coalition (and in particular, the value for those members who are also in the challenger's coalition) is exactly equal to Expression 6.9. Because any incumbent chooses the same transfer, this value is V_I, so

$$V_I = \frac{N}{W} + \delta \left[\frac{W}{S} V_I + \left(1 - \frac{W}{S} \right) V_O \right].$$

Finally, because in equilibrium the incumbent wins in every period, the value V_O of not being in the incumbent's coalition is equal to zero, so that

$$V_I = \left(\frac{1}{1 - \delta \frac{W}{S}} \right) \frac{N}{W}.$$

How does the incumbent provide this value to the members of her coalition? Every period she offers the same transfer T_I, the value of which over an infinite horizon is $V_I = \frac{T_I}{1-\delta}$. Using the expression for V_I just shown, the equilibrium transfer can then be derived as follows:

$$\frac{T_I}{1 - \delta} = \left(\frac{1}{1 - \delta \frac{W}{S}} \right) \frac{N}{W} \Rightarrow$$

$$T_I = \left(\frac{1 - \delta}{1 - \delta \frac{W}{S}} \right) \frac{N}{W}. \tag{6.10}$$

Thus, $T_I < T_C = \frac{N}{W}$. The larger is $\frac{W}{S}$, the closer is the transfer offered by the incumbent to that offered by the challenger. Intuitively, the more credible is the challenger's promise that she will include a member of the transition coalition in the governing coalition (because winning coalitions are large relative to the size of the selectorate), the more the incumbent must surrender to prevent members of her coalition from abandoning her. This is the **loyalty norm**: when $\frac{W}{S}$ is small, members of the incumbent's coalition have less reason to think they will end up in the challenger's future winning coalition, and so they will be more loyal to the incumbent.

The transfer offered by the incumbent is large *relative* to that offered by the challenger when the size of the winning coalition W is large. However, examining the same expression, we see that the absolute size of the transfer is not necessarily increasing in W. Although an increase in W means that members of the incumbent's coalition are less loyal and so means the incumbent must spend more to keep them from supporting the challenger, it also implies that whatever the incumbent spends is divided among a larger number of individuals. The latter effect dominates the former when members of the selectorate place little weight on the future (in particular, for $\delta < \frac{S}{2W}$). By the same logic, equilibrium transfers T_I are decreasing in the discount factor δ: as members of the winning coalition become more patient, they value more highly the future benefits of being in the incumbent's coalition, and so they are less tempted to abandon her for the challenger.

Finally, the proportion of tax revenue retained by the incumbent can be derived as

$$\frac{1}{N}\left[N - W\left(\frac{1-\delta}{1-\delta\frac{W}{S}}\right)\frac{N}{W}\right] = \frac{\delta - \delta\frac{W}{S}}{1-\delta\frac{W}{S}},$$

where total tax revenue is N, out of which the transfer T_I (Equation 6.10) is paid to the W members of the winning coalition. The proportion of tax revenue retained by the incumbent is decreasing in $\frac{W}{S}$, because when coalition members are less loyal more must be spent to keep them from defecting, and increasing in δ, because when coalition members more highly value future benefits the incumbent need pay them less. If we interpret the retention of tax revenue by the incumbent as corruption, then there is less corruption when the winning coalition is large relative to the size of the selectorate.

6.5.3 Public versus Private Goods

Up to now we have considered only pure redistribution. To incorporate public goods into the model, assume that any member i of the selectorate receives utility in each period from private transfers T_i and public goods g equal to $T_i + 2\sqrt{g}$. Further, let the cost of public goods be equal to pg, so that for a coalition of size W, total expenditure out of tax revenue is equal to $pg + WT$, where T is the common transfer to all members of the coalition. Finally, assume that $p > \frac{W^2}{N}$, which ensures an interior solution to the problem to be presented.

In equilibrium, as before, the challenger chooses a coalition of size W, at least one member of which overlaps with the incumbent's coalition. Now, however, the challenger's equilibrium offer divides the available revenue N between private transfers, T_C, and public goods, g_C, to provide the maximum possible utility to her coalition members:

$$\max_{g,T} \ T + 2\sqrt{g} \tag{6.11}$$

$$\text{s.t. } pg + WT = N.$$

Solving for $T = \frac{N-pg}{W}$ from the budget constraint, this problem can be rewritten as

$$\max_{g} \ \frac{N - pg}{W} + 2\sqrt{g}. \tag{6.12}$$

This is a concave problem, and the first-order condition is sufficient for a solution:

$$g_C = \left(\frac{W}{p}\right)^2,$$

$$T_C = \frac{N}{W} - \frac{W}{p}.$$

Thus, the optimal level of public goods provision is increasing in the size of the winning coalition (because private transfers are more expensive when the size of the winning coalition is large) and decreasing in the price of public goods provision. Public goods provision is independent of the revenue to be divided, assumed to be proportional to the size of the population N, but transfers are increasing in N.

In equilibrium the incumbent must match the value of this offer:

$$T_C + 2\sqrt{g_C} + \delta \left[\frac{W}{S} V_I + \left(1 - \frac{W}{S}\right) V_O \right].$$

As in the model presented in the previous section, any promises to provide g_C and T_C to members of the challenger's coalition beyond the transition period are not fully credible: if the challenger wins in period t, she assumes the role of the incumbent in period $t+1$, selecting in that and all following periods a winning coalition of the selectors the challenger most prefers. In contrast to the model of the previous section, however, V_O no longer equals zero but $\frac{2\sqrt{g_I}}{1-\delta}$, the value of the public goods provided by the incumbent in every period. Similarly, V_I equals $\frac{T_I + 2\sqrt{g_I}}{1-\delta}$, the value of the public and private goods received by members of the incumbent's coalition in every period.

This problem can be simplified by noting that in equilibrium the incumbent chooses the same provision of public goods as does the challenger. To see this, note that the incumbent must guarantee a certain

utility (call it $\bar{u}$) in each period for members of her coalition not to abandon her for the challenger. Clearly she wants to do this as cheaply as
possible, so she solves the following expenditure-minimization problem:

$$\min_{g,T} pg + WT$$

$$\text{s.t. } T + 2\sqrt{g} \geq \bar{u}.$$

By the principle of duality, this is the same problem as that faced by
the challenger in maximizing the utility of all members of her coalition,
given a budget constraint (6.11). To see this, substitute $T = \bar{u} - 2\sqrt{g}$
into the objective function, and recall that the minimization of some
function f is equivalent to maximization of $-f$. Then the incumbent's
problem is

$$\max_{g} -pg - W\left(\bar{u} - 2\sqrt{g}\right),$$

which has the same solution as Expression 6.12. The optimal level of
public goods provision is thus $g_I = g_C = \hat{g} \equiv \left(\frac{W}{p}\right)^2$, so that $V_O = \frac{2\sqrt{\hat{g}}}{1-\delta}$.
The value of not being in the winning coalition is larger, the larger is the
winning coalition and the smaller is the price of public goods provision:
in each case the incumbent is more inclined to substitute public for
private goods.

Using $V_O = \frac{2\sqrt{\hat{g}}}{1-\delta}$, the value of being in the challenger's coalition can
be written as

$$T_C + 2\sqrt{\hat{g}} + \delta \left[\frac{W}{S}V_I + \left(1 - \frac{W}{S}\right)\frac{2\sqrt{\hat{g}}}{1-\delta}\right].$$

The incumbent must match this offer to prevent defections from her own
to the challenger's coalition, so

$$V_I = T_C + 2\sqrt{\hat{g}} + \delta \left[\frac{W}{S}V_I + \left(1 - \frac{W}{S}\right)\frac{2\sqrt{\hat{g}}}{1-\delta}\right],$$

that is,

$$V_I = \frac{T_C}{\left(1 - \delta\frac{W}{S}\right)} + \frac{2\sqrt{\hat{g}}}{1-\delta}.$$

In other words, the incumbent must top off the public goods provision
that her coalition members receive every period, regardless of who is in
power, with a large enough transfer to compensate for what her coalition members could receive by defecting to the challenger. Because a

member of the incumbent's coalition receives $T_I + 2\sqrt{\hat{g}}$ every period in equilibrium,

$$V_I = \frac{T_I + 2\sqrt{\hat{g}}}{1 - \delta} = \frac{T_C}{\left(1 - \delta \frac{W}{S}\right)} + \frac{2\sqrt{\hat{g}}}{1 - \delta}.$$

Solving for T_I in terms of T_C then gives

$$T_I = \left(\frac{1 - \delta}{1 - \delta \frac{W}{S}}\right) T_C,$$

which is a generalization of Equation 6.10. For $\frac{W}{S}$ arbitrarily close to one, the incumbent must match the challenger's offer. In contrast, when $\frac{W}{S}$ is close to zero, then the incumbent need only provide a transfer large enough to compensate members of her coalition for what they would receive as members of the challenger's transition (but not governing) coalition, that is, $T_I \approx (1 - \delta) T_C$ (though recall that T_C is a decreasing function of W).

How does the proportion of tax revenue retained by the incumbent depend on W, the size of the winning coalition? Intuitively, the incumbent should have to spend more to retain her coalition as W increases, as the loyalty of members of the governing coalition decreases. To see this, write down the expression for tax revenue retained by the incumbent:

$$N - WT_I - pg_I.$$

Substituting in equilibrium values for T_I and g_I gives

$$N - W \left(\frac{1 - \delta}{1 - \delta \frac{W}{S}}\right) \left(\frac{N}{W} - \frac{W}{p}\right) - \frac{W^2}{p} =$$
$$\left[1 - \left(\frac{1 - \delta}{1 - \delta \frac{W}{S}}\right)\right] \left(N - \frac{W^2}{p}\right).$$

Dividing through by N to give the proportion of tax revenue retained by the incumbent and simplifying gives

$$\left(\frac{\delta - \delta \frac{W}{S}}{1 - \delta \frac{W}{S}}\right) \left(1 - \frac{W^2}{Np}\right),$$

which is decreasing in W. Thus, as the size of the winning coalition increases, there is less corruption in the sense of tax revenue retained by the incumbent for her own use. At the same time, the composition of spending shifts from private to public goods, as transfers become relatively expensive to provide. If large winning coalitions are more common in democracies, we should therefore expect more public goods, less particularistic spending, and fewer rents from holding office in democratic regimes.

Exercises

6.1 Consider a generalization of the Baron-Ferejohn model of Section 6.1 in which the agreement of $K \leq N$ members (N odd) is necessary for a proposal to pass. (For example, if $K = 1$, the agenda setter can implement any proposal on her own, whereas if $K = N$, an agreement can pass only with unanimous agreement.) For simplicity, assume that $p_i = \frac{1}{N}$ and $\delta_i = \delta$ for all legislators i. Restrict attention to equilibria in which any agenda setter chooses a coalition at random from those over which she is indifferent.

   (a) Consider first a two-period version of the model, where $\bar{x}_i = 0$ for all legislators i. What are the qualitative features of any subgame-perfect Nash equilibrium of this game, that is, what is the nature of equilibrium proposals, and what is the expected payoff for any legislator?

   (b) Repeat the analysis for the infinite-horizon version of this game. Restrict attention to stationary equilibria.

   (c) Compare your results for these exercises to each other and to the results for majority rule developed in Section 6.1. Why, intuitively, are the results similar or different in whatever way they are?

6.2 Consider the following variant of the legislative bargaining model presented in Section 6.1. There are three legislators, $i = 1, 2, 3$, who alternate as agenda setter. In particular, legislator 1 is the agenda setter in period 1, followed by legislator 2 in period 2 if no proposal is agreed to in period 1, followed by legislator 3 in period 3 if no proposal is agreed to in period 2. If there is no agreement after three periods, then the status quo policy $\bar{x} = (0, 0, 0)$ is implemented. Legislators have a common discount factor δ.

   (a) What is the outcome if bargaining continues to period 3?

   (b) What is the outcome if bargaining continues to period 2?

   (c) What is the equilibrium distribution?

   (d) How, if at all, would the equilibrium distribution change if there were $N > 3$ periods?

(e) Now consider the status quo policy $\bar{\mathbf{x}} = (x_1, x_2, x_3)$, where $x_1 \neq x_2 \neq x_3$ and $x_i < \frac{1}{2}$ for all i. How does the equilibrium distribution depend on $\bar{x}$?

6.3 Consider the following special case of the model of Banks and Duggan (2000). There are three legislators, $i = 1, 2, 3$, who bargain over policy $x \in [-1, 1]$ using majority rule. If some proposal x is accepted, then the legislators receive an immediate payoff of

$$u_1 = 1 - x,$$
$$u_2 = 1 - |x|,$$
$$u_3 = 1 + x.$$

Thus, legislators 1, 2, and 3 have ideal points of -1, 0, and 1, respectively. All legislators receive a payoff of zero in any period before a proposal is accepted. Assume that legislators have identical recognition probabilities and discount future payoffs according to the common discount factor δ.

We look for a no-delay stationary equilibrium in which legislator 1 offers $-\alpha$, legislator 2 offers 0, and legislator 3 offers α whenever chosen to be agenda setter, where α is a variable for which we will solve.

(a) For each legislator i, derive the continuation payoff V_i (i.e., the expected payoff in equilibrium at the beginning of any period in which a proposal has not already been accepted) as a function of α.

(b) Using your answer to part (a), for each legislator i, find the set of proposals that i would prefer to accept rather than allow bargaining to continue to the next period. Express your answer as "legislator 1 prefers to accept any proposal $x \leq \tilde{x}_1$, legislator 2 prefers to accept any proposal in $[-\tilde{x}_2, \tilde{x}_2]$, and legislator 3 prefers to accept any proposal $x \geq \tilde{x}_3$," where $\tilde{x}_1$, $\tilde{x}_2$, and $\tilde{x}_3$ are values to be derived.

(c) Using your answer to part (b), show that both legislators 1 and 3 prefer to accept legislator 2's proposal of 0 rather than allow bargaining to continue to the next period.

(d) Using your answer to part (b), show that legislator 3 prefers to include legislator 2 rather than legislator 1 in her coalition. (By symmetry, the analogous argument holds for legislator 1.)

(e) Solve for α by setting $\alpha = \tilde{x}_2$. How do the equilibrium proposals depend on the discount factor δ?

6.4   Consider the Baron-Diermeier model of Section 6.3, but now assume the status quo policy $\bar{x} > 1$. As motivation, one might think of there having been an economic crisis, so that there is a consensus among parties that policy should move toward the left.

    (a) What is the equilibrium coalition if the formateur is party 1?
    (b) What is the equilibrium coalition if the formateur is party 2?
    (c) What is the equilibrium coalition if the formateur is party 3?
    (d) Assume that the probability of being chosen formateur is proportional to seat share in parliament and that voters' ideal points are distributed on the interval $[-1, 1]$. Would any voters prefer to vote for a party other than that whose ideal point is closest to their own?

6.5   This exercise explores Weingast's model of legislative norms in Section 6.4, asking whether legislators would be better off with a supermajority norm that falls short of universalism. Define m as the size of the supermajority needed to pass any legislation; a norm of universalism implies $m = N - \frac{N+1}{2} = \frac{N-1}{2}$, whereas a norm of minimum winning coalitions implies $m = 0$.

    (a) For any $m \in \{0, 1, \ldots, \frac{N-1}{2}\}$, derive the probability of being included in some winning coalition, assuming that winning coalitions are chosen with equal probability.
    (b) Derive the expected utility for any legislator, prior to choice of agenda setter, as a function of m. What m maximizes legislators' expected utility? Interpret your result.

6.6   Consider the Groseclose-Snyder vote-buying model in Section 6.4, but now assume that legislators are inclined to oppose the bill even when vote buyer A has promised a slightly higher transfer than vote buyer B. In particular, assume that legislator i votes for the bill if and only if $T_{Ai} \geq T_{Bi} + \frac{1}{2}$.

    (a) Assume that A forms a coalition of $\frac{N+1}{2} + m$ members, where m measures the size of the supermajority. As a function of m, what must A offer to any legislator in her coalition to prevent B from blocking the bill?
    (b) Assume that $N = 7$ and $\varphi = 1$. What $m \in \{0, 1, 2, 3\}$ minimize(s) the cost to A of passing the bill? How would your answer change for different values of φ?

6.7   The Groseclose-Snyder model assumes that vote buyers can condition transfers to some legislator i only on how i votes, not on how

i votes relative to other legislators. In a model with a single vote buyer, Dal Bó (2007) shows that it is possible to minimize the cost of purchasing a majority by making transfer payments conditional on whether a legislator's vote is pivotal.

To see this, assume a legislature of N members, with N even. Any legislator i bears a cost $\theta > 0$ if at least $\frac{N+1}{2}$ legislators vote for the bill, and zero cost otherwise. In what follows, restrict attention to equilibria in weakly undominated voting strategies, which implies that legislators vote as if they are pivotal.

(a) What is the equilibrium of the voting game when the vote buyer offers no transfers?

(b) Now assume that the vote buyer proposes to each legislator i a transfer $\theta + \epsilon$, where $\epsilon > 0$, if exactly $\frac{N+1}{2}$ legislators vote for the bill, including i, and zero transfer otherwise. What is the equilibrium of the subsequent voting game? What is the sum of all transfers paid by the vote buyer in equilibrium?

6.8 Consider the following model of buying legislatures, which is based on Snyder (1991). There is a continuum of legislators with preferences over alternatives $x \in \Re$, where $\bar{x}$ is the status quo and $\hat{x} > \bar{x}$ is a bill supported by a single vote buyer. Assume that legislator i votes for the bill if and only if

$$- (\hat{x} - x_i)^2 + T_i \geq - (\bar{x} - x_i)^2 .$$

Legislators' most-preferred positions x_i are distributed uniformly on the interval $[-1, 1]$; the bill needs the support of one-half of the legislators to pass.

(a) Which legislators must receive positive transfers in order to vote for the bill?

(b) Now assume that $\frac{\bar{x}+\hat{x}}{2} > 0$. Which legislators receive positive transfers when the vote buyer minimizes the cost of passing the bill?

(c) Holding constant the status quo $\bar{x}$, how does the total cost of passing the bill depend on $\hat{x}$?

6.9 Using the selectorate model of Section 6.5, examine the impact of an expansion of the franchise in a democracy. Assume that for any S, $W = \frac{S}{2}$, so that a winning coalition comprises one-half of the selectorate. Now examine the consequences of an increase in S, the size of the selectorate, for:

(a) Equilibrium public goods provision and transfers offered by the challenger.

(b) Equilibrium public goods provision and transfers offered by the incumbent.

(c) The proportion of tax revenue retained by the incumbent.

7

Political Agency

In this chapter we return to electoral competition, but we shift focus from elections as a mechanism for aggregating individual preferences to elections as a means of holding officeholders accountable to voters. The literature on political agency that we survey here has its roots in the economic theory of contracts, where the central question is how contracts govern the relationship between **principals** (e.g., employers or shareholders) and their **agents** (e.g., employees or CEOs). In models of political agency, voters play the role of principals; their agent is a politician elected to govern on their behalf.

In general, voters face two agency problems. First, elected politicians may not bear the full cost or receive the full benefit of their decisions, which can give them an incentive to take actions that are not in voters' best interest. Elections can help voters to alleviate this problem of **moral hazard** by providing them the opportunity to sanction politicians who have behaved poorly. Second, politicians may differ in their competence, preferences, or other characteristics. Elections can encourage the **selection** of politicians who are inclined to act in voters' best interest.

Although elections provide the means by which voters can address these agency problems, two obstacles stand in the way of full accountability. First, voters may not be able to directly observe the actions of elected officials, politicians' characteristics, or the mapping from policy to outcomes. Second, relative to economic contracts, elections are a very crude mechanism by which to reward good behavior and sanction bad behavior, as voters are typically able to tie performance only to a lumpy return from reelection.[1] Many of the costs of democracy are a

---

[1] Meirowitz (2007) shows how this constraint can be relaxed through the use of mixed strategies.

direct consequence of these features of the principal-agent relationship between voters and politicians (Keech, 1995).

We begin our discussion of these issues by presenting a series of models based on Barro (1973) and Ferejohn (1986). As we will see, elections may fail to hold politicians fully accountable, even when there are no selection issues and the actions of politicians are fully observed. We then move to an environment in which both moral hazard and selection play a role. We first present a "career concerns" model, where both the elected politician and voters are uncertain of the politician's competence. As we will see, voters' incentive to select more competent types encourages politicians to act more responsibly. This logic generally carries over to a setting in which politicians possess private information about their type, though, as we will see in our discussion of signaling models, information asymmetries can also encourage good politicians to do the wrong thing.

7.1 The Barro-Ferejohn Model

We begin by examining a simple "two-period" version of the Barro-Ferejohn model. After extending the model to incorporate conflict among voters and conflict among elected officials, we adapt the model to a fully dynamic setting.

7.1.1 A Two-period Model

Consider a model with the following actors:

- A continuum of identical voters, normalized to mass (size) one.
- An incumbent politician.

The question of the model is the extent to which reelection pressure encourages the incumbent to take a costly action in the first period that improves voter welfare.

To make the discussion concrete, assume an infinitely divisible resource of size one. In period 1, the incumbent chooses to keep some proportion $r \in [0, 1]$ of this resource for herself. We refer to r as the *rent* extracted. The amount remaining after rent extraction is divided evenly among all voters; with a population of mass 1, this implies that each voter receives $1 - r$. For simplicity, assume that each voter i receives utility equal to consumption, that is,

$$u_i(r) = 1 - r.$$

The incumbent receives utility from consumption equal to the rent extracted r. Further, if reelected, the incumbent receives an exogenous payoff $R > 0$ from holding office in period 2, discounted according to the discount factor $\delta \in (0, 1)$. Thus, letting $\pi(r)$ refer to the (endogenous) probability that the incumbent is reelected, the incumbent's discounted expected payoff is

$$r + \delta \pi(r) R.$$

To ensure a positive level of rent extraction in equilibrium, we assume $\delta R < 1$.

The sequence of play is as follows:

(i) Each voter i announces a **reservation utility** $\bar{u}_i$, promising to reelect the incumbent if and only if $u_i \geq \bar{u}_i$.
(ii) The incumbent chooses r.
(iii) Voters choose whether to reelect the incumbent.

Implicitly, we assume the existence of a passive challenger, where voters are indifferent over the incumbent and challenger; nothing actually happens in the second period. The strategic logic would be identical if the election winner (incumbent or challenger from period 1) extracted rents or took some other action that affected voter welfare in period 2, so long as the incumbent and challenger had identical preferences and thus took the same action if elected.

Voting in the Barro-Ferejohn model is purely "retrospective" (Key, 1966; Fiorina, 1981), with no subsequent payoff relevance. Consequently, voters' promises to reelect the incumbent if and only if $u_i \geq \bar{u}_i$ are not binding. However, given their indifference between reelecting and not, voters weakly prefer to reelect the incumbent if and only if $u_i \geq \bar{u}_i$, just as they weakly prefer to base their voting decision on any other benchmark, or on no benchmark whatsoever. Given this indifference, there are infinitely many subgame-perfect Nash equilibria of the game. To focus on the ability of elections to hold politicians accountable, we restrict attention to equilibria that satisfy two properties: 1) voters reelect the incumbent if and only if $u_i \geq \bar{u}_i$, as promised, and 2) voters coordinate on a *common* reservation utility, so that $\bar{u}_i = \bar{u}$ for all voters i. Voters thus choose $\bar{u}$ to maximize their utility $1 - r$, anticipating that the incumbent will then choose r to maximize her expected utility, given the constraint that she will be reelected if and only if $1 - r \geq \bar{u}$.

What is the incumbent's optimal level of rent extraction r, given the common reservation utility $\bar{u}$? To answer this question, observe first that any $\bar{u}$ implies a unique level of rent extraction $\bar{r}$ above which voters will vote for the challenger over the incumbent:

$$\bar{r} \equiv 1 - \bar{u}.$$

Clearly, it makes no sense for the incumbent to choose some $r \in (\bar{r}, 1)$: given that voters will vote against the challenger if $r > \bar{r}$, she might as well choose $r = 1$. Further, the incumbent would never adopt any $r < \bar{r}$, as she could extract $\bar{r}$ and still be reelected. Thus, the incumbent chooses between $r = 1$ and $r = \bar{r}$, which provide utility of 1 and $\bar{r} + \delta R$, respectively. In particular, the incumbent chooses $r = \bar{r}$ only if

$$\bar{r} + \delta R \geq 1. \tag{7.1}$$

Given this behavior, what is the optimal $\bar{u}$ for voters to announce? Any reservation utility such that $\bar{r} < 1 - \delta R$ does not satisfy Condition 7.1, so that the incumbent seizes the entire resource and voters are left with nothing, whereas any reservation utility that leaves the incumbent with more than $1 - \delta R$ gives her more than necessary. Voters therefore announce $\bar{u} = \delta R$, which induces the incumbent to choose $r = \bar{r} = 1 - \delta R$.

Elections thus induce partial, but not full, accountability. The incumbent is restricted to extracting $1 - \delta R$, which is less than the maximum possible rent 1. But voters must leave the incumbent with something, as otherwise the incumbent would choose to take everything today, sacrificing the payoff R from holding office tomorrow.

How does the equilibrium level of rents depend on parameters of the model? The politician is more accountable to voters—chooses a smaller r—when she cares more about the future, that is, when δ is large. In addition, equilibrium rent extraction is lower when the payoff R from holding office in period 2 is high. Thus, for example, accountability is greater when politicians' salaries are large, as then incumbents have more to lose from not being reelected. An alternative interpretation, to which we will return later, is that R represents the continuation payoff in an infinite-horizon model that is approximated by the model here.

Although intuitive, these results hinge critically on two assumptions, one of which we employed to narrow the set of equilibria, and the other related to the model itself:

- The assumption that $\bar{u}_i = \bar{u}$ for all voters i. This is a very high degree of coordination among a large population of individuals. In general we should perhaps be skeptical that such coordination is possible. However, in this particular context, coordination on $\bar{u} = \delta R$ might be "focal" (i.e., more likely to attract voters' attention than some other reservation utility), as $\bar{u} = \delta R$ is the most that can be expected from the incumbent.

- The assumption that voters are indifferent between the incumbent and challenger. As Fearon (1999) observes, if voters have even an infinitesimally small preference for one candidate over the other (e.g., because of policy preferences, hair color, or whatever), then they will not vote based on their announced reservation utilities. This suggests that elections hold elected officials accountable to voters not through sanctioning but through selection, a point that we take up in Section 7.2.

Of course, any model is at best a useful fiction. The following extensions illustrate the usefulness of the Barro-Ferejohn model.

7.1.2 Conflict among Voters

The model presented in the previous section assumes that the pool of resources from which the incumbent extracts rents cannot be divided among voters in a discriminatory way, perhaps because of budgetary rules or various administrative constraints. Here we follow Ferejohn (1986) in showing that electoral accountability may be weakened when resources can instead be distributed to voters on a discriminatory basis, as in such environments the incumbent can play one group off against another.

We adapt the model of the previous section in such a way that there are now N voter groups of equal mass, where for notational simplicity we assume N to be even. In addition to choosing a level of rent extraction r, the incumbent decides on a distribution $(t_1, ..., t_N)$ among the N voter groups of the $1 - r$ remaining after rent extraction, where $t_n \geq 0$ is the aggregate (not per capita) transfer to group n, and $\sum t_n = 1 - r$. We assume that the incumbent retains power if she receives the support of at least half the population of voters.

As before, we restrict attention to equilibria in which voters coordinate on a common reservation utility (and vote according to their promises). Now, however, we assume that this coordination takes place at the group level, so that each group n chooses a reservation utility $\bar{u}_n$. Choice of these group voting rules takes place simultaneously and noncooperatively. Thus, in equilibrium, each group's reservation utility must be a best response to every other group's.

In deciding on the appropriate level of rent extraction r and distribution among voters $(t_1, ..., t_N)$, the incumbent faces a choice similar to that discussed in the previous section: she can extract the maximum possible rent, choosing $r = 1$, or she can do exactly what it takes to get reelected. Here, however, the possibility of distributing resources on a discriminatory basis allows the incumbent to win reelection by pleasing only a minimum winning coalition of voters, that is, $\frac{N}{2}$ of the groups. In particular, in assembling a minimum winning coalition, the incumbent chooses the $\frac{N}{2}$ groups with the lowest reservation utility, providing each such group n with a transfer t_n such that their utility is exactly $\bar{u}_n$, while choosing $t_n = 0$ for every other group.

There are multiple equilibria of this game, even after restricting attention to equilibria in which voters in each group coordinate on the best possible reservation utility $\bar{u}_n$, given other groups' reservation utilities. However, in *any* equilibrium the incumbent extracts the maximum possible rent, leaving all voters with nothing. To see this, first recall that the incumbent would never choose $r < 1$ if she expected not to be reelected. Thus, if there is an equilibrium in which the incumbent chooses $r < 1$, she must be reelected. This implies that fewer than $\frac{N}{2}$ groups have named a reservation utility of zero, so that the minimum winning coalition includes at least one group with reservation utility greater than zero. But then some out-coalition group could profitably deviate by reducing its reservation utility to some positive level below that of the in-coalition group with the highest reservation utility (i.e., some out-coalition group could outbid the most "expensive" member of the coalition). Thus, this cannot be an equilibrium.

There is more than one way to construct an equilibrium in which the incumbent extracts the maximum possible rent. Here are two examples:

- At least $\frac{N}{2} + 1$ groups choose a reservation utility of zero, and the incumbent chooses $r = 1$ and is reelected. Clearly, the politician cannot do better than extracting the maximum possible rent and being reelected. Further, no in-coalition group n has an incentive to deviate by instead naming some $\bar{u}_n > 0$, as then the incumbent could still assemble a coalition of $\frac{N}{2}$ groups with reservation utility of zero, leaving the deviating group with nothing as before. Finally, no out-coalition group has an incentive to deviate, as the only way any such group could be brought into the coalition would be by naming a reservation utility of zero, which provides the same payoff as in equilibrium.

- Assume $N \geq 4$. Each group n chooses $\bar{u}_n = 1$, and the incumbent chooses $r = 1$ and is not reelected. Given these demands, the politician cannot assemble a minimum winning coalition (doing so would require more resources than are available); thus, extracting the maximum possible rent is the optimal choice. Further, no group can profitably deviate by choosing a different reservation utility: whatever the deviation, the politician still could not assemble a winning coalition without exhausting the pool of resources, so she would continue to choose $r = 1$.

In summary, conflict among voters can completely eliminate electoral accountability, as the incumbent can play one voter group off against another. The following section shows that the opposite conclusion may hold when there is instead conflict among elected officials.

7.1.3 Conflict among Elected Officials

Most democratic systems involve some separation of powers among elected officials. The key rationale for this this separation—expressed in the political thought of Locke and Montesquieu and forcefully defended in the *Federalist Papers* as an intrinsic feature of the new American republic—is the restraint it places on arbitrary and selfish behavior by those officials. But how does separation of powers function in practice? Persson, Roland, and Tabellini (1997) provide an answer to this question, adapting the Barro-Ferejohn model to incorporate conflict among elected officials.

We return to the model of Section 7.1.1, only we now assume that there are two incumbents rather than one. For concreteness, we refer to a legislature (L) and an executive (E). The legislature has agenda-setting power, choosing a level of rents r_L and r_E for the legislature and executive, respectively, where $r_L + r_E \leq 1$. Define the total rents extracted $r \equiv r_L + r_E$. After the legislature proposes r_L and r_E, the executive may either accept or reject (veto) the proposal. If the proposal is rejected, then the legislature and executive receive an exogenous rent of $\hat{r}_L$ and $\hat{r}_E$, respectively. For simplicity, we assume that $\hat{r}_L = 0$ and $\hat{r}_E \in (0, 1)$, which focuses attention on the role of the executive in constraining the legislature. There is an exogenous payoff from reelection of R_L and R_E

for the legislature and executive, respectively, where $R_L + R_E < 1$. For simplicity, we assume a discount factor $\delta = 1$.[2]

How does the requirement that any legislative proposal be accepted by the executive affect the ability of voters to hold politicians accountable? Surprisingly, perhaps, for certain parameter values it is now an equilibrium for *no* rents to be extracted. Paradoxically, it is the fact that the executive receives *some* rent in the event it rejects the legislature's proposal that makes this possible.

To see this, assume that voters coordinate on the following voting rule:

- Reelect the legislature if and only it proposes $r_L = r_E = 0$.
- Reelect the executive unless it accepts some proposal such that $r > 0$ or rejects some proposal such that $r = 0$.

Thus, each incumbent is rewarded or punished based upon its contribution to the observed level of rents.

By a logic analogous to that in the previous sections, the legislature chooses between proposing 1) $r_L = r_E = 0$, which guarantees the payoff from reelection R_L, and 2) the maximum possible rent $r = 1$, dividing the resource between itself and the executive. The key to the analysis is that the legislature would never propose any $r > 0$ unless it expected that proposal to be accepted by the executive, as its default payoff $\hat{r}_L = 0$ in the event of a veto is less than the payoff from reelection R_L. In particular, if the legislature proposes some division of the resource such that $r_L + r_E = r = 1$, the executive accepts the proposal only if $r_E \geq \hat{r}_E + R_E$ (if the proposal is vetoed, voters retain the executive). Because the legislature would never give the executive more than is necessary for it to accept the proposal, this implies $r_L = 1 - \hat{r}_E - R_E$.

For the legislature to prefer proposing $r_L = r_E = 0$, given that the proposal is accepted, its payoff from reelection must therefore be at least as large as the rent it retains after providing the executive what is necessary not to veto the legislature's proposal, that is, $R_L \geq 1 - \hat{r}_E - R_E$. Further, for this proposal to be accepted, the payoff to the executive from reelection must be at least as large as the rent it receives if it rejects the legislature's proposal, that is, $R_E \geq \hat{r}_E$. Combining these two conditions, we derive the condition for existence of an equilibrium in which no rents

---

[2] Persson et al. (1997) instead assume a two-stage budgeting process, where the executive first decides on the size of the resource to be divided (i.e., decides on the tax rate), following which the legislature determines the division of the resource; each actor has veto power over the other's decision.

are extracted as

$$1 - R_L - R_E \leq \hat{r}_E \leq R_E.$$

The executive's default rent must be large enough that the legislature prefers instead to seek reelection even at the cost of extracting no rents. At the same time, this rent cannot be so large that the executive prefers vetoing a proposal that would ensure her reelection.

7.1.4 An Infinite-horizon Model

In Section 7.1.1, we suggested that the exogenous payoff R from reelection could be thought of as the value of reelection in an infinite-horizon model. In this section we explore that possibility, extending the simple two-period model of Section 7.1.1 to an infinite-horizon setting.

The basic setup follows that of Section 7.1.1, but now in each period $t = 1, 2, \ldots$, every voter i chooses a reservation utility $\bar{u}_{it}$; the incumbent chooses a level of rent extraction r_t; and each voter i decides whether to reelect based on a comparison of u_{it} and $\bar{u}_{it}$. Incumbents remain in office indefinitely, so long as they continue to receive the support of at least half the population, but once voted out of office they may never again run for election. Each period that an incumbent is in office she receives utility equal to r_t; the utility from not being in office is normalized to zero. If voted out of office, the incumbent is replaced by a challenger with identical preferences, who then becomes the incumbent in the next period. Politicians' payoffs are discounted according to the common discount factor $\delta \in (0, 1)$.

As in the two-period model, there are infinitely many subgame-perfect Nash equilibria of this game. As in Section 7.1.1, we restrict attention to equilibria in which voters coordinate on a common reservation utility, that is, $\bar{u}_{it} = \bar{u}_t$ for all i, and vote based on this announcement. In addition, we assume that voters use the same voting rule in each period (i.e., $\bar{u}_t = \bar{u}$ for all t)—that is, their strategies are stationary.

With these restrictions, the analysis is similar to that in Section 7.1.1. Each period, the incumbent faces a choice between extracting the maximum possible rent $r = 1$, thus forfeiting reelection, and choosing $r = \bar{r}$, which leaves voters indifferent between reelecting and not. The expected payoff to the incumbent from choosing $r = \bar{r}$ is $\bar{r} + \delta V$, where V is the value to the incumbent of reelection. For it to be optimal for the incumbent to choose $r = \bar{r}$ thus requires

$$\bar{r} + \delta V \geq 1, \tag{7.2}$$

where 1 is the payoff from choosing $r = 1$ and forfeiting reelection.

If it is an equilibrium for the incumbent to choose $r = \bar{r}$ each period, then the value of reelection $V = \bar{r} + \delta V$, which implies

$$V = \frac{\bar{r}}{1 - \delta}. \tag{7.3}$$

Substituting Equation 7.3 into Condition 7.2 and simplifying gives

$$\bar{r} \geq 1 - \delta.$$

The best possible $\bar{u}$ (implicitly, the best possible $\bar{r}$) leaves the incumbent indifferent between implementing $r = \bar{r}$ and $r = 1$, so that in equilibrium $\bar{r} = 1 - \delta$.

How does this compare to the equilibrium level of rents in the two-period model, which we derived as $1 - \delta R$? We suggested in Section 7.1.1 that the exogenous payoff from reelection R in the two-period model could be thought of as the endogenous continuation payoff in an infinite-horizon model. To explore this idea, note that the value of reelection in equilibrium is

$$V = \frac{\bar{r}}{1 - \delta} = 1,$$

where we use the equilibrium value of $\bar{r} = 1 - \delta$. Then if $R = V$, the equilibrium level of rents in the two-period model is $\bar{r} = 1 - \delta R = 1 - \delta$, which is the same as that in any period in the infinite-horizon model.

7.2 Career Concerns

We now turn attention to models that combine moral hazard and selection.[3] Voting in these models is "prospective," that is, voters compare the incumbent and challenger based on the performance they expect from each following the election. Because politicians differ in their characteristics (type), however, voting to select the best candidate may have the practical effect of inducing incumbents to act responsibly. Intuitively, by behaving in a responsible manner, incumbents hope to fool voters into thinking that they are more competent or well-intentioned than is actually the case.

We first consider a model in which the incumbent has no private information about her type, which we term competence. One interpretation

---

[3] For early work along these lines, see Austen-Smith and Banks (1989) and Banks and Sundaram (1993).

of this assumption is that the incumbent, like voters, is uncertain of the political-economic environment and therefore does not know whether her particular skill set will be useful in solving whatever problems happen to arise. Agency models of this sort—in which the agent (here, incumbent) knows no more about her competence than do the principals (here, voters)—are known in the literature as "career concerns" models, a term that dates to Holmström's (1982) discussion of the role that future career prospects play in managerial discussion making. Numerous applications of this framework to politics have appeared in recent years, in part due to the wide use of career concerns models in Persson and Tabellini (2000).[4]

7.2.1 A Two-period Model

Consider a model with the following actors:

- A population of identical voters.
- An incumbent politician.
- A challenger.

There are two periods: an election period ($t = 1$) and a post-election period ($t = 2$). In the election period the incumbent chooses an effort level $e_1 \in [0, \infty)$, which is unobserved by voters. In the post-election period, whichever politician has been elected (the incumbent or challenger from the election period) chooses an effort level $e_2 \in [0, \infty)$. In each period t, the politician in power bears a cost of effort $\frac{1}{2}(e_t)^2$ and earns an exogenous wage w (this may represent both formal compensation and "ego rents" from holding power). All actors share a common discount factor $\delta \in (0, 1)$.

Although effort itself is unobservable to voters, voters observe the utility they receive from any effort choice. In particular, in each period t, voters receive utility

$$u_t = \theta + e_t,$$

where θ is a random variable that represents the competence of the officeholder in period t. For simplicity, we do not subscript θ by the identity of the officeholder. By further suppressing the time subscript on θ, we signify that the competence of a politician carries over from one period to the next; this gives voters an incentive to reelect incumbents who are perceived to be competent. Later we will consider an alternative approach, where the competence of the officeholder in any period is a

---

[4] See also Lohmann (1998) for an early application.

moving average of shocks to her competence in the previous and current periods.

We assume that the competence of the incumbent politician is drawn from a differentiable distribution function F, with density f and $E(\theta) = 0$. For simplicity, we assume that the support of f is the real number line.[5] As with the incumbent's effort choice, the incumbent's competence θ is unobserved by voters. Further, we assume that θ is drawn after the incumbent's effort choice in period 1, so that the incumbent is herself unaware of her competence level at the time she makes her effort decision. If the incumbent is defeated, the challenger takes power, with $E(\theta) = 0$.

Summarizing, the timing of events is:

(i) $(t = 1)$ The incumbent chooses e_1.
(ii) $(t = 1)$ The incumbent's competence is realized, with voters observing (only) u_1.
(iii) $(t = 1)$ Voters choose whether to reelect the incumbent.
(iv) $(t = 2)$ If the challenger wins, her competence is realized.
(v) $(t = 2)$ The winner of the election chooses e_2.

We begin our analysis with the post-election effort choice. In period 2, whichever politician is in power chooses $e_2 = 0$: without the pressure of an upcoming election, there is no incentive to exert effort. Voter utility in period 2 is therefore $u_2 = \theta$, where θ is the competence of whichever politician won the election in period 1.

Because period-2 utility is a function only of the competence of the politician then holding office, in deciding how to vote in period 1 voters simply compare the incumbent's perceived competence to the challenger's expected competence. Let $\tilde{\theta}$ be voters' (common) perception of the incumbent's competence. Then voters prefer to reelect the incumbent if

$$\tilde{\theta} \geq E(\theta) = 0.$$

How do voters form their perceptions of the incumbent's competence? Recall that voters observe $u_1 = \theta + e_1$. The incumbent's effort level e_1 is itself unobserved, but voters have beliefs about the effort level chosen by the incumbent (in any game, actors have beliefs about the strategies played by other actors). Voters therefore impute competence based on

---

[5] Absent this assumption, multiple equilibria can be supported by implausible beliefs about the incumbent's competence for realizations of u_1 off the equilibrium path; see Gehlbach (2007) for discussion.

these beliefs and their observed utility as follows:

$$\tilde{\theta} = u_1 - \tilde{e}_1,$$

where $\tilde{e}_1$ denotes voters' common belief (correct in equilibrium) about the effort chosen by the incumbent. Voters thus prefer to reelect the incumbent if $u_1 - \tilde{e}_1 \geq 0$.

The incumbent anticipates this voter behavior and takes voters' belief about her effort level $\tilde{e}_1$ as given in solving

$$\max_{e_1} - \frac{(e_1)^2}{2} + w + \Pr\left(u_1 - \tilde{e}_1 \geq 0\right)\delta w,$$

where the payoff to reelection is simply w, because, as we have shown, the incumbent exerts no effort in period 2 if reelected. Substituting $u_1 = \theta + e_1$, the incumbent's problem can be rewritten as

$$\max_{e_1} - \frac{(e_1)^2}{2} + \Pr\left(\theta \geq \tilde{e}_1 - e_1\right)\delta w,$$

where we drop the initial w, because the first-period wage is received regardless of the incumbent's effort choice. Intuitively, the incumbent has an incentive to exert effort to increase her probability of winning, attempting to beat voters' expectations about her effort level so as to appear more competent than she actually is. In fact, this effort is for naught: equilibrium requires that players' beliefs about others' strategies be correct, so that the incumbent cannot fool voters into thinking her more competent than she actually is. Nonetheless, she is forced to exert the expected level of effort, as doing otherwise would lead voters to believe that she is less competent than she actually is.

Using the distribution of θ, the incumbent's problem can be rewritten once again, this time as

$$\max_{e_1} - \frac{(e_1)^2}{2} + \left[1 - F\left(\tilde{e}_1 - e_1\right)\right]\delta w.$$

Differentiating with respect to e_1 gives the first-order condition:

$$-e_1^* + f\left(\tilde{e}_1 - e_1^*\right)\delta w = 0,$$

which is sufficient for a solution if the cost of effort is sufficiently convex, relative to the density f. Finally, we impose the equilibrium condition that voters' beliefs about the incumbent's effort be correct, giving

$$e_1^* = f\left(0\right)\delta w.$$

Examining this condition, we see that the incumbent exerts more effort the more she values the future (i.e., the higher is δ) and the larger her payoff from holding office w. Somewhat loosely, she is also more accountable the less uncertainty there is about her competence—that is, the tighter is the distribution of the random variable θ around $E(\theta) = 0$, as expressed by $f(0)$. Intuitively, there is less incentive to exert effort if the incumbent's reelection is likely to be determined by events beyond her control, whatever her effort choice.

To an outside observer, it looks as though voters are using a pure retrospective-voting rule as in the Barro-Ferejohn model discussed earlier, choosing the incumbent over the challenger only if she delivers a given level of utility. To see this, recall that voters choose to reelect when $\tilde{\theta} = u_1 - \tilde{e}_1 \geq 0$. Given the equilibrium condition that $\tilde{e}_1 = e_1^* = f(0)\delta w$, the condition for voters to reelect the incumbent can be written as

$$u_1 \geq f(0)\delta w. \tag{7.4}$$

However, voters are actually forward-looking, interpreting $u_1 < f(0)\delta w$ to mean that the incumbent is less competent than they expect the challenger to be. Moreover, in contrast to the Barro-Ferejohn model of Section 7.1, this behavior is robust to slight perturbations in voters' preferences. If voters have a slight preference for either the incumbent or the challenger, then they simply use a slightly different voting rule, rather than (as in the Barro-Ferejohn model) abandoning the rule altogether. Exercise 7.3 asks you to verify this fact.

7.2.2 *An Infinite-horizon Model*

We now extend the career concerns model to an infinite-horizon setting. In particular, we modify the two-period model so that the game continues indefinitely, with off-election periods (O) alternating with on-election periods (E). We assume that there is a pool of ex ante identical challengers, with one challenger chosen at random to face the incumbent in any election period. For simplicity, we further assume that once defeated, an incumbent can never regain office.

Much as in the two-period model, voter utility in period t is given by $u_t = \theta_t + e_t$, where θ_t is the competence of the officeholder in period t. Following Persson and Tabellini (2000), however, we now assume that a politician's competence is a moving average of competence shocks

$$\theta_t = y_t + y_{t-1}.$$

where the y_t are serially uncorrelated and distributed according to a differentiable distribution function G with density g and $E(y_t) = 0$. As we will see, this formulation implies that effort follows an electoral cycle, with greater effort in election than in off-election periods. Implicitly, we assume that all potential challengers receive competence shocks in each period, but that voters have no opportunity to infer what these are until a challenger takes office. We assume that in any period t, voters observe y_{t-1} and u_t before deciding whether to reelect the incumbent; the incumbent's current-period competence shock y_t and effort e_t are unobserved.

Clearly, the optimal effort level in off-election periods is $e_O^* = 0$. The utility received by voters in any such period reveals information about the incumbent's current competence, but such information is irrelevant to the voting decision in the election period to follow, as the incumbent's competence in one off-election period is uncorrelated with that in the next. Given that voters are forward-looking, the incumbent therefore has no incentive to exert effort, so that the value in equilibrium of being the incumbent in an off-election period is

$$V_O = w + \delta V_E.$$

The incumbent bears no cost of effort, collects w, and then moves on to an election period, the value of which (V_E) is discounted by δ.

In election periods, voters decide whether to vote for the incumbent by comparing their expected utility from the incumbent's reelection to that if the challenger is elected. For concreteness, consider some election period t. Note first that voters expect the same utility in all periods from $t + 2$ regardless of who is elected, as the incumbent's competence from period t carries over only to period $t + 1$. In contrast, voters' expected utility in period $t + 1$ if the incumbent is reelected is

$$E(u_{t+1}| \text{ incumbent reelected}) = E(\theta_{t+1}| \text{ incumbent reelected}) + e_O^*$$
$$= E(y_{t+1}) + \tilde{y}_t = \tilde{y}_t,$$

where $\tilde{y}_t$ is voters' (common) perception of y_t, versus an expected utility if the challenger is elected of

$$E(u_{t+1}| \text{ challenger elected}) = E(\theta_{t+1}| \text{ challenger elected}) + e_O^*$$
$$= E(y_{t+1}) + E(y_t) = 0,$$

where we recall that a challenger's competence shock in period t cannot be inferred by voters because she is not in office. Voters therefore prefer to reelect the incumbent if $\tilde{y}_t \geq 0$.

Voters impute competence as in the two-period model. Observing u_t and y_{t-1}, and having beliefs $\tilde{e}_t$ about the effort chosen by the politician in period t, voters solve the following equation for $\tilde{y}_t$:

$$u_t = y_{t-1} + \tilde{y}_t + \tilde{e}_t.$$

Thus, the probability that the incumbent wins, which is the probability that $\tilde{y}_t \geq 0$, is given by

$$\Pr\left(\tilde{y}_t \geq 0\right) = \Pr\left(u_t - y_{t-1} - \tilde{e}_t \geq 0\right) = \Pr\left(y_t \geq \tilde{e}_t - e_t\right),$$

where we use $u_t = y_t + y_{t-1} + e_t$.

The incumbent anticipates this voting behavior. Consequently, the value of being the incumbent in any election period is

$$V_E = \max_{e_t} -\frac{(e_t)^2}{2} + w + \Pr\left(y_t \geq \tilde{e}_t - e_t\right)\delta V_O + \left[1 - \Pr\left(y_t \geq \tilde{e}_t - e_t\right)\right]\delta 0.$$

This is an example of a **Bellman equation**, which captures the idea that the optimal course of action is to make the best possible choice in the current period and then follow the optimal course of action thereafter (see also Section 8.3). Here, the value of following the optimal course of action beginning the next period if the incumbent is reelected is given by V_O, which, as already demonstrated, is equal to $w + \delta V_E$. In contrast, there is no decision to be made if the incumbent is defeated, the value of which we have normalized to zero. Using the fact that y_t is distributed according to $G(.)$, this can be rewritten as

$$V_E = \max_{e_t} -\frac{(e_t)^2}{2} + w + \left[1 - G\left(\tilde{e}_t - e_t\right)\right]\delta\left(w + \delta V_E\right).$$

Differentiating with respect to e_t and setting the derivative equal to zero gives

$$e_E^* = g\left(\tilde{e}_E - e_E^*\right)\delta\left(w + \delta V_E\right),$$

where we replace the subscript t with the subscript E to signify that the same effort choice is made in any election period. Finally, imposing the equilibrium condition that voters have correct expectations about the incumbent's effort choice, that is, $\tilde{e}_E = e_E^*$, gives

$$e_E^* = g(0)\delta\left(w + \delta V_E\right). \tag{7.5}$$

The optimal effort choice in election periods looks qualitatively similar to that in the two-period model. But what is V_E? In principle, we could plug the equilibrium level of effort into the Bellman equation for election periods and solve for V_E:

$$V_E = -\frac{[g(0)\,\delta\,(w + \delta V_E)]^2}{2} + w + [1 - G(0)]\,\delta\,(w + \delta V_E).$$

(Note that we have made use of the equilibrium condition $\tilde{e}_E = e_E^*$ to derive the probability of winning in equilibrium as $1 - G(0)$.) The resulting solution would be a complicated function of the parameters of the model.

If, however, we are interested only in how V_E varies qualitatively with parameters of the model (e.g., in whether $\frac{\partial V_E}{\partial w}$ is greater than or less than zero), then there is an alternative approach. The **envelope theorem** says that the effect of a marginal change in a parameter value on the maximized value of a function is the effect of that change on the value of the function, holding the choice variable fixed at its optimum value. More precisely, define

$$V = \max_x \; f(x, \mathbf{p}),$$

where x is a choice variable (the result extends to maximization over a vector of choice variables) and $\mathbf{p}$ is a vector of parameters. Then using the chain rule, the derivative of V with respect to any particular parameter p_i can be derived as

$$\frac{\partial V}{\partial p_i} = \frac{\partial f\,(x^*(\mathbf{p}), \mathbf{p})}{\partial x} \cdot \frac{\partial x^*(\mathbf{p})}{\partial p_i} + \frac{\partial f\,(x^*(\mathbf{p}), \mathbf{p})}{\partial p_i} = \frac{\partial f\,(x^*(\mathbf{p}), \mathbf{p})}{\partial p_i},$$

where $x^*(\mathbf{p})$ is the value of x that maximizes $f(x, \mathbf{p})$, and the second equality follows from the fact that $\frac{\partial f(x^*(\mathbf{p}), \mathbf{p})}{\partial x} = 0$ is the first-order condition to the maximization problem. In other words, all that matters is the direct effect of a change in some parameter of the model. There is no indirect effect, that is, no impact on the value of the function through a change in the optimal value of x.

Here, we can use the envelope theorem to find $\frac{\delta V_E}{\delta w}$. Begin by writing V_E as

$$V_E = -\frac{(e_E^*)^2}{2} + w + [1 - G(\tilde{e}_E - e_E^*)]\,\delta\,(w + \delta V_E).$$

Then implicitly differentiate this equation with respect to w, holding fixed the optimal e_E^*:

$$\frac{\partial V_E}{\partial w} = 1 + [1 - G(\tilde{e}_E - e_E^*)] \delta \left(1 + \delta \frac{\partial V_E}{\partial w}\right)$$

$$= 1 + [1 - G(0)] \delta \left(1 + \delta \frac{\partial V_E}{\partial w}\right).$$

(The second equation follows from the equilibrium condition $\tilde{e}_E = e_E^*$.) Rearranging gives

$$\frac{\partial V_E}{\partial w} = \frac{1 + [1 - G(0)] \delta}{1 - [1 - G(0)] \delta^2} > 0.$$

Thus, an increase in the per-period payoff from holding office results in an increase in the value of being the incumbent in any election period. Examining the expression for the optimal level of effort in any election period (Equation 7.5), we can thus conclude that an increase in w results in an increase in effort in election periods:

$$\frac{\partial e_E^*}{\partial w} = g(0) \delta \left(1 + \delta \frac{\partial V_E}{\partial w}\right) > 0.$$

7.3 Signaling Models of Political Agency

7.3.1 Baseline Model

The model presented in the previous section assumes that the incumbent has no private information about her type at the moment when she chooses her effort level. This assumption is arguably defensible if "type" represents competence, but it is less plausible when politicians differ in their preferences. Incumbents, for example, may have private information about their most-preferred policies or about the degree to which they value policy over personal consumption. When this is the case, voters must infer the incumbent's type from her action, knowing that the incumbent knew her type when taking that action. This is the logic of a signaling game.[6]

We explore this setting by considering a two-period model of political agency that is similar to that developed by Besley (2006). As in the career concerns model, there are three sets of players: voters, an incumbent, and a challenger, with common discount factor δ. We simplify the

---

[6] For a model in which voters are uncertain about both competence and preferences, see Fox and Shotts (2009).

policy environment from that in the previous sections by assuming that, in each period $t = 1, 2$, the officeholder chooses $e_t \in \{0, 1\}$. Both voters and politicians receive a payoff in period t equal to e_t—the interpretation is that $e_t = 1$ represents effort that provides a benefit to all citizens, including politicians. Voters observe e_1 before deciding how to vote.

Politicians are either diligent (d) or lazy (l), where $\pi \in (0, 1)$ is the prior probability that any politician is diligent. Diligent and lazy politicians differ in their cost c_t of choosing $e_t = 1$ in period t; we normalize the cost of choosing $e_t = 0$ to zero for both types. In particular, diligent politicians bear no cost from choosing $e_t = 1$ (i.e., $c_t = 0$), whereas for lazy politicians c_t is a random variable drawn from the distribution F. Assume that F is strictly increasing on $[1, \infty)$, with $F(1) = 0$. Thus, for any realization of c_t, the cost for a lazy politician of choosing $e_t = 1$ is greater than the immediate benefit. Finally, assume that any politician, diligent or lazy, receives a wage $w > 1$ in each period she is in office.

The timing of events and information structure are as follows:

- $(t = 1)$ The incumbent's type (diligent or lazy) is realized, as is the cost of effort if the incumbent is lazy, in each case observed only by the incumbent.
- $(t = 1)$ The incumbent chooses e_1, which is observed by voters.
- $(t = 1)$ Voters choose whether to reelect the incumbent.
- $(t = 2)$ If the challenger wins, her type (diligent or lazy) is realized, as is the cost of effort if the election winner is lazy.
- $(t = 2)$ The winner of the election chooses e_2.

We begin our analysis with the choice of effort in the second period. The optimal e_2 follows directly from the election winner's type: a diligent election winner chooses $e_2 = 1$, whereas a lazy election winner chooses $e_2 = 0$, whatever the realization of c_2. Voters therefore prefer to elect the politician whom they believe is more likely to be diligent. In particular, if voters' posterior belief that the incumbent is diligent is greater than π—the probability that the challenger is diligent—then they vote to reelect the incumbent.

Intuitively, voters should infer that an incumbent who chooses $e_1 = 1$ is more likely to be diligent, as high effort is costless to diligent politicians but costly to lazy politicians. We therefore look for an equilibrium in which voters reelect the incumbent if and only if $e_1 = 1$. Given this anticipated behavior, a diligent incumbent always chooses $e_1 = 1$: doing so provides a higher policy payoff in the current period, and it guarantees reelection, which not only provides the second-period wage w but also ensures that $e_2 = 1$. This behavior, in turn, justifies the reelection of incumbents who choose $e_1 = 1$, as an incumbent who makes this choice is more likely to be diligent than is the challenger (who is diligent with probability π). To see this, use Bayes' Rule to derive the posterior probability that the incumbent is diligent, given that the incumbent has chosen $e_1 = 1$:

$$\Pr(d \mid e_1 = 1) = \frac{\Pr(e_1 = 1 \mid d)\Pr(d)}{\Pr(e_1 = 1)} = \frac{\pi}{\pi + (1 - \pi)\zeta},$$

where $\zeta \equiv \Pr(e_1 = 1 \mid l)$. In contrast, an incumbent who chooses $e_1 = 0$ must be lazy, so that voters prefer to elect the challenger.

We are interested in ζ, the probability that a lazy type chooses $e_1 = 1$, despite the cost of doing so. To derive ζ, first note that the expected payoff to a lazy incumbent from choosing $e_1 = 0$ is

$$w + \delta\left[\pi(1) + (1 - \pi)(0)\right] = w + \delta\pi.$$

A lazy incumbent earns only the wage w in period 1, following which she is replaced by a challenger of unknown type. With probability π, the challenger is diligent and implements $e_2 = 1$, whereas with probability $1 - \pi$, the challenger is lazy and implements $e_2 = 0$. In contrast, the expected payoff to a lazy incumbent from choosing $e_1 = 1$ is

$$w + (1 - c_1) + \delta(w + 0).$$

The incumbent earns $w + (1 - c_1)$ in period 1 (where the latter term is the net benefit of choosing $e_1 = 1$), following which she is reelected, earning the wage w and choosing $e_2 = 0$. Thus, a lazy incumbent chooses $e_1 = 1$ if

$$w + (1 - c_1) + \delta w \geq w + \delta\pi.$$

Using the distribution of c_1, this implies that the probability that a lazy incumbent chooses $e_1 = 1$ is

$$\zeta = F(1 + \delta(w - \pi)). \tag{7.6}$$

Equation 7.6 tells us how political accountability depends on various parameters of the model. Intuitively, lazy incumbents are more accountable—more likely to choose $e_1 = 1$—when they care more about the future and when the wage from holding office is large. More interestingly, accountability is smaller when a lazy incumbent is likely to be replaced by a diligent challenger (i.e., when π is large). Intuitively, a lazy incumbent is more willing to sacrifice reelection if she expects to be replaced by somebody who will subsequently get the job done.

7.3.2 State-dependent Utility

As with the Barro-Ferejohn and career concerns models, the signaling model just presented can easily be extended to an infinite-horizon setting. Here, however, we retain the two-period setting to show how asymmetric information about politician preferences can lead even diligent incumbents to make bad decisions. Intuitively, as Canes-Wrone, Herron, and Shotts (2001) show, high-quality incumbents may "pander" to voters by implementing policies they know to be suboptimal if that is the only way to convince voters that they are deserving of reelection.

Our formalization most closely follows Besley (2006). The single departure from the model of the previous section is that we assume that the benefit to voters and politicians of effort e_t depends on the realization of a random state variable (that is, that voters and politicians have **state-dependent utilities**), which is private information to the incumbent. Let $s_t \in \{0, 1\}$ denote the state in period t, and assume that voters and politicians receive a payoff from effort in period t equal to

$$s_t e_t + (1 - s_t)(1 - e_t).$$

Thus, the policy that maximizes voter welfare is $e_t = 0$ when $s_t = 0$ and $e_t = 1$ when $s_t = 1$. Voters observe e_t but not the state variable s_t or their policy payoff before the election. As an example, e_t might represent the decision to facilitate peace talks between warring states, the benefit of which may depend on factors not easily observed by voters, and the outcome of which may be visible only in the future. Let η denote the probability that $s_t = 1$, where $\eta \in (0, 1)$. All other aspects of the model are the same as before.

For certain parameter values, there exists an equilibrium similar to that in the baseline model, where diligent incumbents always choose $e_1 = 1$, lazy incumbents choose $e_1 = 0$ if c_1 is high and $e_1 = 1$ if c_1 is low, and voters reelect the incumbent if and only if $e_1 = 1$. The analysis for lazy incumbents is analogous to that already presented, though more complicated because we must consider state-dependent choices: see Exercise 7.7. The crucial difference, however, is the calculus for diligent incumbents. We consider each of the two states in turn. If $s_1 = 1$, then the diligent incumbent unambiguously prefers $e_1 = 1$: doing so gives the best policy outcome and ensures reelection. In contrast, if $s_1 = 0$, the diligent incumbent prefers $e_1 = 1$ if

$$w + 0 + \delta(w + 1) \geq w + 1 + \delta[\pi + (1 - \pi)(1 - \eta)]. \tag{7.7}$$

The expression on the left is the payoff from $e_1 = 1$, and the expression on the right is the payoff from $e_1 = 0$. Choosing $e_1 = 1$ produces a lower payoff in period 1, as the appropriate policy given the state is $e_1 = 0$, but a higher expected payoff in period 2: not only does the incumbent receive the wage w in the second period, but with certainty policy is consistent with the state. In contrast, if the incumbent chooses $e_1 = 0$, then with probability $1 - \pi$ a lazy challenger is elected, who subsequently chooses $e_2 = 0$, which matches the state s_2 with probability $1 - \eta$.

Simplifying Condition 7.7 gives

$$w \geq \frac{1}{\delta} - (1 - \pi)\,\eta.$$

Diligent incumbents are more inclined to pander to voters, that is, to choose $e_1 = 1$ when the welfare-maximizing policy is $e_1 = 0$, when the wage w is large. Formal compensation of politicians can thus be a double-edged sword, promoting electoral accountability among lazy types but encouraging pandering among diligent types. In addition, diligent incumbents are more likely to pander when π is small and η is large. Understanding that a loss could lead to the election of a lazy challenger who chooses the "wrong" policy in period 2, incumbents may sacrifice policy before the election so that they are in a position to choose it afterward.

Exercises

7.1 Consider an infinite-horizon model of electoral accountability, identical to the model of Section 7.1.4 but for the following differences:

- Rather than extracting rents, in each period the incumbent chooses an effort level e_t.
- Voters receive utility in each period equal to e_t; politicians do not receive a direct benefit from effort.
- In each period, the incumbent bears a cost of effort equal to e_t. In addition, in each period the incumbent receives an exogenous payoff equal to w. The value of being out of office is normalized to zero.

Derive the equilibrium level of effort when voters always coordinate on the same reservation utility $\bar{u}$ and always vote according to their announcement $\bar{u}$. Relate the predictions of this model to those of Section 7.1.4.

7.2 Consider the following variant of the two-period career concerns model of Section 7.2.1. In each period t, voters receive utility according to

$$u_t = \theta \left(1 + e_t\right).$$

The competence θ of the politician is a random variable, uniformly distributed on the interval $\left[1 - \frac{1}{2\phi}, 1 + \frac{1}{2\phi}\right]$, where the parameter ϕ is large enough to ensure an interior solution to the problem that follows. The challenger has expected competence $E\left(\theta\right) = 1$. Assume the cost of effort to the incumbent to be equal to e_t.

(a) Derive the equilibrium level of effort in period 2 by the election winner. Use this to derive the condition for voters to reelect the incumbent.

(b) Show how voters impute the competence of the incumbent based on their observed utility and on their beliefs about the effort choice of the incumbent in period 1. Use this to derive an expression for the incumbent's reelection probability.

(c) Derive the equilibrium effort choice by the incumbent in period 1. Interpret your result.

7.3 Consider the model of Section 7.2.1, but now assume that voters have an exogenous preference for the challenger over the incumbent represented by the parameter β, which may be greater than or less than zero, such that they support the incumbent over the challenger if

$$\tilde{\theta} \geq E\left(\theta\right) + \beta = \beta.$$

(a) Derive e_1^*, the equilibrium level of effort in the election period.

(b) Assume that the density of θ is single-peaked around $E\left(\theta\right)$, that is, $f\left(\theta\right)$ achieves a maximum at zero and falls away monotonically on either side of zero. In qualitative terms, how does e_1^* depend on the magnitude of voters' bias toward or against the incumbent, that is, on $|\beta|$?

(c) Derive the "retrospective voting rule" (analogous to Condition 7.4) that corresponds to voters' equilibrium behavior.

7.4 Consider a two-period career concerns model in which the survival of a party, comprising many members, depends on the party's ability to convince citizens that it is more competent than some potential challenger. Competence θ is a random variable, initially unknown to party members and unobserved by citizens, with distribution F and density f single-peaked around $E(\theta) = 0$. In a departure from the standard career concerns setup, any citizen's utility in period t is the sum of the performance of N individual party members, indexed by i:

$$u_t = \sum g_{it}.$$

The performance of any member i, in turn, is an additive function of that member's effort and of party competence θ:

$$g_{it} = e_{it} + \theta.$$

The key assumption is that all party members have the same competence, perhaps because they share the same ideology or worldview. Individual effort—like competence—is unobserved by citizens, but citizens observe u_1 before deciding whether to replace the party. To capture incumbency advantage, assume that the party survives if citizens' perception of the party's competence $\tilde{\theta} \geq -\beta$, where $\beta \geq 0$. Finally, let the cost of effort e_{it} be equal to $\frac{(e_{it})^2}{2}$ for any member i, let the payoff to any individual member from survival be w, and assume a common discount factor δ, so that in period 1 any member i solves

$$\max_{e_{i1}} \; \Pr\left(\tilde{\theta} \geq -\beta\right) \delta w - \frac{(e_{i1})^2}{2}$$

where $\tilde{\theta}$ is a function not only of member i's effort but also of the effort of other members.

(a) Derive an expression for $\tilde{\theta}$ (citizens' common perception of the party's competence) as a function of θ, N, $\sum e_{i1}$, and $\sum \tilde{e}_{i1}$, where $\tilde{e}_{i1}$ denotes citizens' common belief about member i's effort choice.

(b) Using your answer to the previous question, rewrite $\Pr\left(\tilde{\theta} \geq -\beta\right)$, the probability that the party survives, as a function of N, $\sum e_{i1}$, $\sum \tilde{e}_{i1}$, and β.

(c) Use this expression to derive the optimum effort by each party member i as a function of other members' effort, voters' beliefs, and parameters of the model.

(d) Impose the equilibrium condition that beliefs about members' actions be correct to find the equilibrium effort for any party member i.

(e) How does equilibrium behavior depend on parameters of the model? What does the model say about accountability (effort) in a centralized political system, where political agents' fortunes rise or fall based on their collective rather than individual reputation?

7.5 Consider the infinite-horizon model of Section 7.2.2. Use implicit differentiation and the envelope theorem to show how e_E^*, the equilibrium level of effort in election periods, depends on the discount factor δ.

7.6 Consider the signaling model of Section 7.3.1. Derive conditions for existence of a pooling equilibrium in which both types choose $e_1 = 0$ and voters reelect the incumbent if and only if $e_1 = 0$, as follows:

(a) What is the diligent type's expected payoff in equilibrium? If the diligent type deviates to $e_1 = 1$? For what parameter values is it a best response for the diligent type to choose $e_1 = 0$?

(b) What is the lazy type's expected payoff in equilibrium? If the lazy type deviates to $e_1 = 1$? For what parameter values is it a best response for the lazy type to choose $e_1 = 0$?

(c) Show that it is a best response for voters to reelect if $e_1 = 0$.

(d) What beliefs off the equilibrium path (i.e., after observing $e_1 = 1$) justify not reelecting if $e_1 = 1$? Do these beliefs satisfy the intuitive criterion of Cho and Kreps (1987), which requires that at any information set off the equilibrium path, the receiver (here, voters) place zero probability on some type if a) the equilibrium payoff for that type is higher than that type's best possible payoff at the off-equilibrium-path information set, and b) this is not true for all types?

7.7 Consider the signaling model with state-dependent utility of Section 7.3.2. For each state $s_t \in \{0, 1\}$, find the probability that a lazy incumbent chooses $e_1 = 1$ if voters reelect the incumbent if and only if $e_1 = 1$.

7.8 Consider the following model of political agency, which is based on Meirowitz and Tucker (2012). In each period t, a representative citizen receives a payoff $\theta \in \{0, 1\}$, where θ is the competence of the politician in power in period t; there is no effort choice in this model. As in the career concerns model of Section 7.2, a politician's competence persists from period to period.

For any politician, $\Pr(\theta = 1) = \pi$. The key assumption is that the citizen is initially uncertain about the value of π. Intuitively, the citizen does not know if she lives in a country where politicians are generally competent or generally incompetent. For concreteness, assume $\pi \in (l, h)$, where $0 < l < h < 1$. The citizen's prior belief is that $\Pr(\pi = h) = q$.

Initially, we assume that there are two periods with no discounting. After observing her payoff in the first period, the citizen decides whether to replace the incumbent with a politician of unknown competence. In contrast to other models of political agency, we assume that acting to replace the incumbent is costly, where the cost to the citizen of replacing the incumbent is $c > 0$.

(a) Use Bayes' Rule to derive $\tilde{\pi}_0$, the citizen's posterior belief that $\pi = h$, given observed competence $\theta = 0$ in the first period.

(b) Under what condition, if any, would citizens choose to replace the incumbent upon observing $\theta = 0$ in the first period?

(c) Use Bayes' Rule to derive $\tilde{\pi}_1$, the citizen's posterior belief that $\pi = h$, given observed competence $\theta = 1$ in the first period.

(d) Under what condition, if any, would citizens choose to replace the incumbent upon observing $\theta = 1$ in the first period?

(e) Now imagine that the game is played for three periods, where in each of the first two periods the incumbent (possibly different in period 2 from the incumbent in period 1) can be replaced by a challenger of unknown competence. For simplicity, assume that the citizen in period 1 survives only to period 2, at which point she is replaced by an identical citizen who observes the full history of the game. Thus, in period 1, the citizen decides whether to replace the incumbent based on her expected payoff in period 2 but not in period 3, whereas in period 2, the citizen decides whether to replace the incumbent based on her expected payoff in period 3.

(1) Would an incompetent incumbent ever be retained in the first period but replaced in the second?

(2) Would an incompetent incumbent ever be retained in the second period after an incompetent incumbent has been replaced in the first period?

7.9 Consider the following model, based on Myerson (1993), which explores the impact of electoral rules on political selection. There are four parties, each of which has a fixed policy platform. Parties

1 and 2 are *left* parties, whereas parties 3 and 4 are *right* parties. Beyond these policy differences, parties are heterogeneous in their propensity for corruption, where parties 1 and 3 are *honest*, whereas parties 2 and 4 are *corrupt*.

There are $N \geq 4$ voters, with N even. Voting is by plurality rule, with ties decided by a fair coin toss. Assume that $\frac{N}{2}$ of these actors (*left* voters) receive a payoff of one if a left party is elected and a payoff of zero otherwise, whereas the other $\frac{N}{2}$ actors (*right* voters) receive a payoff of one if a right party is elected and a payoff of zero otherwise. In addition, assume that any voter bears a cost $\gamma > 0$ if a corrupt party is elected.

(a) Show that it is a Nash equilibrium for all left voters to vote for party 1 and all right voters to vote for party 3.

(b) Show that it is a Nash equilibrium for all left voters to vote for party 2 and all right voters to vote for party 4.

Now assume that voting is by proportional representation, where any party receives seats in parliament in proportion to its share of votes in the election. Voters receive payoffs in proportion to the seat shares of parties elected, given the preferences previously assumed. Thus, for example, if party 1 received one-fourth of the seats and party 4 three-fourths, left voters would receive a payoff of $\frac{1}{4} - \frac{3}{4}\gamma$, whereas right voters would receive a payoff of $\frac{3}{4} - \frac{3}{4}\gamma$.

(c) Show that it is a Nash equilibrium for all left voters to vote for party 1 and all right voters to vote for party 3.

(d) Is there any other Nash equilibrium? Why or why not?

What do your results say about the effectiveness of electoral rules in preventing corruption?

8

Regime Change

In previous chapters, we have largely pushed collective action and institutional change to the background. In this chapter we explore the ability of citizens to force a regime change through coordinated action. We also consider the possibility that political elites respond to the threat of collective action by changing institutions on their own.

We begin by examining the collective action problem itself, focusing first on a coordination game characterized by multiple equilibria—one in which citizens challenge the regime and one in which they do not. Following this, we consider a global-games approach to collective action, where incomplete information about some aspect of the institutional environment generates a unique equilibrium that is continuous in parameters of the model. The two approaches are complementary: the first suggests a greater role for institutions in focusing expectations on particular equilibria, whereas the second emphasizes the relationship between regime type (e.g., the difficulty of regime change) and the likelihood that citizens choose to challenge the regime.

The preceding analysis provides a microfoundation for a discussion of political-regime change, where elites respond to the possibility of collective action by changing the rules of the game.[1] We focus this discussion on a model of political transitions by Acemoglu and Robinson (2000, 2001, 2006). In this model, there is an excluded majority (the poor) that, at some cost, may overthrow a nondemocratic elite (the rich). Critically, the cost to the poor of collective action oscillates from period to period, in such a way that the rich are under pressure to redistribute to the poor only when the cost of collective action is low. As we will see, this pro-

---

[1] North (1990) characterizes institutions as "the rules of the game in a society or, more formally... the humanly devised constraints that shape human interaction" (p. 3).

	Challenge	Not
Challenge	$\beta - \mu, \beta - \mu$	$-\mu, 0$
Not	$0, -\mu$	$0, 0$

Figure 8.1. The payoffs in the two-citizen model in Section 8.1.

vides an incentive for the rich to democratize as a way of more credibly committing to future redistribution.

Formally, the Acemoglu-Robinson model is a Markov game, in which the game transitions among a set of states according to a Markov process. As this may be a new concept for some readers, we precede our discussion of the Acemoglu-Robinson model with a description of Markov games and a related solution concept.

8.1 Collective Action under Complete Information

We begin by considering a simple model of collective action with complete information. There are two citizens, each of whom can *Challenge* the regime or *Not*. The payoffs from each strategy pair are given in Figure 8.1, where $\beta > \mu > 0$. The payoffs here capture the idea that challenging the regime is always costly but that citizens can force a regime change if they both participate.

There are two pure-strategy Nash equilibria of this game: one in which both citizens challenge, and one in which neither does so. (There is also an "unstable" mixed-strategy equilibrium.) Which equilibrium is more compelling as a prediction for behavior in the strategic environment modeled by this game? One approach to equilibrium selection in games of this sort is to look for institutions that help individuals to coordinate on the "good" equilibrium—here, (*Challenge, Challenge*). This approach is especially identified with the work of Barry Weingast, who argues that democratic constitutions can facilitate coordination by setting explicit and commonly known limits on the power of the state (e.g., North and Weingast, 1989; Weingast, 1997; see also Fearon, 2011). From this perspective, a coordination equilibrium is a **focal point**: a transgression of a constitutional limit on state power creates the expectation that citizens will challenge the regime, which in turn justifies the decision to challenge.[2] As a corollary, authoritarian institutions that make such

---

[2] Weingast (1997) considers in particular the possibility that constitutions can serve

transgressions common knowledge within an elite group (e.g., a party) can check autocratic behavior, perhaps to the benefit of the ruler himself (Myerson, 2008; Gehlbach and Keefer, 2011).

Although an important perspective, one puzzle in this story is that the parameters of the model play no role in determining equilibrium selection. Intuitively, if β is small relative to μ, then we might expect either citizen to play it safe (i.e., given strategic uncertainty about the other citizen's behavior) by choosing *Not*. This idea is not captured by the institutions-as-coordination-devices argument. Terminologically, we say that if $\beta < 2\mu$, then (Not, Not) is (strictly) **risk-dominant**.[3] In contrast, $(Challenge, Challenge)$ is **payoff-dominant**, by which we mean that it Pareto dominates the other equilibrium. A coordination game with one risk-dominant and one payoff-dominant equilibrium is known as a **stag hunt**, after Jean-Jacques Rousseau's suggestion that civilization began when individuals learned to cooperate in pursuit of large game—in his example, a dangerous stag.

The two-citizen game can easily be generalized. To foreshadow the discussion in the following section, assume a continuum of citizens of mass one, each of whom decides to *Challenge* the regime or *Not*. As before, any citizen who challenges incurs a cost μ. Now, however, assume that the benefit of challenging is $\beta > \mu$ if more than k citizens challenge, and 0 otherwise. As in the two-player game, there are two pure-strategy equilibria: one where all citizens challenge, and one where none do. To see that there are no other equilibria in which h citizens challenge and $1 - h$ do not, observe that if $h > k$, then all citizens strictly prefer to challenge, whereas if $h \leq k$, then none do.

To incorporate the idea that characteristics of the political environment represented by parameters of the model should affect participation (beyond determining the basic structure of the game), we can proceed in one of two directions. First, we can relax the assumption that all elements of the game are common knowledge. The following section takes up this approach. Second, and not mutually exclusively, we can assume that individuals have heterogeneous preferences (e.g., Kuran, 1991a,b; Lohmann, 1994). Exercise 8.1 provides an example.

---

as coordination devices when there is no "natural" focal point, unlike the situation here, where one equilibrium Pareto dominates the other.

[3] In a 2×2 coordination game, one equilibrium risk dominates another if the product of each player's loss from deviating from the first equilibrium is greater than the product of each player's loss from deviating from the second. Here, this requires $\mu^2 > (\beta - \mu)^2$, or $\beta < 2\mu$.

8.2 *Collective Action under Incomplete Information*

We now modify the model of the previous section in such a way that some feature of the political environment is not common knowledge. Intuitively, one might think of this unknown characteristic as regime type. Each citizen forms her own impression of regime type based upon her everyday experience: what she reads in the newspapers, what happens when she needs something from the government, and so forth. Given that citizens live under the same regime, however, their private signals of regime type are correlated.

As we will see, this change in modeling strategy has two consequences. First, given the information and payoff structure to be developed here, there is a unique equilibrium of the game.[4] Second, the proportion of citizens who challenge in equilibrium is continuous in parameters of the model. This **global games** approach has its origins in the work of Carlsson and van Damme (1993) and Morris and Shin (2003). Our treatment is similar in some respects to that of Edmond (2008) and especially Boix and Svolik (2012), each of whom embeds a global game in a larger model where an autocrat has the ability to manipulate collective action.

We continue to assume a continuum of citizens of mass one, indexed by i. For each citizen, the benefit of challenging is $\beta > 0$ if more than k citizens challenge, and 0 otherwise. The parameters β and k are common knowledge. In contrast, citizens have private but correlated costs of challenging the regime. In particular, we assume that each citizen i receives a private signal $s_i = \mu + \epsilon_i$, where μ is the common component and ϵ_i the idiosyncratic component of citizen i's cost of challenging s_i. We assume that citizens have a common prior belief that μ is distributed uniformly on the real number line. Although this prior belief is "improper," having infinite probability mass, the posterior belief (i.e., having received a private signal of μ) is well defined. Further, for simplicity, we assume that ϵ_i is drawn from a uniform distribution with support $[-\psi, \psi]$. Then, given the flat prior belief, citizen i's posterior belief is that μ is uniformly distributed on the interval $[s_i - \psi, s_i + \psi]$.

---

[4] In particular, the payoff structure satisfies **global strategic complementarities**, which says that the incentive to take some action is (weakly) greater, the more that others do so, and **two-sided limit dominance**, which says that there are private signals such that some citizens strictly prefer to challenge, and others not to challenge, whatever they expect other citizens to do. See Bueno de Mesquita (2010) and Shadmehr and Bernhardt (2011) for models of collective action without global strategic complementarities and two-sided limit dominance.

Clearly, if s_i is low enough, then citizen i prefers to challenge, whatever she expects others to do. Moreover, because the private signals are correlated, the lower is s_i, the more likely it is that other citizens also find challenging to be a dominant strategy, which in turn justifies challenging even if s_i is not so low that challenging is a dominant strategy for citizen i. Taken together, these considerations suggest a **cutpoint strategy**, where any citizen i challenges if $s_i < \bar{s}$ and does not challenge if $s_i > \bar{s}$.

For this strategy to be optimal, any citizen i with $s_i = \bar{s}$ must be indifferent between challenging and not. Denoting by h the mass of individuals who challenge, this requires

$$\bar{s} = \Pr\left(h > k \mid s_i = \bar{s}\right)\beta. \tag{8.1}$$

Regardless of turnout, any citizen i with $s_i = \bar{s}$ bears a cost of challenging equal to $\bar{s}$, whereas she receives the benefit β if and only if $h > k$.

To solve for $\bar{s}$, we need to derive $\Pr\left(h > k \mid s_i = \bar{s}\right)$. We begin by noting that the proportion of individuals who challenge, given μ, is

$$\begin{array}{ll} 1 & \text{if } \mu < \bar{s} - \psi, \\[2mm] \dfrac{\bar{s} - (\mu - \psi)}{2\psi} & \text{if } \mu \in [\bar{s} - \psi, \bar{s} + \psi], \\[2mm] 0 & \text{if } \mu > \bar{s} + \psi, \end{array} \tag{8.2}$$

which follows from the cutpoint strategy and the signal-generating process. From the perspective of an individual who has received the signal $s_i = \bar{s}$, μ is a random variable with distribution $[\bar{s} - \psi, \bar{s} + \psi]$. Thus,

$$\Pr\left(h > k \mid s_i = \bar{s}\right) = \Pr\left(\frac{\bar{s} - \mu + \psi}{2\psi} > k \mid s_i = \bar{s}\right) =$$

$$\Pr\left(\mu < \bar{s} + \psi - 2\psi k \mid s_i = \bar{s}\right) = \frac{(\bar{s} + \psi - 2\psi k) - (\bar{s} - \psi)}{2\psi} = 1 - k.$$

(The first equality uses Expression 8.2; the second is algebra; the third uses the posterior distribution of μ, given $s_i = \bar{s}$; and the fourth is algebra.) Finally, substituting this probability into Equation 8.1 gives $\bar{s} = (1 - k)\beta$.

Thus, in equilibrium, any citizen i challenges if her signal $s_i < (1 - k)\beta$ and does not challenge if $s_i > (1 - k)\beta$. As Morris and Shin (2003) demonstrate, this is the unique equilibrium. Moreover (and more strongly), it is the unique strategy consistent with common knowledge of rationality, that is, with iterated elimination of strictly dominated strategies.

Intuitively, the more citizens (k) are needed in order for regime change to take place, and the smaller the benefits (β) of that outcome, the less costly challenging must be in order for citizens to prefer taking that action.

Although finding this strategy seems to ask a lot of citizens, there is an interpretation consistent with minimal rationality: assume that h is distributed uniformly on the unit interval (so that the probability that $h > k$ is $1 - k$) and compare the expected utility of challenging and not challenging. Then the condition for any citizen i to challenge is

$$(1 - k)\beta - s_i > 0,$$

which is precisely the cutpoint strategy just derived. Morris and Shin (2003) refer to the beliefs about h in this interpretation as **Laplacian beliefs**, after Pierre-Simon Laplace's idea that the uniform prior is the natural way to represent complete ignorance.

8.3 Markov Games

In the following section, we consider political transitions that take place due to the threat of collective action. To preview that discussion, we define a discrete-time **Markov game**, which is an infinite-horizon game with the following elements:

- A set of players, indexed by i.
- A set of **states** K, where in each period t, the game is in some state $k \in K$.
- For each player i, an action space $A_i(k)$.
- A **transition function** $g\left(k^{t+1} \mid k^t, a^t\right)$, which for each state k gives the probability that the game transitions to that state in period $t{+}1$, given the state and actions taken by all players in period t.
- For each player i, preferences represented by the discounted sum of payoffs

$$\sum_{t=0}^{\infty} \delta^t u_i\left(k^t, a^t\right).$$

The key feature to note from this definition is that, in any period t, the action spaces, the transition function, and the utility functions are functions only of the state and (for g and u_i) the actions taken in that period.

	C	D
C	1,1	-1,2
D	2,-1	0,0

	C	D
C	3,3	4,0
D	0,4	1,1

Figure 8.2. The payoffs in the states PD and NPD, respectively, in the example in Section 8.3.

To illustrate, consider the following example, a simple two-player Markov game. There are two states, PD (prisoner's dilemma) and NPD (not prisoner's dilemma). In each state, each player can choose either C (cooperate) or D (defect). The game begins in the state PD. In any period in which the state is PD, if both players cooperate, then the game transitions to the state PD (i.e., remains in the same state in the following period) with probability q and to the state NPD with probability $1-q$. In any period in which the state is PD, if any player defects, then the game transitions to the state PD in the following period with certainty. Finally, once the game enters the state NPD it stays there regardless of what the players do; we say that NPD is an **absorbing state**, meaning that it transitions to itself with probability one. Thus, the transition probabilities are:

- $g\left(PD \mid PD, (C, C)\right) = q$;
- $g\left(PD \mid PD, (C, D)\right) = g\left(PD \mid PD, (D, C)\right) = g\left(PD \mid PD, (D, D)\right)$ $= 1$;
- $g\left(PD \mid NPD\right) = 0$,

with complementary probabilities for $g\left(NPD \mid .\right)$. Payoffs are given according to the payoff matrices in Figure 8.2.

We are familiar with the idea that repetition can facilitate cooperation in a repeated game through credible threats of punishment if any player defects. In this game, cooperation may be possible for a different reason: so long as each player cooperates, there is some probability that the game transitions to a state (NPD) in which cooperation is the dominant strategy. In particular, the payoff from the action profile (C, C) in the state NPD is higher than the payoff from defection in the state PD when the other player cooperates, giving players an incentive to cooperate in the state PD.

To explore this idea, we restrict attention to **Markov strategies**, in which players' actions may be conditioned only on the current state.[5]

---

[5] Our usage follows much applied work. In the game theory literature, a distinction is sometimes drawn between Markov strategies, in which actions may be conditioned

Intuitively, Markov strategies capture the idea that players' behavior is conditioned only on the payoff-relevant history of the game, as captured by the current state. A subgame-perfect Nash equilibrium in which players' strategies satisfy this condition is a **Markov perfect equilibrium**. In particular, in a Markov perfect equilibrium, the requirement of subgame perfection that players' strategies be a Nash equilibrium in every subgame reduces to the requirement that they be a Nash equilibrium in every state.

We ask whether there is a Markov perfect equilibrium in which each player plays C, whatever the state. Examine first the state NPD. Because this state is absorbing, players anticipate that whatever they do the game will be in the same state in the following period. Consequently, the value to either player (since the players are symmetric) of being in the state NPD, given that each player optimally chooses C in that state, is

$$V\left(NPD,(C,C)\right) = 3 + \delta V\left(NPD\right).$$

This **Bellman equation** expresses the idea that the value (V) of playing C whenever the state is NPD and one's opponent plays C is equal to the sum of a) the payoff from (C,C) in this period, and b) the discounted payoff of being in the state NPD in the following period, given that each player adheres to her equilibrium strategy. If it is an equilibrium for each player to play (C,C) whenever the state is NPD, then the value at the beginning of the next period is the same as the value at the beginning of the current period, that is, $V\left(NPD\right) = V\left(NPD,(C,C)\right)$. We can therefore solve for the value at the beginning of the current period as

$$V\left(NPD,(C,C)\right) = \frac{3}{1-\delta}.$$

To check that this is a best response, we need only to verify that there is no incentive to deviate to D in the current period, holding constant the equilibrium strategy profile in all subsequent periods, i.e.,

$$V\left(NPD,(C,C)\right) = \frac{3}{1-\delta} \geq 0 + \delta V\left(NPD,(C,C)\right) = \frac{3\delta}{1-\delta},$$

which clearly holds. The idea that we need only check for profitable deviations in the current period is known as Bellman's **principle of optimality**, which in game theory we learn as the **one-deviation property**.

on the current state and length of the history, and stationary Markov strategies, in which actions may be conditioned only on the current state; see, e.g., Mailath and Samuelson (2006, p. 177). When we refer to Markov strategies, stationarity is implied.

In contrast, the Bellman equation when the players optimally play (C, C) whenever the state is PD is the more complicated expression

$$V(PD, (C, C)) = 1 + \delta \left[qV(PD) + (1 - q) V(NPD) \right].$$

The payoff from the action profile (C, C) is 1 in the current period, following which the game transitions either to the state PD (with probability q) or the state NPD (with probability $(1 - q)$). In either case the value of being in that state is discounted by δ. As the value of being in the state PD in the next period is the same as that in the current period when (C, C) is always played in that state, $V(PD, (C, C))$ can be solved for as

$$V(PD, (C, C)) = \frac{1 + \delta(1 - q) V(NPD)}{1 - \delta q},$$

which is a function of the value of being in the state NPD. In the equilibrium in which the players choose (C, C) whatever the state, $V(NPD) = \frac{3}{1-\delta}$, derived earlier. Substituting in this value gives

$$V(PD, (C, C)) = \frac{1 - \delta + 3\delta(1 - q)}{(1 - \delta q)(1 - \delta)}.$$

To verify that players are playing a mutual best response (i.e., that their strategies are a Nash equilibirum in this state), we check the one-deviation property, showing that there is no incentive to deviate to D in any period when the state is PD, given that the players adhere to equilibrium strategies thereafter:

$$V(PD, (C, C)) = \frac{1 - \delta + 3\delta(1 - q)}{(1 - \delta q)(1 - \delta)} \geq 2 + \delta V(PD, (C, C)).$$

If a player deviates to D, she receives an immediate payoff of 2, following which the game transitions to the state PD with certainty, as given by the transition probabilities presented earlier. After simplifying, the condition is

$$\delta(2 - q) \geq 1.$$

Thus, it is an equilibrium for the players to play C in both states if δ is sufficiently large (so that the payoff from the eventual transition to the state NPD is more valuable) and q is sufficiently small (so that transition to the state NPD is expected to take place sooner rather than later).

8.4 Political Transitions

The discussion in Sections 8.1 and 8.2 suggests that citizens might force a regime change through collective action. An established tradition in political science, however, emphasizes that many regime changes are initiated by elites (e.g., O'Donnell, Schmitter, and Whitehead, 1986). Intuitively, collective action is costly, which implies that elites may be able to find a compromise that leaves all actors better off than if political institutions were changed by force.

Acemoglu and Robinson (2000, 2001, 2006) capture this idea by considering two types of concessions by a nondemocratic elite (the "rich") that may forestall collective action by an excluded majority (the "poor"). First, the rich can compromise on policy by redistributing to the poor whenever the latter are able to overcome their collective action problem— which is to say, not always. Second, the rich can "expand the franchise" by democratizing.

The key assumption of the Acemoglu-Robinson model is that the majority chooses policy in a democracy. Following Meltzer and Richard (1981), an expansion of the franchise therefore increases redistribution relative to what could be consistently expected in a nondemocracy. This implies that democratization is more effective than simple redistribution in preventing a revolution by the poor. A similar logic motivates Ticchi and Vindigni (2008), who show that democratization can improve war effort by the poor by increasing the credibility of post-war redistribution. In contrast, Lizzeri and Persico (2004) trace expansions of the franchise to a desire by the elite to undermine special interest politics and increase spending on public goods. Finally, Boix (2003) analyzes a model in which the poor are incompletely informed about how costly repression is to the rich. As in international relations models of war, this introduces inefficiency into the bargaining process, so that violent regime change is possible in equilibrium.

8.4.1 Dictatorship and Revolution

We begin discussion of the Acemoglu-Robinson model by building a Markov game of dictatorship and revolution, deferring for the moment the possibility that the elite democratizes as a way of credibly committing to policies preferred by the majority. In this section we show that even in a dictatorship the elite is never unconstrained in choice of policy, as on occasion the majority has the opportunity to seize power from the

elite. The knowledge that the majority has this option can spur the elite
to buy off the majority through policy compromise. However, the fact
that the elite cannot credibly promise to compromise in periods when
the majority does not pose a threat limits the extent to which the majority can be bought off, possibly leading to a revolution even when that
is worse for the elite than compromising in every period.

Consider, in particular, a Markov game in which in each period the
political system is either a dictatorship (N, for "nondemocracy") or a
post-revolutionary regime (R, for "revolution"). There is an elite (r, for
"rich") and a majority (p, for "poor"). Initially, the political system is a
dictatorship in which the rich are in control and the poor may attempt
a revolution. The key assumption of the model is that there are periods
in which the revolutionary threat is real and those in which it is not.
The Acemoglu-Robinson framework handles this in a reduced-form way
by assuming that the cost of revolution to the poor varies from period
to period, though one might alternatively assume that there are periods
in which the poor manage to overcome the collective action problem
and those in which they do not. We denote the cost of revolution (to
be defined later) by $\mu \in \{\mu^H, \mu^L\}$, where μ^H refers to a relatively *low*
cost so that the attractiveness of revolution is *high*, and μ^L refers to a
relatively high cost so that the attractiveness of revolution is low.[6]

The transition among states follows a particularly simple Markov process, in which the only action on which the transition probabilities depend is the decision of the poor to initiate a revolution or not. Figure 8.3
illustrates this process. Initially, the game is in either the state (N, μ^H)
or the state (N, μ^L). Assuming no revolution has taken place, the state
in any future period is (N, μ^H) or (N, μ^L), with probability q and $1 - q$,
respectively. However, should a revolution take place, the state transitions immediately to (R, μ), where $\mu \in \{\mu^H, \mu^L\}$ corresponds to the
state—(N, μ^H) or (N, μ^L)—at the time when revolution was initiated.
The states (R, μ^H) and (R, μ^L) are absorbing, as defined in the previous
section.

In each period in which the political system is nondemocratic, the rich
receive an income normalized to one and the poor receive no income; we
relax this assumption in the following section. The rich may redistribute
any portion $x \in [0, 1]$ of their income to the poor. Both rich and poor
are risk-neutral, and we normalize their payoffs from this policy to $1 - x$
and x, respectively. Following this decision, the poor decide whether to

---

[6] Our notation follows Acemoglu and Robinson (2000, 2001, 2006).

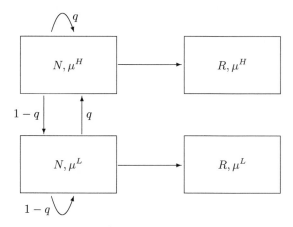

Figure 8.3. The structure of the game with dictatorship and revolution.

initiate a revolution. (We thus slightly extend the definition of Markov games from the last section to incorporate sequential decision making *within* a period.) Should the poor revolt, then the economy suffers a permanent negative productivity shock, so that total income in that and any subsequent period is $1 - \mu$, where $\mu \in \{\mu^H, \mu^L\}$ is determined by the cost of revolution at the time when the revolution took place. Any decision made by the rich about redistribution is rendered moot by revolution, and the poor receive the entirety of income produced by the economy $(1 - \mu)$ in that and all later periods. For simplicity, we assume that $\mu^L = 1$, so that only when $\mu = \mu^H < 1$ might the poor be tempted to initiate a revolution.

We are primarily interested in the following question: when are the rich able to buy off the poor and avoid a revolution? As in the previous section, we look for a Markov perfect equilibrium of the game, where players' actions may be conditioned only on the current state. Here, the restriction to Markov strategies captures in an especially simple way the idea that the rich cannot commit to pursuing redistribution in periods when the poor do not pose a revolutionary threat: because the actions of the rich may be conditioned only on the current state, any past promises are meaningless.

We begin the analysis by deriving the value to the poor of being in a post-revolutionary regime. Because proportion μ of the wealth-producing capacity of the economy is destroyed in a revolution, the payoff to the poor (which is the total income produced by the economy) in any post-revolutionary period is $1 - \mu$. Thus, the value to the poor of being in the two post-revolutionary states is

$$V_p \left(R, \mu^H \right) = \frac{1 - \mu^H}{1 - \delta},$$

$$V_p \left(R, \mu^L \right) = \frac{1 - \mu^L}{1 - \delta} = 0.$$

Clearly, the poor would never strictly prefer to initiate a revolution when the state is $\left(N, \mu^L \right)$, even when provided with nothing by the rich, as all wealth would be destroyed in the process. We say that the "revolution constraint" is not binding when the state is $\left(N, \mu^L \right)$. In this state the rich therefore optimally keep all income for themselves, choosing $x = 0$. The value to the poor of being in this state is then given by the following Bellman equation:

$$V_p \left(N, \mu^L \right) = 0 + \delta \left[q V_p \left(N, \mu^H \right) + (1 - q) V_p \left(N, \mu^L \right) \right].$$

The poor receive a payoff of zero in the current period, after which the state transitions to $\left(N, \mu^H \right)$ with probability q and to $\left(N, \mu^L \right)$ with probability $1 - q$. The value $V_p \left(N, \mu^L \right)$ can thus be solved for as

$$V_p \left(N, \mu^L \right) = \frac{\delta q V_p \left(N, \mu^H \right)}{1 - \delta (1 - q)}, \tag{8.3}$$

which is a function of the value to the poor of being in the state $\left(N, \mu^H \right)$.

In contrast, when the state is $\left(N, \mu^H \right)$, the revolution constraint is binding: the poor prefer revolution when the state is $\left(N, \mu^H \right)$ to never receiving anything from the rich:

$$\frac{1 - \mu^H}{1 - \delta} > \frac{0}{1 - \delta}.$$

Because the rich lose everything in revolution, they may try to buy off the poor through redistributive transfers in this state. The question is whether the maximum possible transfer ($x = 1$, which leaves the rich just indifferent between revolution and redistribution) is sufficient to dissuade the poor from revolting.

Let $V_p \left(N, \mu^H, x = \hat{x} \right)$ be the value to the poor when the rich choose $x = \hat{x}$ whenever the state is $\left(N, \mu^H \right)$ and the poor do not revolt:

$$V_p \left(N, \mu^H, x = \hat{x} \right) = \hat{x} + \delta \left[q V_p \left(N, \mu^H, x = \hat{x} \right) + (1 - q) V_p \left(N, \mu^L \right) \right].$$

This Bellman equation is the mirror image of that for the case when the state is (N, μ^L): the poor receive $\hat{x}$ in any period when the state is (N, μ^H), after which the state transitions to either (N, μ^H) (where again the poor receive $\hat{x}$) or (N, μ^L). Solving for $V_p(N, \mu^H, x = \hat{x})$ gives

$$V_p\left(N, \mu^H, x = \hat{x}\right) = \frac{\hat{x} + \delta\left(1 - q\right) V_p\left(N, \mu^L\right)}{1 - \delta q}. \tag{8.4}$$

Thus, the value to the poor of being in the state (N, μ^H) when the rich always transfer $\hat{x}$ in that state and the poor never initiate a revolution is a function of $V_p(N, \mu^L)$ (Equation 8.3), which is itself a function of $V_p(N, \mu^H)$. If it is an equilibrium for the rich to offer $\hat{x}$ in every period when the state is (N, μ^H) and for the poor not to revolt, then $V_p(N, \mu^H) = V_p(N, \mu^H, x = \hat{x})$ and we can use Equations 8.3 and 8.4 to solve for $V_p(N, \mu^H, x = \hat{x})$:

$$V_p\left(N, \mu^H, x = \hat{x}\right) = \hat{x}\left(\frac{1 - \delta\left(1 - q\right)}{1 - \delta}\right).$$

Given this, we can now answer the question: when will the rich be able to prevent a revolution through redistribution? The maximum possible redistribution is $x = 1$, so in order for the poor to be willing to accept whatever they are offered by the rich rather than revolting it must be the case that $V_p(N, \mu^H, x = 1) \geq V_p(R, \mu^H)$, or

$$1\left(\frac{1 - \delta\left(1 - q\right)}{1 - \delta}\right) \geq \frac{1 - \mu^H}{1 - \delta}.$$

Simplifying gives the following condition for the poor to prefer the maximum possible redistribution over revolution:

$$\mu^H \geq \delta\left(1 - q\right).$$

Trivially, a revolution can be avoided when the cost of revolution in the state (N, μ^H) is relatively high. Less obviously, the rich find it easier to avoid a revolution the *more* often the poor pose a credible revolutionary threat, that is, the higher is q. Promises to redistribute in the future are credible only if the poor expect to be in a position to extract concessions at a later date. The paradoxical conclusion is that the rich may be better off if the poor pose a frequent revolutionary threat. Finally, revolution is less likely when the discount factor δ is low, as then the poor care less about those future periods (when the state is (N, μ^L)) in which they receive nothing from the elite.

8.4.2 Inequality

In the model of the previous section only the rich had income. We now extend the model by assuming that both the rich and the poor have income, but that the income distribution is skewed toward the rich. This extension is important for what follows, where we will ask how the likelihood of dictatorship, revolution, and democracy depend on economic inequality.

Assume as before that total income is normalized to one, but that the rich receive only proportion θ of this income, with the remaining $1 - \theta$ received by the poor. The parameter θ represents income inequality. (In the model in the previous section, θ implicitly equaled one.) Further, let the proportion of the total population—normalized to mass one—that is rich be η, so that proportion $1 - \eta$ is poor. We can then define the per capita income of the rich and poor, respectively, as

$$y^r \equiv \frac{\theta}{\eta},$$

$$y^p \equiv \frac{1 - \theta}{1 - \eta}.$$

Let $\theta > \eta$, so that $y^r > y^p$, and $\eta < \frac{1}{2}$, so that the poor are more numerous than the rich. The latter assumption implies in particular that the median individual is poor, so that if policy is chosen by the median individual (as we will assume to be the case in a democracy), it will be chosen by the poor.

Further, rather than letting the rich choose a direct transfer to the poor as assumed in the previous section, assume that policy takes the form of a linear tax on pre-tax income $\tau \in [0, \bar{\tau}]$, where $\bar{\tau} \in (0, 1)$. Tax revenue is returned to individuals as a lump sum transfer; given that both total income and the population are normalized to one, the per capita transfer thus equals τ. The upper bound $\bar{\tau}$ on the tax rate captures in a reduced-form way the idea that there is a limit to how high taxes can be before individuals stop working, owners of capital stop investing, and so forth. The after-tax income of any rich citizen is thus

$$(1 - \tau) y^r + \tau = \frac{(1 - \tau) \theta + \tau \eta}{\eta},$$

whereas that for any poor citizen is

$$(1 - \tau) y^p + \tau = \frac{(1 - \tau) (1 - \theta) + \tau (1 - \eta)}{1 - \eta}.$$

We can verify that the first expression is decreasing in τ (as by assumption $\theta > \eta$), whereas the second is increasing in τ. Thus, the preferred tax rate for the rich is $\tau = 0$, whereas the preferred tax rate for the poor is $\tau = \bar{\tau}$. Further, we can define the "tax burden" on the rich—the net transfer away from the rich—as

$$\frac{\tau\theta}{\eta} - \tau,$$

which is clearly increasing in θ. Thus, for any tax rate τ, redistribution away from the rich is greater the more unequal is society. When inequality is large, the rich may therefore be more inclined to hold onto power through force (an option we consider in Section 8.4.4), rather than to redistribute or democratize.

As before, the revolution constraint is not binding when the state is (N, μ^L), so in this state the rich always choose $\tau = 0$. The value to the poor of being in this state is

$$V_p\left(N, \mu^L\right) = y^p + \delta\left[qV_p\left(N, \mu^H\right) + (1 - q)V_p\left(N, \mu^L\right)\right]$$
$$= \frac{y^p + \delta qV_p\left(N, \mu^H\right)}{1 - \delta(1 - q)}, \tag{8.5}$$

which is a function of the value of being in the state (N, μ^H). In contrast to the model in the previous section, however, the revolution constraint may or may not be binding when the state is (N, μ^H), as the poor now receive some income even when there is no redistribution. To see whether the constraint is binding, we redefine the value of revolution to the poor when the cost of revolution is μ^H to be the *per capita* payoff

$$V_p\left(R, \mu^H\right) = \frac{1 - \mu^H}{(1 - \eta)(1 - \delta)}.$$

Then the poor strictly prefer revolution to receiving no redistribution in any period if

$$\frac{1 - \mu^H}{(1 - \eta)(1 - \delta)} > \frac{y^p}{1 - \delta},$$

which, given $y^p = \frac{1-\theta}{1-\eta}$, simplifies to

$$\theta > \mu^H.$$

Intuitively, the poor are unwilling to accept the status quo of no redistribution when inequality is large (so that the poor are relatively worse off) and the cost of revolution is small. In the analysis to follow we assume that this condition holds. Further, for reasons that will be apparent, we assume that $\mu^H > \eta$, which implies that the cost of revolution is sufficiently large that for at least some levels of inequality the rich can dissuade the poor from revolting.

Assuming that the revolution constraint is binding when the state is (N, μ^H), when can the rich avoid revolution by redistributing? To answer this question, we begin by deriving the value to the poor in the state (N, μ^H) when the rich maximally redistribute whenever the revolution constraint is binding:

$$
\begin{aligned}
V_p \left(N, \mu^H, \tau = \bar{\tau} \right) \\
= y^p + (\bar{\tau} - \bar{\tau} y^p) + \delta \left[q V_p \left(N, \mu^H, \tau = \bar{\tau} \right) + (1 - q) V_p \left(N, \mu^L \right) \right] \\
= \frac{y^p + (\bar{\tau} - \bar{\tau} y^p) + \delta (1 - q) V_p \left(N, \mu^L \right)}{1 - \delta q}.
\end{aligned}
$$

In any period in which the state is (N, μ^H), the poor receive their per capita income y^p and a net transfer $(\bar{\tau} - \bar{\tau} y^p)$, following which the state transitions to either (N, μ^H) or (N, μ^L). Substituting $V_p \left(N, \mu^L \right)$ from Equation 8.5, where $V_p \left(N, \mu^H \right) = V_p \left(N, \mu^H, \tau = \bar{\tau} \right)$ in the equilibrium where the rich always choose $\tau = \bar{\tau}$ whenever the state is (N, μ^H) and the poor do not revolt, gives

$$
\begin{aligned}
V_p \left(N, \mu^H, \tau = \bar{\tau} \right) = \frac{y^p + (\bar{\tau} - \bar{\tau} y^p)}{1 - \delta q} \\
+ \frac{\delta (1 - q)}{1 - \delta q} \cdot \frac{y^p + \delta q V_p \left(N, \mu^H, \tau = \bar{\tau} \right)}{1 - \delta (1 - q)}.
\end{aligned}
$$

Multiplying through by $(1 - \delta q) [1 - \delta (1 - q)]$ gives

$$
\begin{aligned}
V_p \left(N, \mu^H, \tau = \bar{\tau} \right) (1 - \delta q) [1 - \delta (1 - q)] = \\
[1 - \delta (1 - q)] [y^p + (\bar{\tau} - \bar{\tau} y^p)] + \delta (1 - q) \left[y^p + \delta q V_p \left(N, \mu^H, \tau = \bar{\tau} \right) \right],
\end{aligned}
$$

which after simplifying is

$$
V_p \left(N, \mu^H, \tau = \bar{\tau} \right) = \frac{y^p + [1 - \delta (1 - q)] (\bar{\tau} - \bar{\tau} y^p)}{1 - \delta}.
$$

Intuitively, the poor receive y^p in every period but $(\bar{\tau} - \bar{\tau} y^p)$ only in periods when the state is (N, μ^H), which happens with probability q. As q becomes arbitrarily close to one, the value to the poor of being in the state (N, μ^H) and receiving in that state the maximal redistribution is simply the discounted value of receiving y^p plus the net transfer

$(\bar{\tau} - \bar{\tau}y^p)$ in every period:

$$\lim_{q \to 1} V_p\left(N, \mu^H, \tau = \bar{\tau}\right) = \frac{y^p + (\bar{\tau} - \bar{\tau}y^p)}{1 - \delta}.$$

As we will show, this is precisely the value to the poor in a democracy: when the poor are almost always able to threaten revolution, then the rich can credibly promise nearly as much as the poor could receive if they themselves held power.

To see whether revolution can be averted, we compare the payoff to the poor from maximal redistribution when the state is $\left(N, \mu^H\right)$ to the payoff from revolution. Redistribution is sufficient to prevent revolution when

$$V_p\left(N, \mu^H, \tau = \bar{\tau}\right) \geq V_p\left(R, \mu^H\right),$$

that is, when

$$\frac{y^p + [1 - \delta(1 - q)](\bar{\tau} - \bar{\tau}y^p)}{1 - \delta} \geq \frac{1 - \mu^H}{(1 - \eta)(1 - \delta)}.$$

Using $y^p = \frac{1-\theta}{1-\eta}$ gives, after some simplification,

$$\mu^H \geq \theta - [1 - \delta(1 - q)]\bar{\tau}(\theta - \eta).$$

Thus, as was the case in the previous section, revolution can be averted when μ^H is high, when δ is low, and when q is high. New to the model of this section, however, are three additional comparative-static results, which are perhaps easier to see if this condition is rewritten in terms of θ:

$$\theta \leq \frac{\mu^H - [1 - \delta(1 - q)]\bar{\tau}\eta}{1 - [1 - \delta(1 - q)]\bar{\tau}}. \tag{8.6}$$

(Note that the right-hand side of this expression is strictly greater than η if $\mu^H > \eta$, which we have assumed. Thus, for some $\theta > \eta$ the condition is satisfied.)

- Revolution is easier to avert when inequality θ is low. Intuitively, that there are limits to redistribution matters more to the poor when there is greater inequality, thus making revolution relatively more attractive.
- Revolution is easier to avert when tax evasion is more difficult (i.e., when $\bar{\tau}$ is high), as then more may be redistributed to the poor.
- Revolution is easier to avert when the proportion η of the population that is rich is small, as then the gains from revolution must be

divided among a larger population of poor individuals. (The same is true, of course, for redistributed funds, but this is outweighed in the model by the effect of dividing the spoils of revolution.)

8.4.3 Democratization

As shown in the previous section, the rich are limited in their ability to redistribute to the poor and prevent revolution, in part because any promises to redistribute in future periods when the poor do not pose a threat are not credible. Democratization is a solution to this commitment problem. Policies can easily be reversed, but institutions are sticky. Thus, an expansion of the franchise to include the poor can solve the commitment problem of the rich.

We extend the model as shown in Figure 8.4. Rather than redistributing, the rich may choose to democratize. We assume that the median individual chooses policy in a democracy; because the median individual is poor, this means that democratization transfers control over policy from the rich to the poor. Once democratization has occurred, the political system may not revert to dictatorship (this possibility is examined in Acemoglu and Robinson, 2001, 2006), though the poor may initiate a revolution. Thus, democratization—like redistribution—must be preferable for the poor to revolution.

What is value to the poor of democracy? With policy chosen by the median (poor) individual, the tax rate is $\bar{\tau}$ in every period, so that

$$V_p(D) = \frac{(1-\bar{\tau})y^p + \bar{\tau}}{1-\delta}.$$

Each period the poor are taxed at the rate $\tau = \bar{\tau}$, and receive the lump sum transfer $\bar{\tau}$. As noted in the previous section, this is precisely what the rich can credibly promise to the poor in a dictatorship as the probability q that the state transitions to (N, μ^H) in any period becomes arbitrarily large. Thus, democratization is more useful to the rich as a commitment mechanism when the poor are not typically able to threaten revolution, that is, when q is small.

The poor prefer democracy to revolution when

$$V_p(D) \geq V_p(R, \mu^H),$$

that is, when

$$\frac{(1-\bar{\tau})y^p + \bar{\tau}}{1-\delta} \geq \frac{1-\mu^H}{(1-\eta)(1-\delta)}.$$

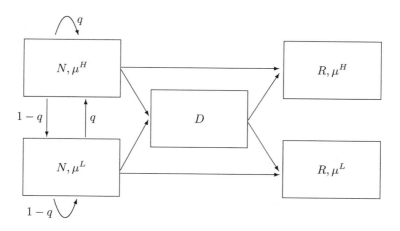

Figure 8.4. The structure of the game with democratization.

As before, this condition may be written in terms of θ:

$$\theta \le \frac{\mu^H - \bar{\tau}\eta}{1 - \bar{\tau}}. \tag{8.7}$$

Note that the right-hand term in Condition 8.7 is larger than that in Condition 8.6 given the assumption that $\mu^H > \eta$.

With these conditions in hand, we can explore the relationship between democratization and inequality, as captured by the parameter θ, the proportion of income received by the rich:

- When $\theta \le \mu^H$, the revolution constraint is not binding in any period, so that the poor are content with no redistribution.
- When $\mu^H < \theta \le \frac{\mu^H - [1-\delta(1-q)]\bar{\tau}\eta}{1-[1-\delta(1-q)]\bar{\tau}}$, the rich buy off the poor through redistribution.
- When $\frac{\mu^H - [1-\delta(1-q)]\bar{\tau}\eta}{1-[1-\delta(1-q)]\bar{\tau}} < \theta \le \frac{\mu^H - \bar{\tau}\eta}{1-\bar{\tau}}$, redistribution is insufficient to prevent revolution and the rich democratize.
- When $\theta > \frac{\mu^H - \bar{\tau}\eta}{1-\bar{\tau}}$, not even democracy is sufficient to prevent revolution, so the poor revolt.

Thus, democratization occurs only when the level of inequality is moderately high. When inequality is low, the poor are either content with no redistribution or can be bought off through periodic redistribution.

When inequality is high, the gains from revolution outweigh even what the poor receive in a democracy, so that revolution is unavoidable.

What this analysis perhaps misses is that democratization is more costly to the rich when inequality is high. Thus, when inequality is high, the rich may choose to hang onto power by force, if that option is available. The following section explores this possibility.

8.4.4 Repression

To incorporate the possibility that the rich hang onto power by force, assume that in any period the rich can choose to repress at cost $\phi > 0$. If the rich repress, revolution is impossible in the current period. There is no direct impact of repression on the players' payoffs or action spaces in future periods.

Given the cost, the rich never repress when the state is (N, μ^L), as in that state the revolution constraint is not binding. However, when the state is (N, μ^H), the rich may choose to repress. Let $V_r(N, \mu^H, O)$ be the value to the rich from repressing (where O signifies "oppress") whenever the state is (N, μ^H):

$$V_r\left(N, \mu^H, O\right) = y^r - \phi + \delta \left[q V_r\left(N, \mu^H, O\right) + (1 - q) V_r\left(N, \mu^L\right)\right].$$

Employing the same sort of substitution as before gives

$$V_r\left(N, \mu^H, O\right) = \frac{y^r - [1 - \delta(1 - q)]\phi}{1 - \delta},$$

which says that the rich receive y^r in every period and lose ϕ in those periods when the state is (N, μ^H).

The rich therefore prefer repression to democratization when

$$V_r\left(N, \mu^H, O\right) > V_r(D),$$

that is, when

$$\frac{y^r - [1 - \delta(1 - q)]\phi}{1 - \delta} > \frac{y^r + (\bar{\tau} - \bar{\tau} y^r)}{1 - \delta}.$$

The right-hand side of the inequality uses the fact that in a democracy the rich are taxed at the maximum possible tax rate in each period. Simplifying gives

$$\phi < \frac{\bar{\tau}(\theta - \eta)}{[1 - \delta(1 - q)]\eta}.$$

The expression on the right-hand side of the inequality is increasing in θ:

as inequality increases, democratization becomes more costly to the rich, so that they are more likely to hang onto power by force. Of course, the rich also prefer repression to revolution, as they lose everything in revolution. Thus, when inequality is high, either the rich repress rather than democratize, or they repress in order to avoid a revolution that (because inequality is high) cannot be prevented through democratization.

Exercise 8.3 considers the analogous choice between repression and redistribution.

Exercises

8.1 Consider the following model of collective action under complete information. There are N citizens, indexed by i, where N is arbitrarily large. The benefit from challenging is $\beta > 0$ for all citizens. The cost of challenging is idiosyncratic, though related to the number of citizens who challenge. In particular, for citizen i, the cost of challenging is $i + \frac{\mu}{M}$ when M citizens challenge, where the parameter $\mu > 0$. The idiosyncratic component of the cost (i) may represent psychological factors or the opportunity cost of time spent challenging. The common component $\left(\frac{\mu}{M}\right)$ can be interpreted as follows: any citizen who challenges faces the possibility of being punished by the regime, where the probability of punishment is inversely proportional to the number of citizens who challenge. As a function of β and μ, how many citizens challenge in equilibrium?

8.2 Consider the following variant of the model of Section 8.2. For each citizen, the cost of challenging is zero if more than k citizens challenge, and $\mu > 0$ otherwise. The parameters μ and k are common knowledge. In contrast, citizens have private but correlated benefits of challenging the regime $s_i = \beta + \epsilon_i$, where citizens have a common prior belief that β is distributed uniformly on the real number line and ϵ_i is drawn from a uniform distribution with support $[-\psi, \psi]$.

In equilibrium, each citizen i challenges if $s_i > \bar{s}$, where $\bar{s}$ is some common cutpoint, and does not challenge if $s_i < \bar{s}$. Following the procedure outlined at the end of Section 8.2, find $\bar{s}$ by applying a Laplacian prior to the proportion of individuals who challenge.

8.3 Consider the environment described in Sections 8.4.2 and 8.4.4.

(a) Assume that Condition 8.6 holds. Solve for the tax rate τ_H that leaves the poor just indifferent between revolting and not revolting when the state is $\left(N, \mu^H\right)$.

(b) Derive $V_r\left(N, \mu^H, \tau = \tau_H\right)$, the value to the rich in the state $\left(N, \mu^H\right)$ if they always choose τ_H in that state and the poor never revolt.

(c) Now compare $V_r\left(N, \mu^H, \tau = \tau_H\right)$ to $V_r\left(N, \mu^H, O\right)$, the value to the rich in the state $\left(N, \mu^H\right)$ if they always repress in that state. How, if at all, does income inequality θ affect the choice between redistribution and repression?

8.4   Consider the following extension of the Acemoglu-Robinson model. As before, the rich choose the tax rate in a nondemocracy. In a democracy, the tax rate is chosen by a politician who values the welfare of the poor but may be lobbied by the rich. With some modification of the policy environment as presented earlier, we model this process using the approach of Section 3.4:

- In either a nondemocracy or a democracy, the tax rate τ may take any value in $[0, 1]$, where there is a deadweight loss of taxation of $\frac{\omega}{2}\tau^2$, with $\omega > \theta$. Net tax revenue is returned as a lump sum transfer to poor residents only. Thus, the transfer paid to any poor citizen is

$$\frac{\tau - \frac{\omega}{2}\tau^2}{1 - \eta}.$$

- In each period that the state is a democracy, a lobby representing the rich names a contribution function $C\left(\tau\right)$, credibly promising a particular contribution $C \geq 0$ to the politician for every tax rate $\tau \in [0, 1]$ that the politician could choose.
- The lobby maximizes the aggregate welfare of the rich, represented by the expression

$$\eta\left(1 - \tau\right)y^r - C.$$

- The politician values both the welfare of the poor and contributions, with preferences represented by

$$\gamma\left(1 - \eta\right)\left[\left(1 - \tau\right)y^p + \left(\frac{\tau - \frac{\omega}{2}\tau^2}{1 - \eta}\right)\right] + C,$$

where $\gamma > 1$. Implicitly, the parameter γ measures the influence of the poor in a democracy.

Analyze the impact of lobbying in a democracy as follows:

(a) Derive τ_D, the equilibrium tax rate in a democracy. How does τ_D depend on various parameters of the model?

(b) Using your answer to part (a), derive $V_p(D)$, the value of democracy to any poor citizen.

(c) Using your answer to part (b), derive the condition for the poor to prefer democracy to revolution.

(d) How does the likelihood of democratization depend on γ, which measures the influence of the poor in a democracy? If the rich had control over γ (e.g., through control of the constitutional process during a political transition), what γ would they choose upon democratizing?

8.5 Consider the following extension to the Acemoglu-Robinson model of political transitions, which is based on Dunning (2008). The environment is identical to that in Sections 8.4.2–8.4.4, but for the following differences:

- Whichever group is in power chooses a tax rate $\tau \in [0,1]$.
- Total government spending is $g = \tau + R$, where R is an exogenous resource rent under the control of the government.
- Government spending is devoted entirely to a public good that benefits all citizens, where the payoff from public goods spending g is equal to $\ln(g)$. Thus, any citizen i receives a payoff from policy τ of $(1-\tau)y^i + \ln(\tau + R)$, where y^i is citizen i's pre-tax income.

To focus on the interesting case, assume $\frac{1}{y^r} < R < \frac{1}{y^p} < 1 + R$.

(a) Show that the rich most prefer $\tau = 0$ if unconstrained by the possibility of revolution.

(b) Derive the tax rate τ_p most preferred by the poor.

(c) Derive $V_r(D)$, the value of democracy to any rich citizen.

(d) Derive $V_r(N, \mu^H, O)$, the value to the rich if they repress when the state is (N, μ^H).

(e) Do resource rents increase or decrease the attractiveness to the rich of democratization, relative to repression? Interpret your result.

8.6 This problem analyzes political conflict in Ukraine in 2004 using a stylized variant of the Acemoglu-Robinson model. Power is contested by Leonid Kuchma (K), through his chosen successor Viktor Yanukovich, and Viktor Yushchenko (Y). At the beginning of the game Kuchma is in power. Assume that in every period that Kuchma is in power he chooses some policy $x \in [0,1]$, where

Kuchma and Yushchenko receive payoffs from x of

$$U_K = x - 1,$$
$$U_Y = -x,$$

respectively. Thus, Kuchma has an ideal point of 1 and Yushchenko has an ideal point of 0. Kuchma and Yushchenko discount future payoffs according to the common discount factor δ.

Assume that Kuchma can be removed from power only by an "orange revolution." In each period in which Kuchma is in power, the cost to Yushchenko of initiating an orange revolution is $\mu \in \{\mu^C, \mu^W\}$, where μ^C is the cost of organizing street protests when the weather is cold and μ^W is the cost when the weather is warm, with $\mu^C > \mu^W > 0$. Assume for the sake of simplicity that μ^C is prohibitively high, so that an orange revolution never occurs when the weather is cold. Every warm period is followed by a cold period with probability one, and every cold period is followed by a warm period with probability one.

If there is an orange revolution, then policy immediately and permanently switches to $x = \bar{x}$, where $\bar{x} \in (0, 1)$. Thus, an orange revolution leads to some policy that falls between Kuchma's and Yushchenko's ideal points. Further (and in contrast to the Acemoglu-Robinson model), assume that the cost of revolution is borne only in the period in which it occurs.

We represent the game graphically in Figure 8.5, where (K, μ) refers to the state when Kuchma is in power and the cost of revolution is μ, and R is the absorbing state when there has been a revolution.

Explore the possibility that Kuchma avoids an orange revolution by looking for a Markov perfect equilibrium of the game, as follows:

(a) Write down the Bellman equation for Yushchenko in state (K, μ^C).

(b) Derive the condition for the revolution constraint to be binding when $\mu = \mu^W$, that is, for Yushchenko to prefer revolution to always receiving Kuchma's most-preferred policy.

(c) Write down the Bellman equation for Yushchenko in state (K, μ^W) when Kuchma sets policy equal to some $x = \hat{x}$ whenever $\mu = \mu^W$ and Yushchenko never initiates an orange revolution.

(d) Assume that the revolution constraint is binding. Derive the

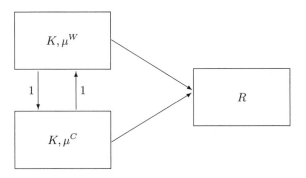

Figure 8.5. The structure of the game in Exercise 8.6.

condition for it to be possible for Kuchma to avoid an orange revolution by offering $x = 0$ whenever $\mu = \mu^W$. Explain how your result depends on parameters of the model.

(e) Will Kuchma always want to avoid a revolution when that is possible? Explain.

(f) Implicitly, this is a model where winter and summer each last for six months. Discuss how the model might be modified to account for a longer winter or summer, and how this would affect your results.

References

Acemoglu, Daron, and Robinson, James A. 2000. Why Did the West Expand the Franchise? Growth, Inequality and Democracy in Historical Perspective. *Quarterly Journal of Economics*, **115**(4), 1167–1199.

Acemoglu, Daron, and Robinson, James A. 2001. A Theory of Political Transitions. *American Economic Review*, **91**(4), 938–963.

Acemoglu, Daron, and Robinson, James A. 2006. *Economic Origins of Dictatorship and Democracy*. Cambridge: Cambridge University Press.

Adams, James F., Merrill III, Samuel, and Grofman, Bernard. 2005. *A Unified Theory of Party Competition*. Cambridge: Cambridge University Press.

Aghion, Philippe, and Tirole, Jean. 1997. Formal and Real Authority in Organizations. *Journal of Political Economy*, **105**(1), 1–29.

Aldrich, John H. 1995. *Why Parties? The Origin and Transformation of Political Parties in America*. Chicago: University of Chicago Press.

Alesina, Alberto, and Spear, Stephen E. 1988. An Overlapping Generations Model of Electoral Competition. *Journal of Public Economics*, **37**(3), 359–379.

Ansolabehere, Steven, de Figueiredo, John M., and Snyder, James M. 2003. Why Is There So Little Money in U.S. Politics? *Journal of Economic Perspectives*, **17**(1), 105–130.

Ashworth, Scott. 2006. Campaign Finance and Voter Welfare with Entrenched Incumbents. *American Political Science Review*, **100**(1), 55–68.

Ashworth, Scott, and Bueno de Mesquita, Ethan. 2009. Elections with Platform and Valence Competition. *Games and Economic Behavior*, **67**(1), 191–216.

Austen-Smith, David. 1987. Interest Groups, Campaign Contributions, and Probabilistic Voting. *Public Choice*, **54**(2), 123–139.

Austen-Smith, David, and Banks, Jeffrey S. 1988. Elections, Coalitions, and Legislative Outcomes. *American Political Science Review*, **82**(2), 405–422.

Austen-Smith, David, and Banks, Jeffrey S. 1989. Electoral Accountability and Incumbency. In Ordeshook, Peter (ed.), *Models of Strategic Choice in Politics*. Ann Arbor: University of Michigan Press.

Austen-Smith, David, and Banks, Jeffrey S. 1990. Stable Governments and the Allocation of Policy Portfiolios. *American Political Science Review*, **84**(3), 891–906.

Austen-Smith, David, and Banks, Jeffrey S. 1999. *Positive Political Theory I: Collective Preference*. Ann Arbor: University of Michigan Press.

Austen-Smith, David, and Banks, Jeffrey S. 2005. *Positive Political Theory II: Strategy and Structure*. Ann Arbor: University of Michigan Press.

Banks, Jeffrey S. 1990. Monopoly Agenda Control and Asymmetric Information. *Quarterly Journal of Economics*, **105**(2), 445–464.

Banks, Jeffrey S. 2000. Buying Supermajorities in Finite Legislatures. *American Political Science Review*, **94**(3), 677–681.

Banks, Jeffrey S., and Duggan, John. 2000. A Bargaining Model of Collective Choice. *American Political Science Review*, **94**(1), 73–88.

Banks, Jeffrey S., and Duggan, John. 2006a. A General Bargaining Model of Legislative Policy-making. *Quarterly Journal of Political Science*, **1**(1), 49–85.

Banks, Jeffrey S., and Duggan, John. 2006b. A Social Choice Lemma on Voting over Lotteries with Applications to a Class of Dynamic Games. *Social Choice and Welfare*, **26**(2), 285–304.

Banks, Jeffrey S., and Sundaram, Rangarajan. 1993. Adverse Selection and Moral Hazard in a Repeated Elections Model. In Barnett, William A., Hinich, Melvin J., and Schofield, Norman J. (eds.), *Political Economy: Institutions, Competition, and Representation*. New York: Cambridge University Press.

Baron, David P. 1994. Electoral Competition with Informed and Uninformed Voters. *American Political Science Review*, **88**(1), 33–47.

Baron, David P., and Diermeier, Daniel. 2001. Elections, Governments, and Parliaments in Proportional Representation Systems. *Quarterly Journal of Economics*, **116**(3), 933–967.

Baron, David P., and Ferejohn, John A. 1989. Bargaining in Legislatures. *American Political Science Review*, **83**(4), 1181–1206.

Barro, Robert. 1973. The Control of Politicians: An Economic Model. *Public Choice*, **14**(1), 19–42.

Barry, Brian. 1978. *Sociologists, Economists, and Democracy*. Chicago: University of Chicago Press.

Bawn, Kathleen. 1995. Political Control versus Expertise: Congressional Choices about Administrative Procedures. *American Political Science Review*, **89**(1), 62–73.

Beck, Thorsten, Clarke, George, Groff, Alberto, Keefer, Philip, and Walsh, Patrick. 2001. New Tools in Comparative Political Economy: The Database of Political Institutions. *World Bank Economic Review*, **15**(1), 165–176.

Bendor, Jonathan, and Meirowitz, Adam. 2004. Spatial Models of Delegation. *American Political Science Review*, **98**(2), 293–310.

Bendor, Jonathan, Glazer, Ami, and Hammond, Thomas H. 2001. Theories of Delegation. *Annual Review of Political Science*, **4**, 235–269.

Bernhardt, Dan, Duggan, John, and Squintani, Francesco. 2009. The Case for Responsible Parties. *American Political Science Review*, **103**(4), 570–587.

Bernheim, Douglas B., and Whinston, Michael D. 1986. Menu Auctions, Resource Allocation, and Economic Influence. *Quarterly Journal of Economics*, **101**(1), 1–31.

Besley, Timothy. 2006. *Principled Agents?* Oxford: Oxford University Press.

Besley, Timothy, and Coate, Stephen. 1997. An Economic Model of Representative Democracy. *Quarterly Journal of Economics*, **112**(1), 85–114.

Besley, Timothy, and Coate, Stephen. 2001. Lobbying and Welfare in a Representative Democracy. *Review of Economic Studies*, **68**(1), 67–82.

Black, Duncan. 1948. On the Rationale of Group Decision Making. *Journal of Political Economy*, **56**(1), 23–34.

Boardman, Anthony E., Greenberg, David H., Vining, Aidan R., and Weimer, David L. 2010. *Cost-Benefit Analysis: Concepts and Practice*. Upper Saddle River, NJ: Prentice-Hall.

Boix, Carles. 2003. *Democracy and Redistribution*. Cambridge: Cambridge University Press.

Boix, Carles, and Svolik, Milan W. 2012. The Foundations of Limited Authoritarian Government: Institutions and Power-sharing in Dictatorships. *Journal of Politics*, **Forthcoming**.

Brady, David W., and Volden, Craig. 1998. *Revolving Gridlock: Politics and Policy from Carter to Clinton*. Boulder, CO: Westview Press.

Brown, J. David, Earle, John S., and Gehlbach, Scott. 2009. Helping Hand or Grabbing Hand? State Bureaucracy and Privatization Effectiveness. *American Political Science Review*, **103**(2), 264–283.

Brym, Robert J., and Gimpelson, Vladimir. 2004. The Size, Composition, and Dynamics of the Russian State Bureaucracy in the 1990s. *Slavic Review*, **63**(1), 90–112.

Buchanan, James M., and Tullock, Gordon. 1962. *The Calculus of Consent*. Ann Arbor: University of Michigan Press.

Bueno de Mesquita, Bruce, Morrow, James D., Siverson, Randolph M., and Smith, Alastair. 1999. An Institutional Explanation of the Democratic Peace. *American Political Science Review*, **93**(4), 791–807.

Bueno de Mesquita, Bruce, Morrow, James D., Siverson, Randolph M., and Smith, Alastair. 2002. Political Institutions, Policy Choice and the Survival of Leaders. *British Journal of Political Science*, **32**(4), 559–590.

Bueno de Mesquita, Bruce, Smith, Alastair, Siverson, Randolph M., and Morrow, James D. 2003. *The Logic of Political Survival*. Cambridge, MA: MIT Press.

Bueno de Mesquita, Ethan. 2010. Regime Change and Revolutionary Entrepreneurs. *American Political Science Review*, **104**(3), 446–466.

Callander, Steven. 2005. Duverger's Hypothesis, the Run-Off Rule, and Electoral Competition. *Political Analysis*, **13**(3), 209–232.

Callander, Steven. 2008a. Political Motivations. *Review of Economic Studies*, **75**(3), 671–697.

Callander, Steven. 2008b. A Theory of Policy Expertise. *Quarterly Journal of Political Science*, **3**(2), 123–140.

Calvert, Randall L. 1985. Robustness of the Multidimensional Voting Model: Candidate Motivations, Uncertainty, and Convergence. *American Journal of Political Science*, **29**(1), 69–95.

Calvert, Randall L., McCubbins, Mathew D., and Weingast, Barry R. 1989. A Theory of Political Control and Agency Discretion. *American Journal of Political Science*, **33**(3), 588–611.

Cameron, Charles M. 2000. *Veto Bargaining: Presidents and the Politics of Negative Power*. New York: Cambridge University Press.

Canes-Wrone, Brandice, Herron, Michael C., and Shotts, Kenneth W. 2001. Leadership and Pandering: A Theory of Executive Policymaking. *American Journal of Political Science*, **45**(3), 532–550.

Carlsson, Hans, and van Damme, Eric. 1993. Global Games and Equilibrium Selection. *Econometrica*, **61**(5), 989–1018.

Cho, In-Koo, and Kreps, David. 1987. Signaling Games and Stable Equilibria. *Quarterly Journal of Economics*, **102**(2), 179–221.

Cho, Seok-ju, and Duggan, John. 2003. Uniqueness of Stationary Equilibria in a One-Dimensional Model of Bargaining. *Journal of Economic Theory*, **113**(1), 118–130.

Coase, Ronald. 1937. The Nature of the Firm. *Economica*, **4**(16), 386–405.

Coase, Ronald. 1960. The Problem of Social Cost. *Journal of Law and Economics*, **3**, 1–31.

Coate, Stephen. 2004. Pareto-Improving Campaign Finance Policy. *American Economic Review*, **94**(3), 628–655.

Coughlin, Peter. 1992. *Probabilistic Voting Theory*. New York: Cambridge University Press.

Coughlin, Peter, and Nitzan, Shmuel. 1981. Electoral Outcomes with Probabilistic Voting and Nash Social Welfare Maxima. *Journal of Public Economics*, **15**(1), 113–121.

Cox, Gary W. 1987a. Duverger's Law and Strategic Voting. Unpublished manuscript.

Cox, Gary W. 1987b. Electoral Equilibrium under Alternative Voting Institutions. *American Journal of Political Science*, **31**(1), 82–108.

Cox, Gary W. 1997. *Making Votes Count: Strategic Coordination in the World's Electoral Systems*. New York: Cambridge University Press.

Cox, Gary W., and McCubbins, Mathew D. 1994. *Legislative Leviathan: Party Government in the House*. Berkeley: University of California Press.

Cox, Gary W., and McCubbins, Mathew D. 2005. *Setting the Agenda: Responsible Party Government in the U.S. House of Representatives*. Cambridge: Cambridge University Press.

Crawford, Vincent P., and Sobel, Joel. 1982. Strategic Information Transmission. *Econometrica*, **50**(6), 1431–1451.

Crombez, Christophe, Groseclose, Tim, and Krehbiel, Keith. 2006. Gatekeeping. *Journal of Politics*, **68**(2), 322–334.

Dal Bó, Ernesto. 2007. Bribing Voters. *American Journal of Political Science*, **51**(4), 789–803.

Denzau, Arthur T., and Mackay, Robert J. 1983. Gatekeeping and Monopoly Power of Committees. *American Journal of Political Science*, **27**(4), 740–761.

Dewan, Torun, and Spirling, Arthur. 2011. Strategic Opposition and Government Cohesion in Westminster Democracies. *American Political Science Review*, **105**(2), 337–358.

Diermeier, Daniel, and Feddersen, Timothy J. 1998. Cohesion in Legislatures and the Vote of Confidence Procedure. *American Political Science Review*, **92**(3), 611–621.

Diermeier, Daniel, and Merlo, Antonio. 2004. An Empirical Investigation of Coalitional Bargaining Procedures. *Journal of Public Economics*, **88**(3-4), 783–797.

Dixit, Avinash, and Londregan, John. 1996. The Determinants of Success of Special Interests in Redistributive Politics. *Journal of Politics*, **58**(4), 1132–1155.

Downs, Anthony. 1957. *An Economic Theory of Democracy*. New York: Harper and Row.

Dunning, Thad. 2008. *Crude Democracy: Natural Resource Wealth and Political Regimes*. New York: Cambridge University Press.

Duverger, Maurice. 1954. *Political Parties: Their Organization and Activity in the Modern State*. New York: Wiley.

Edmond, Chris. 2008. Information Manipulation, Coordination, and Regime Change. Unpublished manuscript.

Eguia, Jon X. 2007. Citizen Candidates under Uncertainty. *Social Choice and Welfare*, **29**(2), 317–331.

Elkins, Zachary, Ginsburg, Tom, and Melton, James. 2009. *The Endurance of National Constitutions*. New York: Cambridge University Press.

Enelow, James M., and Hinich, Melvin J. 1982. Nonspatial Candidate Characteristics and Electoral Competition. *Journal of Politics*, **44**(1), 115–130.

Epstein, David, and O'Halloran, Sharyn. 1994. Administraive Procedures, Information, and Agency Discretion. *American Journal of Political Science*, **38**(3), 697–722.

Epstein, David, and O'Halloran, Sharyn. 1999. *Delegating Powers: A Transaction Cost Politics Approach to Policy Making under Separate Powers*. New York: Cambridge University Press.

Eraslan, Hülya. 2002. Uniqueness of Stationary Equilibrium Payoffs in the Baron-Ferejohn Model. *Journal of Economic Theory*, **103**(1), 11–30.

Evans, Peter, and Rauch, James E. 1999. Bureaucracy and Growth: A Cross-National Analysis of the Effects of 'Weberian' State Structures on Economic Growth. *American Sociological Review*, **64**(5), 748–765.

Fearon, James D. 1999. Electoral Accountability and the Control of Politicians: Selecting Good Types versus Sanctioning Poor Performance. In Przeworski, Adam, Stokes, Susan C., and Manin, Bernard (eds.), *Democracy, Accountability, and Representation*. New York: Cambridge University Press.

Fearon, James D. 2011. Self-Enforcing Democracy. *Quarterly Journal of Economics*, **126**(4), 1661–1708.

Feddersen, Timothy J., Sened, Itai, and Wright, Stephen G. 1990. Rational Voting and Candidate Entry under Plurality Rule. *American Journal of Political Science*, **34**(4), 1005–1016.

Ferejohn, John A. 1986. Incumbent Performance and Electoral Control. *Public Choice*, **50**(1–3), 5–26.

Fey, Mark. 1997. Stability and Coordination in Duverger's Law: A Formal Model of Preelection Polls and Strategic Voting. *American Political Science Review*, **91**(1), 135–147.

Fiorina, Morris P. 1981. *Retrospective Voting in American National Elections*. New Haven, CT: Yale University Press.

Fox, Justin, and Shotts, Kenneth W. 2009. Delegates or Trustees? A Theory of Political Accountability. *Journal of Politics*, **71**(4), 1225–1237.

Gailmard, Sean. 2009. Discretion rather than Rules: Choice of Instruments to Control Bureaucratic Policy Making. *Political Analysis*, **17**(1), 25–44.

Gailmard, Sean, and Patty, John W. 2007. Slackers and Zealots: Civil Service, Policy Discretion, and Bureaucratic Expertise. *American Journal of Political Science*, **51**(4), 873–889.

Gans, Joshua S., and Smart, Michael. 1996. Majority Voting with Single-Crossing Preferences. *Journal of Public Economics*, **59**(2), 219–237.

Gehlbach, Scott. 2007. Electoral Institutions and the National Provision of Local Public Goods. *Quarterly Journal of Political Science*, **2**(1), 5–25.

Gehlbach, Scott, and Keefer, Philip. 2011. Investment without Democracy: Ruling-Party Institutionalization and Credible Commitment in Autocracies. *Journal of Comparative Economics*, **39**(2), 123–139.

Gehlbach, Scott, and Malesky, Edmund J. 2010. The Contribution of Veto Players to Economic Reform. *Journal of Politics*, **72**(4), 957–975.

Gehlbach, Scott, Sonin, Konstantin, and Zhuravskaya, Ekaterina. 2010. Businessman Candidates. *American Journal of Political Science*, **54**(3), 718–736.

Gerber, Alan. 1996. *Rational Voters, Candidate Spending, and Incomplete Information: A Theoretical Analysis with Implications for Campaign Finance Reform*. Working paper, Institution for Social and Policy Studies.

Gerber, Elizabeth R., Lupia, Arthur, and McCubbins, Mathew D. 2004. When Does Government Limit the Impact of Voter Initiatives? The Politics of Implementation and Enforcement. *Journal of Politics*, **66**(1), 43–68.

Gilligan, Thomas W., and Krehbiel, Keith. 1987. Collective Decisionmaking and Standing Committees: An Informational Rationale for Restrictive Amendment Procedures. *Journal of Law, Economics, and Organization*, **3**(2), 287–335.

Green, Donald, and Shapiro, Ian. 1996. *Pathologies of Rational Choice: A Critique of Applications in Political Science*. New Haven, CT: Yale University Press.

Groseclose, Tim, and Snyder, James M. 1996. Buying Supermajorities. *American Political Science Review*, **90**(2), 303–315.

Groseclose, Tim, and Snyder, James M. 2000. Vote Buying, Supermajorities, and Flooded Coalitions. *American Political Science Review*, **94**(3), 683–684.

Grossman, Gene M., and Helpman, Elhanan. 1994. Protection for Sale. *American Economic Review*, **84**(4), 833–850.

Grossman, Gene M., and Helpman, Elhanan. 1996. Electoral Competition and Special Interest Politics. *Review of Economic Studies*, **63**(2), 265–286.

Grossman, Gene M., and Helpman, Elhanan. 2001. *Special Interest Politics*. Cambridge, MA: MIT Press.

Hellman, Joel S. 1998. Winners Take All: The Politics of Partial Reform in Postcommunist Transitions. *World Politics*, **50**(2), 203–234.

Henisz, Witold J. 2000. The Institutional Environment for Economic Growth. *Economics and Politics*, **12**(1), 1–31.

Hinich, Melvin J. 1977. Equilibrium in Spatial Voting: The Median Voter Result Is an Artifact. *Journal of Economic Theory*, **16**(2), 208–219.

Hinich, Melvin J., Ledyard, John O., and Ordeshook, Peter C. 1972. Nonvoting and the Existence of Equilibrium under Majority Rule. *Journal of Economic Theory*, **4**(2), 144–153.

Holmström, Bengt. 1982. Managerial Incentive Problems - A Dynamic Perspective. In *Essays in Economics and Management in Honor of Lars Wahlbeck*. Helsinki: Swedish School of Economics.

Horn, Murray J., and Shepsle, Kenneth A. 1989. Commentary on 'Administrative Arrangements and the Political Control of Agencies': Administrative Process and Organizational Form as Legislative Responses to Agency Costs. *Virginia Law Review*, **75**(2), 499–508.

Hotelling, Harold. 1929. Stability in Competition. *Economic Journal*, **39**(153), 41–57.

Huber, John D. 1996. The Vote of Confidence in Parliamentary Democracies. *American Political Science Review*, **90**(2), 269–282.

Huber, John D., and McCarty, Nolan. 2004. Bureaucratic Capacity, Delegation, and Political Reform. *American Political Science Review*, **98**(3), 481–494.

Huber, John D., and Shipan, Charles R. 2002. *Deliberate Discretion? The Institutional Foundations of Bureaucratic Autonomy*. New York: Cambridge University Press.

Keech, William R. 1995. *Economic Politics: The Costs of Democracy*. New York: Cambridge University Press.

Keefer, Philip. 2007. Clientelism, Credibility, and the Policy Choices of Young Democracies. *American Journal of Political Science*, **51**(4), 804–821.

Keefer, Philip, and Stasavage, David. 2003. The Limits of Delegation: Veto Players, Central Bank Independence, and the Credibility of Monetary Policy. *American Political Science Review*, **97**(3), 407–423.

Key, V. O. 1966. *The Responsible Electorate: Rationality in Presidential Voting 1936–1960*. Cambridge, MA: Belknap Press.

Krehbiel, Keith. 1998. *Pivotal Politics: A Theory of U.S. Lawmaking*. Chicago: University of Chicago Press.

Krishna, Vijay, and Morgan, John. 2001. Asymmetric Information and Legislative Rules: Some Amendments. *American Political Science Review*, **95**(2), 435–452.

Kuran, Timur. 1991a. The East European Revolution of 1989: Is It Surprising that We Were Surprised? *American Economic Review,* **81**(2), 121–125.

Kuran, Timur. 1991b. Now Out of Never: The Element of Surprise in the East European Revolution of 1989. *World Politics,* **44**(1), 7–48.

Laver, Michael, and Shepsle, Kenneth A. 1990. Coalitions and Cabinet Government. *American Political Science Review,* **84**(3), 873–890.

Laver, Michael, and Shepsle, Kenneth A. 1996. *Making and Breaking Governments: Cabinets and Legislatures in Parliamentary Democracies.* Cambridge: Cambridge University Press.

Lin, Tse-Min, Enelow, James M., and Durussen, Han. 1999. Equilibrium in Multicandidate Probabilistic Spatial Voting. *Public Choice,* **98**(1–2), 59–82.

Lindbeck, Assar, and Weibull, Jorgen. 1987. Balanced Budget Redistribution as the Outcome of Political Competition. *Public Choice,* **52**(3), 273–297.

Lizzeri, Alessandro, and Persico, Nicola. 2004. Why Did the Elites Expand the Suffrage? Democracy and the Scope of Government, with an Application to Britain's "Age of Reform." *Quarterly Journal of Economics,* **119**(2), 705–763.

Lohmann, Susanne. 1994. The Dynamics of Informational Cascades: The Monday Demonstrations in Leipzig, East Germany, 1989-91. *World Politics,* **47**(1), 42–101.

Lohmann, Susanne. 1998. Rationalizing the Political Business Cycle: A Workhorse Model. *Economics and Politics,* **10**(1), 1–17.

Lupia, Arthur. 1992. Busy Voters, Agenda Control, and the Power of Information. *American Political Science Review,* **86**(2), 390–403.

Lupia, Arthur, and McCubbins, Mathew D. 1994. Learning from Oversight: Fire Alarms and Police Patrols Reconstructed. *Journal of Law, Economics, and Organization,* **10**(1), 96–125.

Mailath, George J., and Samuelson, Larry. 2006. *Repeated Games and Reputations: Long-Run Relationships.* New York: Oxford University Press.

Matthews, Steven A. 1989. Veto Threats: Rhetoric in a Bargaining Game. *Quarterly Journal of Economics,* **104**(2), 347–369.

McCarty, Nolan. 1997. Presidential Reputation and the Veto. *Economics and Politics,* **9**(1), 1–26.

McCarty, Nolan, and Meirowitz, Adam. 2007. *Political Game Theory: An Introduction.* New York: Cambridge University Press.

McCubbins, Mathew D., and Schwartz, Thomas. 1984. Congressional Oversight Overlooked: Police Patrols versus Fire Alarms. *American Journal of Political Science,* **28**(1), 165–179.

McCubbins, Mathew D., Noll, Roger G., and Weingast, Barry R. 1987. Administrative Procedures as Instruments of Political Control. *Journal of Law, Economics, and Organization,* **3**(2), 243–277.

McCubbins, Mathew D., Noll, Roger G., and Weingast, Barry R. 1989. Structure and Process, Politics and Policy: Administrative Arrangements and the Political Control of Agencies. *Virginia Law Review,* **75**(2), 431–482.

McKelvey, Richard D., and Patty, John W. 2006. A Theory of Voting in Large Elections. *Games and Economic Behavior,* **57**(1), 155–180.

Meirowitz, Adam. 2007. Probabilistic Voting and Accountability in Elections with Uncertain Policy Constraints. *Journal of Public Economic Theory*, **9**(1), 41–68.

Meirowitz, Adam. 2008. Electoral Contests, Incumbency Advantages, and Campaign Finance. *Journal of Politics*, **70**(3), 681–699.

Meirowitz, Adam, and Tucker, Joshua A. 2012. People Power or a One Shot Deal? A Dynamic Model of Protest. *American Journal of Political Science*, **Forthcoming**.

Meltzer, Allan H., and Richard, Scott F. 1981. A Rational Theory of the Size of Government. *Journal of Political Economy*, **89**(5), 914–927.

Morris, Stephen, and Shin, Hyun Song. 2003. Global Games: Theory and Applications. In Dewatripont, Mathias, Hansen, Lars Peter, and Turnovsky, Stephen J. (eds.), *Advances in Economics and Econometrics: Theory and Applications, 8th World Congress of the Econometric Society*. New York: Cambridge University Press.

Morrow, James D. 1994. *Game Theory for Political Scientists*. Princeton, NJ: Princeton University Press.

Myerson, Roger B. 1979. Incentive Compatability and the Bargaining Problem. *Econometrica*, **47**(1), 61–74.

Myerson, Roger B. 1993. Effectiveness of Electoral Systems for Reducing Government Corruption: A Game-Theoretic Analysis. *Games and Economic Behavior*, **5**(1), 118–132.

Myerson, Roger B. 2008. The Autocrat's Credibility Problem and Foundations of the Constitutional State. *American Political Science Review*, **102**(1), 125–139.

Nichter, Simeon. 2008. Vote Buying or Turnout Buying? Machine Politics and the Secret Ballot. *American Political Science Review*, **102**(1), 19–31.

Niskanen, William. 1971. *Bureaucracy and Representative Government*. Chicago: Aldine Transaction.

North, Douglass C. 1990. *Institutions, Institutional Change, and Economic Performance*. Cambridge: Cambridge University Press.

North, Douglass C., and Weingast, Barry R. 1989. Constitutions and Commitment: The Evolution of Institutions Governing Public Choice in Seventeenth-Century England. *Journal of Economic History*, **49**(4), 803–832.

O'Donnell, Guillermo, Schmitter, Philippe C., and Whitehead, Laurence. 1986. *Transitions from Authoritarian Rule: Prospects for Democracy*. Baltimore: Johns Hopkins University Press.

Ordeshook, Peter C. 1986. *Game Theory and Political Theory: An Introduction*. New York: Cambridge University Press.

Osborne, Martin J. 1993. Candidate Positioning and Entry in a Political Competition. *Games and Economic Behavior*, **5**(1), 133–151.

Osborne, Martin J. 2004. *An Introduction to Game Theory*. Oxford: Oxford University Press.

Osborne, Martin J., and Slivinski, Al. 1996. A Model of Political Competition with Citizen Candidates. *Quarterly Journal of Economics*, **111**(1), 65–96.

Palfrey, Thomas R. 1984. Spatial Equilibrium with Entry. *Review of Economic Studies*, **51**(1), 139–156.

Palfrey, Thomas R. 1989. A Mathematical Proof of Duverger's Law. In Ordeshook, Peter C. (ed.), *Models of Strategic Choice in Politics*. Ann Arbor: University of Michigan Press.

Persson, Torsten, Roland, Gérard, and Tabellini, Guido. 1997. Separation of Powers and Political Accountability. *Quarterly Journal of Economics*, **112**(4), 1163–1202.

Persson, Torsten, and Tabellini, Guido. 2000. *Political Economics: Explaining Economic Policy*. Cambridge, MA: MIT Press.

Prat, Andrea. 2002. Campaign Advertising and Voter Welfare. *Review of Economic Studies*, **69**(4), 999–1017.

Primo, David M. 2002. Rethinking Political Bargaining: Policymaking with a Single Proposer. *Journal of Law, Economics, and Organization*, **18**(2), 411–427.

Rauch, James E., and Evans, Peter. 2000. Bureaucratic Structure and Bureaucratic Performance in Less Developed Countries. *Journal of Public Economics*, **75**(1), 49–62.

Riker, William H. 1962. *The Theory of Political Coalitions*. New Haven, CT: Yale University Press.

Riker, William H. 1982. The Two-Party System and Duverger's Law: An Essay on the History of Political Science. *American Political Science Review*, **76**(4), 753–766.

Riker, William H., and Ordeshook, Peter C. 1968. A Theory of the Calculus of Voting. *American Political Science Review*, **62**(1), 25–42.

Robinson, James A., and Verdier, Thierry. 2002. *The Political Economy of Clientelism*. CEPR Working Paper 3205.

Roemer, John E. 1994. A Theory of Policy Differentiation in Single-Issue Electoral Politics. *Social Choice and Welfare*, **11**(4), 355–380.

Roemer, John E. 1997. Political-Economic Equilibrium When Parties Represent Constituents: The Unidimensional Case. *Social Choice and Welfare*, **14**(4), 479–502.

Roemer, John E. 2001. *Political Competition: Theory and Applications*. Cambridge, MA: Harvard University Press.

Romer, Thomas, and Rosenthal, Howard. 1978. Political Resource Allocation, Controlled Agendas, and the Status Quo. *Public Choice*, **33**(4), 27–43.

Rubinstein, Ariel. 1982. Perfect Equilibria in a Bargaining Model. *Econometrica*, **50**(1), 97–109.

Schiavo-Campo, Salvatore, de Tommaso, Giulio, and Mukherjee, Amitabha. 1997. *An International Statistical Survey of Government Employment and Wages*. World Bank Policy Research Working Paper 1806.

Schwartz, Thomas. 1987. Your Vote Counts on Account of the Way It Is Counted: An Institutional Solution to the Paradox of Not Voting. *Public Choice*, **54**(2), 101–121.

Shadmehr, Mehdi, and Bernhardt, Dan. 2011. Collective Action with Uncertain Payoffs: Coordination, Public Signals, and Punishment Dilemmas. *American Political Science Review*, **105**(4), 829–851.

Shepsle, Kenneth A. 1978. *The Giant Jigsaw Puzzle: Democratic Committee Assignments in the Modern House.* Chicago: University of Chicago Press.

Shepsle, Kenneth A. 1979. Institutional Arrangements and Equilibria in Multidimensional Voting Models. *American Journal of Political Science*, **23**(1), 27–59.

Shepsle, Kenneth A. 1991. *Models of Multiparty Electoral Competition.* Chur, Switzerland: Harwood Academic Publishers.

Shepsle, Kenneth A., and Weingast, Barry R. 1981a. Political Preferences for the Pork Barrel: A Generalization. *American Journal of Political Science*, **25**(1), 96–111.

Shepsle, Kenneth A., and Weingast, Barry R. 1981b. Structure-Induced Equilibrium and Legislative Choice. *Public Choice*, **37**(3), 503–519.

Shepsle, Kenneth A., and Weingast, Barry R. 1987. The Institutional Foundations of Committee Power. *American Political Science Review*, **81**(1), 85–104.

Shirk, Susan. 1993. *The Political Logic of Economic Reform in China.* Berkeley: University of California Press.

Simpser, Alberto. 2012. *Why Governments and Parties Manipulate Elections: Theory, Practice, and Implications.* New York: Cambridge University Press.

Snyder, James M. 1989. Election Goals and the Allocation of Campaign Resources. *Econometrica*, **57**(3), 637–660.

Snyder, James M. 1991. On Buying Legislatures. *Economics and Politics*, **3**(2), 93–109.

Spiller, Pablo T., and Tiller, Emerson H. 1997. Decision Costs and the Strategic Design of Administrative Process and Judicial Review. *Journal of Legal Studies*, **26**(2), 347–370.

Stephenson, Matthew C. 2007. Bureaucratic Decision Costs and Endogenous Agency Expertise. *Journal of Law, Economics, and Organization*, **23**(2), 469–498.

Ticchi, Davide, and Vindigni, Andrea. 2008. War and Endogenous Democracy. Unpublished manuscript.

Ting, Michael M. 2002. A Theory of Jurisdictional Assignments in Bureaucracies. *American Journal of Political Science*, **46**(2), 364–378.

Ting, Michael M. 2003. A Strategic Theory of Bureaucratic Redundancy. *American Journal of Political Science*, **47**(2), 274–292.

Tsebelis, George. 2002. *Veto Players: How Political Institutions Work.* Princeton, NJ: Princeton University Press.

Verba, Sidney, Schlozman, Kay Lehman, and Brady, Henry E. 1995. *Voice and Equality: Civic Voluntarism in American Politics.* Cambridge, MA: Harvard University Press.

Volden, Craig. 2002. A Formal Model of the Politics of Delegation in a Separation of Powers System. *American Journal of Political Science*, **46**(1), 111–133.

Volden, Craig, and Wiseman, Alan E. 2007. Bargaining in Legislatures over Particularistic and Collective Goods. *American Political Science Review*, **101**(1), 79–92.

Weber, Max. 1978. *Economy and Society.* Berkeley: University of California Press.

Weingast, Barry R. 1979. A Rational Choice Perspective on Congessional Norms. *American Journal of Political Science,* **23**(2), 245–262.

Weingast, Barry R. 1997. The Political Foundations of Democracy and the Rule of Law. *American Political Science Review,* **91**(2), 245–263.

Weingast, Barry R., and Marshall, William. 1988. The Industrial Organization of Congress; or Why Legislatures, Like Firms, Are Not Organized as Markets. *Journal of Political Economy,* **96**(1), 132–163.

Weingast, Barry R., and Wittman, Donald A. (eds). 2006. *The Oxford Handboook of Political Economy.* Oxford, UK: Oxford University Press.

Williamson, Oliver. 1985. *The Economic Institutions of Capitalism.* New York: Free Press.

Wittman, Donald A. 1973. Parties as Utility Maximizers. *American Political Science Review,* **67**(2), 490–498.

Author Index

Subject Index